Also by GABRIEL JACKSON

THE SPANISH REPUBLIC AND THE CIVIL WAR, 1931–39
[1965]

THE SPANISH CIVIL WAR: DOMESTIC CRISIS OR
INTERNATIONAL CONSPIRACY
[1967]

Historian's QUEST

Historian's QUEST

Gabriel Jackson

New York Alfred · A · Knopf

1969

THIS IS A BORZOI BOOK
PUBLISHED BY ALFRED A. KNOPF, INC.

First Edition
 Published in the United States by Alfred A. Knopf, Inc., New York, and simultaneously in Canada by Random House of Canada Limited, Toronto. Distributed by Random House, Inc., New York.

Library of Congress Catalog Card Number: 73-79332

Manufactured in the United States of America

TO Elizabeth

PREFACE

I should like to begin by explaining the title of this book. During the years 1960–4, while I was writing *The Spanish Republic and the Civil War,* I frequently regretted the amount of material in my notes which was not appropriate to the kind of objective, scholarly history I was then composing. I knew very well that my conversations with veterans of the war, my visits to historic monuments and orphanages, had no place in such a history. Yet when I thought in terms of human value, of what was worth retaining and communicating, it seemed to me that many of those materials were as important as anything currently entering the scholarly book. My original impulse, then, was that after completing the formal history I would write a short book or a series of loosely connected essays based upon those facets of my work in Spain which were not to be included under the heading of scholarship.

When I began directly to plan that new writing, it seemed to me desirable, and even necessary, that my Spanish experience be related to my principles and practices as a historian, and also to the portions of my personal life which I knew to have affected my work as a historian. The germ of this further purpose may well have come from my repeated readings of the endlessly stimulating and suggestive work of Américo Castro, *The Structure of Spanish History*. The great Spanish scholar had shown that much of the passion and humor of his nation's literature flows from a current of "personal integralism," definable as the effort to absorb all experience into the self, not for purposes of narrative or anecdote, but as a way of comprehending a world in which the individual finds it extremely difficult to arrive at reliable, unfluctuating, objective criteria of understanding. Hence, in works both of fiction and of nonfiction, the writer could not be satisfied to express himself entirely in the third person. Completeness, intellectual and emotional honesty, required him to present the specific "I" for whom the poem, the narrative, the philosophical or religious reflection was an attempt to comprehend the world. This personal integralism deliberately erased the conventional boundaries between the personal and the impersonal. It also tended to erase the distinctions between the appropriate and the inappropriate (arbitrary in any school of thought), the spiritual and the material, the tragic and the comic.

A further motive had to do with my relation to colleagues and students in several colleges and universities. No sensitive human being today can be unaware of the desperate uncertainty of purpose that afflicts a high proportion both of his contemporaries and of his juniors. I myself became a historian largely by accident, and not until my late twenties. In recent years I have felt an increasing rather than decreasing sense of purpose, and I am aware of the contrast between my good fortune in this regard and the painful situation of many of my friends and acquaintances. I think I might give courage to other people by discussing the nature of my involvement and my increasing commitment to the work of a historian. But I do not want to speak in the abstract of training, purposes, projects. Like every other professional man I have a *curriculum vitae* which lists institutions, degrees earned, prizes, jobs, fellowships, publications, work in progress. If I were to use that *curriculum vitae* as the basis of my present writing, I would surely give the reader a general impression of smoothness, regularity, quantitative stepwise progress in a career. But it would be a set of half-truths, in which the various practical obstacles and attainments would be reflected, but in which neither the elation nor the doubts and hesitations would appear.

The *quest* has included the slowly developed sense of purpose, the inner uncertainties, the emotional reactions to many different kinds of people and circumstances, the dialectic between teaching and writing, between being a citizen and being an objective scholar, between the wide gamut of personal interests and the discipline of professional work, between manifold hopes and limited practical possibilities in the future. The more I concentrated on the attempt to define principles and practices of work, the more it seemed to me that intellectual experience must constantly be related to personal experience, that I could not in fact be honest about what I mean in general, abstract terms without seeking to know how far what I felt, and what I had lived through, had modified my principles and affected my interpretation of history. Hence the partially autobiographical character of this book, and the choice of the word "quest" in its title.

I am very happy to acknowledge a generous fellowship from the American Council of Learned Societies and the granting of an early sabbatical year by the University of California at San Diego, two forms of aid which made it possible for me to write the present book.

January 1969 G. J.

CONTENTS

Historian's QUEST

1

The Discovery of a Mission

When in 1942 I graduated from Harvard College with an A.B. in history and literature I was not thinking either of becoming a historian or of writing about Spain. The Spanish Civil War of 1936–9, together with Nazi outrages against the Jews and the Soviet purge trials, had awakened a strong political consciousness while I was still in high school. But Spain for me had simply been the locus of the most protracted single struggle among the forces of fascism, communism, and democracy. I knew nothing of Spanish language or culture, and my knowledge of Spanish history was confined to the era of the Counter Reformation as seen through the eyes of English and Dutch Protestants. I should, however, suggest one possible modification of the above statement. In December 1940, I had been seriously injured in an automobile accident, and my tutor, the late F. O. Matthiessen, had sent to the hospital the Phaidon Press edition of El Greco. He wrote that he had found great solace and inspiration in those paintings, and hoped that they might also help me through a difficult period. I believe that at the time Matty's thoughtfulness meant more to me than did El Greco. In any case, when I had recovered sufficiently to return to Cambridge, my whole energy was absorbed in preparing for final examinations in American history and literature.

All this was to change as a result of a Sheldon Traveling Fellowship to Mexico in the summer of 1942. Our group of a dozen Harvard, Princeton, and Wellesley students were housed among Spanish Republican exiles. Although I had not studied Spanish, I enjoyed languages, could read French and German fluently, and remembered some Latin. The rapid acquisition of grammar and vocabulary thus presented no problem. My host in Mexico City, Dr. Joaquin Sanz Astolfi, had been one of the directors of a tropical medicine laboratory in Morocco. He had been a friend of the Republican High Commissioner Álvarez Buylla, who was shot by the Nationalist forces during the Civil War; and the widow of Álvarez Buylla had a small apartment in the same building as the Astolfis. The doctor and his Argentine-born wife had four very energetic, excitable children between the ages of six and sixteen. At the dinner table he regarded them with a kind of wry aloofness. I am sure that, other things being equal, he would rather not have had *pensionnaires* in the already noisy apartment, but I believe he enjoyed conversation with slightly older and more mature company. In any event he was very patient and helpful with the two American college boys, a Princeton fellow and myself, who shared a room in his apartment.

I would sometimes accompany him after dinner to the Mexican public health laboratory where he now worked. During these walks he would explain systematically the significance of Spanish phrases with which I had had trouble either in reading or in conversation. Dr. Astolfi was the author of a short book of satirical poems, of which he gave me a copy. He loved words and all their associations. At the same time he never betrayed the slightest pain at my mauling of his beloved language, and whenever I could not make myself clear he acted as though the cause of misunderstanding somehow lay in his failure to catch my entire sentence. Once or twice a week we would also play dominoes after supper, in company with his wife, Sra. Álvarez Buylla, and occasionally some other friend. The mood of the game was restful and intimate. The conversation proceeded slowly, with frequent pauses, and I was thus able both to understand more of what was said and to think out my own sentences before speaking.

Most of the long evenings, both before and after the nine o'clock supper, I devoted to reading Spanish essays and novels in the Austral and Losada paperback editions which had made a rich selection of fine literature available at low prices several decades before the paperback revolution reached the United States. Azorín's *Trasuntos de España* evoked magically the great variety of landscapes and local cultural traits of Spain. At the same time his short sentences and his precise use of words made him an ideal author for a beginning reader. Dr. Astolfi recommended to me Unamuno's *Por tierras de Portugal y de España,* much more complex in vocabulary, full of irony and of cryptic allusions which the doctor delighted in explaining to me.

From Unamuno's intensely moving novella *San Manuel Bueno, martír* I received my first inkling of the religious agony of modern Spain. The hero of the story is a village priest whose devotion and sacrifices have given him the reputation of a veritable saint. In his heart, however, the priest has lost his faith, and his martyrdom consists in the fact that he guards the terrible secret and continues, for the sake of his parishioners, to act as though he were a fully believing priest. There was no mistaking the connotations of the story. Spain had lost its spiritual certainty. But Spain needed a powerful religious ideal, and in the absence of any new faith it must continue to live by the Christian ideals of its great past.

In all three essayists whom I read, Azorín, Unamuno, and Dr. Marañon, there was a large component of bitter-sweet nostalgia. At a certain level they seemed to recognize that the past was past, and that Spain needed to find new directions in the twentieth century. But emotionally they were tied to an ideal, and much idealized, past. Unamuno's essays exemplified the contradictions the most dramatically: on the one hand self-conscious defensiveness concerning the economic and educational backwardness of Spain; on the other hand a fierce pride in Spanish austerity, in the triumph of metaphysical ideals over material prosperity.

The great philologist and historian Ramón Menéndez Pidal wrote more calmly than Unamuno, but with the same preoccupations in the background. In *La idea imperial de Carlos V* he claimed that the Emperor's aim had not been to enforce the harsh Counter Reformation as it was experienced in Belgium or Hungary. Rather he had envisioned a unified Christian world, tolerant and pluralistic in all matters except the fundamental faith. Menéndez Pidal's argument was quite convincing as to ideal intentions, but it necessarily glossed over the harsh truths concerning dynastic and religious imperialism in the sixteenth century. Moreover, always coloring the tone of the prose was a defensive nostalgia in the face of Spain's inadaptability to secular capitalist civilization as it has developed since the Renaissance. From these writers I became aware, as of the summer of 1942, of a Spanish predicament which has virtually no equivalent in American life: the attachment to a long and rich tradition which had become a heavy obstacle to the solution of contemporary problems.

By no means all that I read shared this pessimistic character. The novels of Galdós celebrated the common man more joyously and vividly than any literature I had previously known. Dostoevsky could depict superstitious peasants, and Zola could almost convince me that his carefully studied workmen were flesh-and-blood individuals, but Galdós was unique for the variety of completely natural, intuitively understood personalities drawn from among the lower middle classes, the peasantry, and the workers. Later I was to experience the candor, the pride, and the verbosity of ordinary Spaniards which made it possible for a great novelist to know his countrymen without self-conscious study. For the moment it was an exhilarating introduction to a master of prose fiction who has yet to receive the attention he deserves in the English-speaking world.

In the course of two crowded months I also came to know a number of remarkable and highly individual Spanish exiles. As it happened, the Wellesley professor who was in charge of the housing arrangements became ill and asked me to help her with rent payments and with several "culture conflicts" between American students and their hosts. In this way I not only met people, but was introduced to their angle of vision. They could permit young children to be noisy and undisciplined, as did the Astolfis, but they did not understand the American teen-ager's custom of raiding the icebox at midnight. Some of them were mystified by what they called the inexpressiveness of their *pensionnaires.* They wanted me to tell them whether the students were satisfied with the rooms and meals. In these instances I could see that the Spaniards, who were used to more voluble reactions, felt confused by the smooth, polite exterior of middle-class Anglo-Saxon girls. They were also persuaded, I am afraid with frequent justification, that the Americans were scornful of simple furnishings, and of soups made with leftover vegetables and chunks of bread. In more general terms they resented what seemed to them a callous indifference to the meaning of war, concentration camps, and the trials of being a refugee. I could only reply that most Americans had had absolutely no comparable experience by which to comprehend the Spaniards.

From these interviews I became very conscious, perhaps exaggeratedly conscious, of the cultural differences between one nation and another, and of the alacrity with which people will attach a national label to traits which they dislike or misunderstand. But more important than the conflicts was the feeling I had of being able successfully to communicate with Spaniards. I use that verb deliberately because the level of my speaking knowledge was very elementary. Nor did I in all cases sympathize with the Spaniards' criticisms of my compatriots. Quite the contrary, I thought that some of them had too exalted a view of their personal worth, and that they were expecting a kind of worshipful respect based solely on their recent sufferings or their political stance.

However, I felt that I was living in an environment and dealing with people I could understand. At Harvard, despite the brilliant professors I had known and fine experiences I had had on my house committee and on the student council, I had never felt "at home." There were invisible rules of decorum which I had more or less learned, but which never felt natural to me. I had performed Bach cantatas in Unitarian churches and played Mozart flute quartets in the most appreciative Cambridge homes. Yet on these occasions I had almost always missed the spontaneous expression of emotion, as against the fluttering expression of cultivated appreciation. No one who acted like the Cambridge intellectuals could possibly have created the music we were playing.

At the end of four years at Harvard I felt a mixture of gratitude for a rich intellectual training and impatience to escape from an unsatisfying emotional context. Unexpectedly, in Mexico I found myself much more attuned to my surroundings than in Massachusetts. People said exactly what was on their minds. They were unabashed in the expression of their own biological and spiritual impulses, and openly curious about, and respectful of, the impulses of others. They expressed pleasure quickly when they felt it. They became angry quickly and recovered just as quickly. They were people with whom I did feel at home.

As a direct result of my Mexican experience, I became interested both in the Spanish past generally and in the history of the recent Republic and Civil War. But for seven years thereafter I was otherwise occupied; I spent four years in the army, first as an aircraft mechanic and later as a photo interpreter and cartographer, and then three years teaching English, Spanish, and flute at the Putney School in Vermont. My army career had a curiously negative relationship to my past education and to my future profession. As a mechanic I was living with men who were belligerently proud to have quit school at the minimum legal age and who never looked into a book unless it happened to be a manual dealing with the metal trades. I enjoyed my work as a "salvage" mechanic, removing usable instruments from wrecked planes. I liked my companions and spent the off-hours much as they did: playing volleyball in the late afternoon and devoting the evenings to every movie turned out by Hollywood in the years 1943 and 1944. I took part in long bull sessions concerning army life, baseball players, Hollywood stars, and women. I read almost nothing except a few novels, and remembered the Jewish intellectual world of my boyhood and the Harvard University world of my college years as though they were phenomena of a distant planet.

Later, as part of my work in mapping the Caroline

Islands and Saipan from aerial photographs, I read a number of American and German accounts of whaling voyages in the Pacific. These records had been sent to Military Intelligence, and they served to help interpret coastlines, offshore depths, fresh-water supplies, and the like in the photos. The narratives were often interesting, and they inspired in me a temporary desire to join the Coast and Geodetic Survey after the war. But far and away the strongest impression from my army experience was the sensation of how little the vast majority of men knew or cared about the subjects I had been studying in high school and college. My own values were temporarily submerged when I could not establish any meaningful contact between my intellectual training and my present environment.

However, in 1944 I was assigned to teach map reading to groups of noncommissioned officers in combat divisions. I discovered that I enjoyed teaching, and thus I was very happy in 1946 to accept a position at the Putney School, whose lively and informal atmosphere I had tasted briefly during a Harvard Orchestra trip before the war. At Putney my interest in history, literature, and music revived as rapidly as it had wilted in the army. In addition, the inspiring headmistress, Mrs. Carmelita Hinton, and several of my older colleagues set an example of qualitative excellence and humane concern for students which I have never seen surpassed anywhere. In later years I was often to be impotently angry when it was obvious that the craft-guild psychology of college and university administrators placed a very low professional evaluation on my Putney experience. In point of fact no course I have ever taken and no teaching I have ever observed elsewhere has contributed as much to my professional formation as did the Putney years.

Nevertheless, there were two factors in the Putney situation which made me realize, even at the moments of greatest satisfaction, that I would not stay there indefinitely. For one thing, I wanted eventually to marry and have a family. As a bachelor receiving room and board I was not pinched by the smallness of the salary. But it was clear to me that all the married couples with children depended in some degree on a private supplementary income or on generous relatives. The second factor had to do with the implications of the complete informality in personal relations. Students and faculty were all called by their first names. I recognized that this had great advantages for establishing confidence and candor in the teaching relationship. But I was not pleased to have the parents place me, however unconsciously, on the same level with their children. For the time being I found it more amusing than bothersome. However, I did not relish the thought that at the age of forty or fifty I would habitually be treated by the adult world as if I were Jonnie's camp counselor. Parenthetically I might say that one of the obstacles to improving secondary education in the United States is the almost universal tendency to treat secondary-school teachers, economically and socially, as somehow less than adult.

In December 1948 I married the recently arrived geometry teacher, thereby fulfilling a prediction of Mrs. Hinton, who had told me in the previous spring that "you're going to like the new math teacher very much, Gabe." Elizabeth had majored in economics and minored in mathematics, largely to prove to her father that girls can be just as "practical" as boys. However, she was much more interested in literature and was thinking of doing graduate work in French. For me, the question of graduate school was complicated by my memories of Harvard. As a top student in American history and literature I had had the almost unique good fortune to have as my tutors in successive years Perry Miller and F. O. Matthiessen. They were the most brilliant men under whom I ever studied—though I did not appreciate the fact as fully then as I do now.

They were also tortured souls, as I was quite aware. One afternoon I had circled Harvard Yard three times with Miller, who was preparing to deliver his annual lecture on *The Scarlet Letter* and kept saying in hopeless desperation: "What the hell am I going to say about that f—— masterpiece that I haven't said ten times already?" During that same year he had come to a virtual halt in his major scholarly work on the Puritans. He was sick and tired of hairsplitting sermons and scholastic debates within the Calvinist fold. Besides these intellectual difficulties I knew that he was unhappy in his personal life and that he drank too much.

Matthiessen was an even more anguished soul. Simultaneously a Marxist and an Anglican, he suffered constant doubts about the validity of both positions, taken separately and in combination. He was convinced that his political beliefs had hurt him in his academic career. He was nasty to the wives of his graduate students, and then would flay himself for his waspish tongue and jealousy. I had stayed several times at his home in Kittery, Maine. On the last occasion, in 1948, he had brought the conversation back repeatedly to two themes: one, that he could not conceive how anyone who had reached maturity after the dropping of the atom bomb could have faith in *anything;* the other, the fate of several noncommunist Czech professors whom he had worked with in 1947 and of whom he had heard nothing since the February 1948 Communist party coup in Prague.

On this same occasion I told him I was thinking of doing graduate work in European history but that I was haunted by the memory of the graduate students I had known, groaning over theses topics which seemed trivial to them even as they did their research, and hastily reading the prefaces and dust jackets of hundreds of books they had no time to read but might be asked about on the orals. Matty listened silently, and offered no defense whatever of the existing graduate programs. He said only that if I wanted to teach at the college level I would need a doctorate, and that hopefully there might be some real value in some of the seminars I would take.

With such memories of my two great tutors I felt that graduate training, and a college or university career, would make sense only if I had a long-term project which I could really enjoy, and of whose ultimate value I could be sure while going through the hurdles of academic apprenticeship. One of the subjects I was teaching at Putney was elementary Spanish. After a lapse of five years I began again to read widely in Spanish history and literature. There was a former Spanish journalist and diplomat on the faculty; I had conversational practice sessions with him several times weekly, and our conversations dealt frequently with the Civil War. I also remembered the wonderful months in Mexico before my military service, and I began to think definitely of making twentieth-century Spain my principal field of scholarship.

After our marriage my wife and I left Putney to go to Stanford University as graduate students. I knew that the Hoover Library contained an immense quantity of materials on the Spanish Civil War and its antecedents. My first conversation with my adviser, Professor Ralph Lutz, augured well for the future. When I told him that I would like to work on the Spanish Republic he expressed immediate pleasure at the choice, remarking that the topic was well worth detailed study and that almost no scholarly work had been done on it. Then, after reflecting a moment, he added: "Of course that subject is rather controversial. If anyone asks you why you chose it, just say that your graduate adviser put you on to it." The "Cold War" had already placed liberals on the defensive, and Lutz himself was a conservative, in fact a close personal friend of former President Hoover. I deeply appreciated his consideration, and later his help was to be very important in my obtaining a student Fulbright fellowship to the University of Toulouse.

For my Master's degree at Stanford I wrote a thesis on the educational reforms and Church policies of the Spanish Republic during the years 1931–3. These were the first two years of the new regime, and Spain was being governed, in the midst of the world depression, by a Republican-Socialist coalition under the leadership of the Left Republican Manuel Azaña. Azaña was presiding over a species of New Deal some two years before the start of the Roosevelt era in the United States. Through deficit financing a strong start was made in the building of schools and hospitals and the extension of irrigation and hydroelectric development. Azaña had also reduced the size of Spain's swollen, inefficient army. His government had separated Church and state and had granted a statute of internal autonomy to the province of Catalonia.

It was an enlightened, reformist government with generous long-range plans and important practical accomplishments to its credit in the areas of education, economic "pump priming," and Catalan autonomy. But it lacked administrative experience, was constantly sniped at by the anarchist Left and the monarchist Right, and in its dogmatic anticlericalism it underestimated the strength of Catholic sentiment. The complexities of the situation reminded me of the ambiguous feelings toward the Spanish heritage which had characterized the work of Spain's best twentieth-century writers. At the same time, the economic problems of an "underdeveloped" but proud and energetic nation during the depression and the ideological ferment involving monarchists, Jacobin republicans, reformist and revolutionary Socialists, Communists, Trotskyites, and anarchists all served to maintain high interest in the subject.

While I enjoyed the research and writing of my thesis, I must confess that I experienced no intellectual stimulation from the seminars, occupied as they were with technical detail. My neglect of one such detail caused a minor crisis in the editing of my thesis. When I submitted my first draft, I thought that I had carefully followed the rules of the departmental pamphlet on the preparation of theses, and from my earlier conversations with Professor Lutz I had reason to anticipate that he would approve the contents of my essay. When I went to pick up the draft my adviser looked at me severely and said: "I see you haven't bothered to look at the Stanford rules on punctuation." My heart sank as he demonstrated, impatiently and curtly, that I had repeatedly used semicolons at a point in my bibliographical listings which called for commas. I left the office in speechless dismay. In practical terms it was not difficult to make the necessary changes, but he had said nothing about the content of the thesis, and several weeks passed before he offered me any reassurance in that regard. The uninitiated reader may well think that my anxiety on this occasion was somewhat exaggerated. But the fact is that in most graduate schools the majority of professors devote more attention and more emotional energy to details of form than to content, much less ideas. Never before or after was I to see

Professor Lutz so excited, and while the incident seems absurd in retrospect it was traumatic at the time. I believe it played a considerable role in my desire later to avoid the universities, and now that I am teaching in a university I am determined not to bore or terrorize my graduate students on matters of formal detail.

For several reasons my wife and I were relieved as well as grateful when I received a student Fulbright fellowship to the University of Toulouse. Neither of us had enjoyed the first year of graduate school enough to want to continue for another two or three. At the same time we each felt that to become bilingual would be a positive result of studying in Toulouse, regardless of what the courses might be like. Since she was studying French literature and I Spanish history, Toulouse, with its proximity to Spain and its large Spanish-speaking community, would be an excellent location for our joint interests. By combining the GI Bill subsidies with the Fulbright fellowship, and by deciding not to have children immediately, we would be able to manage two years abroad.

Having written a Master's essay on one aspect of the Spanish Republic, I now hoped to write my doctoral thesis on another aspect of the same period. However, my adviser, Professor Jacques Godechot, firmly refused to consider the years 1931–6 as "history." In order to do a proper thesis I should choose a subject on which more complete data and a longer perspective would be available than for anything as recent and controversial as the 1930s. At the moment I was disappointed, but afterward I felt very grateful because my eventual thesis on Joaquín Costa enabled me to know the background of the Republic and the Civil War in much greater depth than I would have learned it by working directly on the events of the 1930s.

In view of the semicolon crisis at Stanford, I was anxious to have a clear understanding as soon as possible concerning the formal details of my doctoral thesis. In reading the work of French scholars I noticed that even official manuals, such as the "Clio" series put out by the Presses Universitaires, differed substantially as to organization, capitalization, and punctuation of bibliographies. I would have felt foolish going to Professor Godechot's office specifically to ask him about such details. But one day I happened to pass his apartment while he was dusting the hood of his car (this being a frequent ritual with the French). I asked him whether, from the point of view of form, he would be satisfied if I prepared my thesis in accordance with the standards of the University of Chicago *Manual of Style*. He looked puzzled, or perhaps amused, for a moment and then said: "*Mon cher* Jackson, anything reasonably clear and consistent will be quite all right." I could have kissed the ground he walked on, but Professor Godechot was a very mild and reserved gentleman, so I thanked him politely and expressed my elation elsewhere.

In the course of the following two years, under his flexible and critical guidance, I wrote my doctoral thesis: *Joaquín Costa et les grands problèmes de l'Espagne moderne*. Costa was one of the intellectual giants of late nineteenth-century Spain. He can be characterized roughly as a cross between Thorstein Veblen and Henry George. Like Veblen, he was deeply learned and intensely individual in his approach to the newly developing social sciences of economics and anthropology. He employed the same teasing, ironic tone, and he possessed a similar gift for striking phrases. As with Henry George, a generous idealism and an impatient desire for conclusive solutions led him to preach a panacea. What the single tax was to Henry George, the irrigation and reforestation of Spain were to Costa. He was a "self-made" man, and, in contrast with most Spanish intellectuals of the time, an ardent admirer of modern science and technology. Throughout the 1890s, and especially after his country's humiliating defeat in the Spanish-American War of 1898, Costa pointed to the domestic accomplishments of Republican France and Bismarckian Germany and advised his compatriots to put a *doble llave al sepulcro del Cid,* a double lock on the tomb of the Cid. He demanded public education and land reform. Above all, in order to raise standards of living and to bring Spain abreast of the most progressive European nations, he called for a gigantic national program of *política hidráulica,* the harnessing of

Spain's vast water resources for the combined benefit of agriculture, electric power, and water transport.

In all matters relating to education and economic development Costa was close in spirit to the European democratic Left, and the leading economic officials of the Spanish Republic, notably Indalecio Prieto and Jaime Carner, drew much of their inspiration from him. But Costa also had a penchant for hero worship and one-man rule. He admired Cromwell more than he admired British parliamentary institutions. He attributed the success of the young American republic far more to the personality of George Washington than to the Constitution of 1787. In Spain he saw only the shortcomings of the Cortes and the press. He consented once to be a candidate for the Cortes, and never recovered from his pride-searing defeat. Increasingly between 1898 and his death in 1911 he called for an "iron surgeon" to cure the Spanish body politic of its ills. Thus, his double lock on the Cid's tomb referred strictly to Spanish imperialism, not to authoritarian domestic rule.

While working on my thesis I had several conversations in Madrid with the late Manuel Lorenzo Pardo, an engineer who was Costa's leading disciple and who had supervised the irrigation works constructed in the Ebro Valley under both the Primo de Rivera dictatorship and the Republic. I was not surprised to find that Lorenzo Pardo's political ideal was the quiet civilian dictatorship of Salazar in Portugal. The study of Joaquín Costa was thus invaluable preparation for my later work. His personality embodied most of the contradictory impulses which were to dominate the politics of the Republic and the Civil War. His writings furnished a brilliant analysis of Spain's social and economic problems within a context of Spanish history, ideals, habits, reflexes.

At the same time, during my several research trips from Toulouse, I became acquainted with the post-Civil War Spain of hunger and repression. In 1951 no tourist boom or foreign investments had yet begun to relieve the worst poverty. Tens of thousands of Republican veterans were still in prison, and many of those on the outside were unemployed. The railroad stations were full of able-bodied, underfed men competing to carry your suitcase and guide you to a hotel from which they would receive a pitiful commission. Gypsy women carrying babies, or dolls covered to look like babies, pursued you on every sidewalk. At each corner the blind were selling lottery tickets, shoelaces, or American cigarettes (one at a time, not by the pack). When in Barcelona I met the late Jaime Vicens Vives, probably the finest historian produced by Spain in the present century, I must have startled him by the extent of my dismay at the ubiquitous poverty. He recommended to me a history of social work in Spain, from which I learned that the international beggars' fraternities in the sixteenth and seventeenth centuries had considered Spain the most profitable country in which to practice the mendicant trade—and also that as of 1950 Spain was far behind the rest of Europe in matters of social security. I took the hint, did my best to overcome my instinctive American reaction against beggars, and distributed my change freely.

Alongside the poverty I also experienced the spontaneous dignity, the true sense of honor, of the Spanish pueblo. Once on a windy day in Madrid I passed a blind lottery salesman who was losing all his tickets without realizing that the wind was carrying them off. I collected as many as I could off the sidewalk. When I tried to return them he insisted vehemently that I keep them all, and would not accept a peseta. Only by asserting with equal vehemence that I would be leaving Spain before the drawing and that I had no family or friends in the country could I finally induce him to accept the return of the tickets.

A few weeks later I was changing buses in Bilbao at 8 P.M., hungry, and still several hours from my destination. I walked over to a small fruit stand, where there was nothing left except two winter pears. The woman looked apologetic, but I told her I would be glad to buy them. She picked them up and was going to wrap them in a piece of newspaper when she noticed a dark spot, which she pointed out to me. I said that a small bad spot would not matter, but she shook her head, saying "Young man, you don't want to buy this one," and she sliced it open to show me how it was spoiled throughout. Very well, there was the second, smaller pear. As she weighed it, I discovered that I had nothing smaller in my wallet than a fifty-peseta note. Seeing that I had to run for my bus, and not having change herself, she laughingly ordered me to take the pear and *Vayate con Dios, joven,* "Go with God, young man." For such people I was determined, after completing my doctorate, to write the best history of which I was capable.

During the three years I spent on the faculty of Goddard College in Vermont I had time only for infrequent trips to the Dartmouth Library, but at Wellesley College between 1955 and 1960 I was able to read and take notes on the enormous mass of materials in the Harvard Library. Equally important in these years was the friendship and the frequent conversations of my colleague, the eminent poet Jorge Guillén. I was able to audit his course on Spanish poetry in the twentieth century. He had known Unamuno, Juan Ramón Jiménez, Federico García Lorca, and Antonio Machado. He had been a lifelong friend of Pedro Salinas. He was a marvelous mimic, and read in class each man's poems in the voice and rhythm of the poet. Neither of us had a class the following hour, and so we could discuss both poetry and politics at leisure.

For pleasure, and to learn better both the man and the Spanish language, I made translations of several of Guillén's poems. At the same time he, whose subject matter had never been political until about 1950, was now writing the intensely political poems which appeared subsequently in the volumes entitled *Clamor* and *Maremagnum.* Several months after the course was over he asked me, in the lobby of the library, who was my favorite among the poets we had read. I answered Machado, and tears filled his eyes as he pieced together his scattered memories of this man who had never visited the literary cafes and whom, consequently, the young Guillén had not known as well as he had known lesser but more sociable poets. Suddenly he paused, took hold of my coat lapels, and, looking directly into my eyes, said: "We didn't know yet what a master he was. *Era un hombre que no se daba importancia* [he was a man who did not give himself importance]."

Although the Wellesley years were rich in both human and intellectual experience, I was constantly anxious about the bleak prospects of my professional future. I had been offered an assistant professorship with the very clear stipulation that I could not expect tenure, i.e., permanent employment. This stipulation was regretfully explained to me in terms of what the administration called the age-in-grade problem. There were already two members of the department who were the same age as I, and these two persons were in line for tenure. Several departments in recent years had been badly hurt by having two or three members reach retirement age in quick succession. It was necessary to avoid such difficulties in the future, and therefore it was hoped that I would understand why, without any prejudice against me as an individual, there was no room for me beyond a maximum of five years. An accidental advantage of this situation was that as a temporary colleague I was not appointed to any important committees and was therefore free to use almost all my nonteaching time for research. I made fortnightly trips to the Harvard Library and was thus able, before returning to Spain, to know the bibliography of the Republic and the Civil War better than I could have known it from study in Spain itself, there being no Spanish, or indeed, European, library comparable in completeness to the best American libraries.

As of 1960 I had published several scholarly articles and had discussed the project for a history of the Republic and the Civil War with a number of leading Hispanists. When Fulbright exchanges were finally initiated that year between Spain and the United States, I was awarded a faculty fellowship, and, planning in terms of a two-year stay abroad, I was permitted simultaneously to hold a fellowship of the Social Science Research Council. At the same time, I had been unable during the five years at Wellesley to locate any college teaching job with permanent prospects. I do not know how much this was due to my foreign doctorate, how much to the inevitably suspicious fact (from an outsider's point of view) that I was not receiving tenure at Wellesley, how much to the extremely tight employment situation of the late 1950s for young professors, particularly in English and history. The committees awarding the research fellowships surely knew from my dossier that I had no job to return to, and perhaps they were trying, among other things, to help me through a difficult season.

In any event it was a strange feeling simultaneously to be awarded two highly competitive fellowships and to have no salaried position in a profession I had been exercising with reasonable qualitative success for eleven years. With my wife's full support we decided, in effect, to risk everything on the results of the next two years. I would write the book toward which my Mexican experience, my Master's and doctoral study, my reading and writing of the late 1950s had all pointed. She, on our second two-year stay in Europe, would complete her own doctorate in French literature. We would leave the future to work itself out.

2

The Intellectual Baggage of a Historian

In each of the very different institutions in which I have taught students have asked me, challengingly and candidly, in the privacy of my office: "Why do we have to study history?" Developing the general question, they say that they cannot see the relevance to their lives of such matters as the organization of the medieval Church, the nature of the Bourbon monarchy, or the growth of Prussia in the seventeenth and eighteenth centuries. Anyone, they opine, can learn the "facts" (pronounced scornfully) in order to "regurgitate" them on an examination, but what have those facts got to do with life in the contemporary world? They find it easy to recognize that the study of psychology can help them understand themselves as individuals and perhaps help them to live happier, more "adjusted" personal lives. They see that sociology helps them understand such critical problems as juvenile delinquency and racism. They see the immediate relevance of political science to the improvement of local government or the achievement of international peace. But history seems, precisely for some of the most ethically motivated students, to be remote, irrelevant, almost frivolous.

I do not wish to exaggerate the issue. Actually, history is a very popular major in most colleges, and many of the students who asked me why they had to study history nevertheless went on to elect an occasional course in history after fulfilling their minimal "distribution requirements." However, a serious question deserves a serious answer, and those who, like myself, teach required courses under the rubrics "Western Civilization" or "Humanities" have a special responsibility to justify their subject matter to the students who are obliged to take their courses. Many professors take refuge in such plausible assertions as that a knowledge of history will enable one to understand current political issues "in perspective" or that graduate schools are looking for the well-rounded man. The second of these assertions is nothing but a form of blackmail, and the first of them attributes value to history only as a partial means to another end.

Slightly more dignified in tone, and employed by many professors and deans who are not historians, is the argument that a knowledge of history is "the mark of an educated man." I have colleagues who are shocked when freshmen betray a total ignorance of the Roman republic. Personally I do not find this any more shocking than a total ignorance of molecular biology or Mayan Indian culture. There is nothing sacrosanct about the education of a pre-1914 European gentleman, and the constantly accelerating accumulation of knowledge makes it absolutely essential to create a place in the curriculum for concepts and disciplines which have developed in the last few decades.

Besides not wishing to give a trivial answer to the question "Why study history?" I also remembered how, in the military service during World War II, I had lost my own intellectual bearings. Some people can, out of desire to shine or out of pure gamesmanship, study carefully whatever materials are required of them. But I could never concentrate on my own studies without some feeling of relevance to the interests and problems of the people among whom I lived. I assumed that this was the fundamental problem for my students. They could see the direct relationship of the social sciences, and sometimes of literature, to their own lives, but not that of history. If today I can answer the question confidently, it is only as a result of many probing conversations with students over the years. The substance of my answer lies in the following paragraphs.

I define my own interest in history by reference to three

broad ideas concerning motivation, method, and value. As to motivation, I study history out of curiosity and concern for human conduct as a whole, and as manifested under widely differing conditions of geography, social organization, economic development, and spiritual ideals. The emphasis on human conduct as a whole is what makes history feel different to me from the social sciences. With regard to method: the mass of data which composes the raw material of history must be organized in at least roughly chronological and narrative form, so that events can be understood in their context and so that the reader senses how each new situation develops out of a previous situation. Much of the value, and most of the joy, of studying history comes from the stimulus to one's imagination, the recognition in concrete, specific terms of the enormous variety of forms that human enterprise can take.

If the study of history is inspired by curiosity concerning human conduct as a whole, then the raw materials become, simply and overwhelmingly, all the reliable evidence one can find concerning human activities anywhere, any time: political documents, literary and artistic productions, architectural remains, primitive tools, oral traditions—literally everything that can enable us to know what men have done. I recognize that in stressing the totality of human affairs I am contradicting received ideas about the nature of history. Prior to the twentieth century it was generally the case that historians, reflecting their own background as members of the "establishment," were concerned primarily with leaders, systems of government, and international relations. Most historical "classics" are indeed narratives of politics, war, and diplomacy.

But in recent decades historians, responding to the growth of democracy, the impact of science, and the needs of general education, have greatly broadened their conception of their own discipline. Since the appearance in the United States of such figures as James Harvey Robinson and Charles and Mary Beard, in France of Charles Seignobos and the magnificent, collectively written *Peuples et Civilisations* series, and under the influence of such cultural historians as Jacob Burckhardt and Jan Huizinga, historians on both shores of the

Atlantic have bent every effort to relate all aspects of human conduct, and not content themselves with politics, war, and diplomacy. Today the textbooks used all over Europe and the United States contain chapters on the scientific, cultural, and artistic accomplishments of the periods and nations with which they deal. Anyone who rejects history today on the grounds that it deals merely with past politics is knocking over a straw man.

History differs from the social sciences in the breadth of its subject matter and in the methodological consequences resulting from that greater breadth. The social sciences, like the natural sciences on which they are modeled, abstract out of the total of human activity those aspects they have chosen to analyze. Roughly speaking, the economist concentrates on systems of production, exchange, and distribution; the psychologist concentrates on the behavior of the individual; and the sociologist on the behavior of the class, caste, or other definable group. Such special disciplines yield increasingly accurate data and, more important, superior tools for the analysis of complex problems within a deliberately limited context. Their quantitative techniques can best be applied to the recent history of highly developed societies, because these are the societies for which it is possible to collect accurate quantitative data. But an analysis, for example, of urban social structure in a contemporary industrial city will surely throw some light on the nature of cities in general. The more intelligently the sociologist has defined the limiting factors in his own results, the greater the chances that a historian can make an accurate partial analogy to earlier urban conditions. Certainly my own note packets contain at least as much material from journals of economics, political science, and sociology as from historical journals.

However, life cannot be understood in cross section only, and the partial aspects of reality revealed by the various scholarly disciplines must somehow be placed in the total human context. Whenever reading past history or current politics, I am struck by the role of contingency. Analyses of the market economy and the managerial revolution greatly help one to understand the several "economic miracles" which have occurred since World War II, but they do not explain why the Japanese economy has developed so much more rapidly than the French. To take a more limited, and agonizing, example: the computers in the Pentagon undoubtedly supply the President's military chiefs with accurate information about a great variety of possible military courses and their probable consequences; but a man, the President, decides whether or not Hanoi shall be bombed.

No matter how much data can be brought to bear concerning a single public event, the historian who tries to interpret that event must reckon with the accidents of personal and group character, the contradictory desires and choices of the moment, and the sequence in which related events have occurred. This is why chronology and narrative are so crucial to the writing of history, and also why historians cannot deal exclusively with objective factors. Relatively speaking, for the social scientist quantifiable data and abstract models will be more important than individual cases. For the historian the primary emphasis must fall on the specific sequence of events: What happened? Who did what? In what circumstances? With what motives? Quantifiable data and repeated patterns of behavior will undoubtedly serve to explain a great deal of what has happened. But it will always be necessary to understand individual idiosyncrasies and unique contexts. This latter principle applies to scientific and artistic events quite as much as to political history. It is significant that Dr. Freud discovered the immense role of the subconscious while dealing with symptoms of hysteria among middle-class women in late nineteenth-century Vienna. It is likewise significant that the concept of the brain as a data-processing system developed from physiological experiments proving the electrical nature of brain activity, and that the analogies between brains and electronic machines have influenced both the design of computers and the design of psychological experiments.

The above example may also be used to illustrate my third point, the value of history as a stimulus to the imagination. From the moment when the first primitive men, helpless to control their environment, created gods of fire and flood, men have been reasoning from the appearances and knowledge of their surroundings to the appearances and knowledge of their inner lives. It is a joyful and liberating experience, one which stretches the individual's conception of human possibilities, to learn how variously human beings have responded to different conditions. I will mention several examples from my own teaching experience.

Alert students are always puzzled and intrigued by the evidence of homosexuality in parts of the *Iliad* and in the Platonic dialogues. Everything in their own cultural background makes them tend to laugh at, or scorn, or hide such practices. But were Achilles and Patrocles "fairies"? Did the guests at Plato's banquet waggle their hips at one another? If the students read some of the political and biographical literature of the Greek city-states they learn that the Greek "man in the street" scorned homosexuals, but just as clearly they see that homosexuality was tolerated, that it did not cause the reactions of moral outrage which it has constantly aroused in the modern West. It is a broadening, truly liberal and liberating, experience for American students, especially those from Midwestern towns and suburbs, to learn that sexual deviations were generally tolerated, if not necessarily admired, in one of the supreme civilizations thus far created by man.

A profound broadening of perspective on race relations often occurs when students have an opportunity to compare the nineteenth-century expansion of the United States with that of the Russian and Brazilian empires. They know that the United States repeatedly signed solemn treaties with the Indians and later proceeded to despoil them of their lands. They know that for the westward-pressing pioneers the only good Indian was a dead Indian, that in general the Indians who resisted were killed, and that the remainder were placed on reservations. They feel that all this was "too bad" from a humane standpoint. However, since the Indians were primitive, illiterate, often warlike, and since their hunting economy required absurdly large amounts of land to support a very small population, was it not inevitable that the white pioneers should push them off that land?

In nineteenth-century Russia an eastward expansion of white Muscovite control took place across the thinly populated plains of Siberia. These too were inhabited by illiterate tribes of hunters and herdsmen, racially different from the invading Europeans, and just as incapable as the American Indians of understanding Western concepts of private property. We do not know in detail about the Russian settlement of Siberia, but we do know that there was no such wholesale decimation of the native population as with the Great Plains Indians. And it is evident from the racial composition, and from the absence of racial tension, in modern Siberia that Russian administrators, farmers, businessmen, miners, and railroad builders did not hesitate to marry Siberian women. The evidence of this phenomenon alone is enough to suggest to American students that civilized men establishing themselves in a large area formerly inhabited by primitive men do not necessarily have to exterminate or quarantine the indigenous population.

The case of nineteenth-century Brazil is equally illuminating. The semitropical areas of Brazil, like the southern states before the Civil War, had a plantation economy dependent on the labor of Negro slaves. In United States history every American reads that the multiple economic, political, and moral struggles between the North and the South took on the character of an "irrepressible conflict." Wherever his sentimental sympathies may lie, the average American tends to "learn" from the Civil War and its aftermath (1) that the question of slavery versus freedom could be settled only by war; (2) that Negroes and whites can live peacefully on the same territory only if there are clear physical and social boundaries between the two racial communities.

However, in Brazil slavery was abolished gradually, and without war. For about fifteen years prior to 1889 "the womb was freed," i.e., all children born to slave women became free at the age of twenty-one; and in 1889 slavery was entirely abolished. Furthermore, there was never any question of practicing segregation. The mass of Brazilian Negroes suffered, and to this day suffer, the disadvantages that result from poverty and lack of education. In the competition for economic and social standing they are disadvantaged in the same sense as are Italian or East European immigrants in the United States. But there is no absolute color bar in matters of education, professional opportunity, or marriage. The Brazilian census has long since dropped the various terms formerly used to name groups of the population with differing proportions of white and Negro ancestry. They have done so because no one today can accurately identify the mixtures and because there is no political or ideological desire to perpetuate racial castes of any sort.

In my teaching experience the history of nineteenth-century Brazil is an eye opener for American students. It is not a question of romanticizing a country whose history is laden with poverty and social conflict and whose general economic and health standards are abysmally low, but it is a salutary challenge to inertial assumptions to learn that slavery can be abolished and that a multiracial community can develop without the traumatic conflicts which have accompanied these changes in the United States. If the students notice somewhat similar phenomena in the history of Spanish America, Southeast Asia, and Indonesia, they may be led to a general reversal of assumptions. Instead of supposing that color prejudice is "normal" to the human race they may begin to wonder why color feeling has been so much stronger among Anglo-Saxons than among other human groups.

I have stated that for me the distinctive characteristics of history are the interest in human conduct as a whole and the organization of the data in sequential, narrative form. In preparing to teach or write, I ask myself a rather formidable list of fundamental questions. I might say parenthetically that the pursuit of these questions guarantees me, ideally at least, against boredom and triviality. One of the dangers of a lifetime of professional scholarship is that one gets to know more and more about less and less. A professor can protect himself somewhat against this danger by deliberately choosing to teach a variety of courses rather than confining himself to his specialty. But the strongest safeguard, I think, against becoming merely a retailer of anecdotes, chronological outlines, and bibliographical data is to keep returning to fundamental questions concerning both the areas one knows a lot about and those one is newly studying. These questions are the core of my intellectual baggage.

First of all, to what extent is a given society pastoral, agricultural, commercial, industrial, or—in the circumstances of the rapidly developing electronic and computer revolution—postindustrial? In placing first the question of economic organization, of the "modes of production," I gladly acknowledge the immense influence of Karl Marx, not only on me personally but on thousands of historians and social scientists who may be very decidedly anti-Marxist in their political sentiments. Any careful reader can, of course, separate Marx's insistence on economic structure as the most basic characteristic of a society from his political program. Nor was Marx's insistence a novelty. When Madison and Hamilton in the *Federalist Papers* spoke of "factions," they were pointing to economic and class pressure groups, and they constantly assumed that the most important determinants of a man's political attitudes are the way he makes his living and the extent of his wealth.

The next question is to understand the conscious ideals, religious and secular, by which a given society lives. To what extent are men propitiating the gods, or preparing for an afterlife? Do they aspire to military glory? to absolute equality? to the "pursuit of happiness"? The other side of this coin is equally important, to wit, the assumptions and motives that move men so constantly that they rarely bother to verbalize them. At Knox College I learned how universally Americans think of all men as having conscious "goals" in life. At the end of a Western Civilization course I asked a class of over one hundred students to compare the careers of Socrates, Caesar, and Saint Francis. They had a couple of days to think about the question, and then they wrote their essays, without notes, in the examination room. For the vast majority the most important single thing to prove about each of these men was that he had "goals." Socrates spent his life teaching the Athenians to use words more carefully and to love truth above any other reward that life might offer. Caesar devoted his career to the conquest of Gaul, and then to ending the civil disorder in Rome. St. Francis' goal was to live an ascetic life and to set an example of Christian charity. However accurate or inaccurate their accounts, however crude or subtle their perception of the three individuals, they all saw these great figures as "goal oriented," and clearly, from the essays, it is a very good thing to have goals, whatever those goals may be and wherever they may lead—whether to military dictatorship or to sainthood.

My third question concerns the way in which a society organizes its many activities. What acts are determined by custom, and what activities allow for choice? How much is decided by individuals, by families, by tribes, by class or caste membership, by the state? My students have always begun by assuming that the individual and the state are really all that count in modern civilization. They are surprised to learn that in Europe and in Japan the family still plays a large role in marriages and business partnerships. They are liable to think I am kidding if I ask them whether their church-going and dating habits are matters of custom or individual choice. For myself, I am endlessly puzzled by the relationship between political democracy and social discipline. Apropos of the functioning of political democracy in the United States: How much depends upon the federal form of organization? How much upon the prestige of courts and the rule of law? How much upon the proportion of people participating in elections? How much upon voluntary office holding at the local level? How much upon the "advice and consent" of the economic elites? How much upon the relations between "amateur" elective officials and professional administrators? I ask myself such questions, thinking not just in terms of a cross section or profile but of the evolution of each of the factors over decades.

My fourth question concerns the extent to which a country is dependent upon war, or, to put it more politely, desires to dominate its neighbors. All the world's great nations share a monumental tradition of hypocrisy and self-deception in this matter. Louis XIV bled France white in order to establish her "natural borders" and maintain such sacred principles as French diplomatic primacy in all international ceremonies. In the 1790s and under Napoleon, France claimed merely to be defending the Revolution against its enemies. Neither Kaiser Wilhelm II in 1914 nor Hitler in 1939 acknowledged a taste for war; each was merely defending Germany against "encirclement." When the Soviet army crushed the Hungarian revolution in 1956 it was merely assisting the patriotic Hungarian government to suppress counterrevolutionary banditry. When the United States intervenes repeatedly in Latin America and Asia, it insists, more in sorrow than in anger, that it is regretfully employing force to defend itself against "international communism." Whole peoples have identified themselves with the military glory of their rulers, and the great majority of national heroes are generals or admirals. Yet no nation acknowledges the thirst to dominate its neighbors. History is everywhere taught from a "patriotic" point of view, and school textbooks have as one of their most important tasks the justification of each country's past wars. In order to clear away the multiple self-deceptions of the past and to achieve a world in which men can live at peace, any historian should deal candidly with the degree to which a given society strives to coerce its neighbors.

A fifth fundamental question is the degree to which a society tries to control the lives of its citizens, and to what extent it is able to exercise control. Everyone knows the strong contrast between ancient Sparta and Athens, the former exercising rigid discipline in both military and civil affairs, the latter priding itself on the spontaneous and voluntary nature of both military service and civil government. Out of polemical motives, the contrast has probably been overdrawn, both by the ancient Greeks and by the pro-Spartan and pro-Athenian classicists of the nineteenth century. In countries for which we have more complete information than we have about ancient Greece, the situation appears more complex. The Spanish Empire in the seventeenth century tried to exercise absolute control over religion, political administration, and seaborne commerce. Presumably a Spaniard must be a Roman Catholic, he must obey the decrees of the king or the king's viceroy, and he must not trade with the English except at the annual trade fair at Porto Bello. However, the government had no way of knowing how many of its subjects were practicing Catholics; officials big and little applied the famous "I obey but do not comply" to a host of royal directives; and smuggling was both an honorable and a profitable career. The whole context of Spanish history, from imperial times to the present, suggests that except for an officially designated religion, Spaniards have been pretty free to live their professional and private lives as they see fit.

The Spain of Philip II has often been portrayed by foreign historians as a rigidly authoritarian regime, but it never really tried to establish the degree of control that has been exercised by twentieth-century authoritarian regimes. This is partly because the only orthodoxy it truly cared about was religious orthodoxy, and partly because it did not have the personnel or the means of communication to exercise tight control. No nation in the past has attempted to control its people as completely as the Soviet government under Stalin. The Soviets wanted not only to revolutionize the entire economy but to create a new Soviet man, free of religious "superstition" and differently motivated from the war-making and profit-seeking man of European history. At the same time they met tremendous resistance to the collectivization of agriculture, had to force a nation of peasants to become a nation of punctual and efficient industrial workers, and had to fight a war of survival against Nazi Germany. The combination of immense practical problems and ideological zeal led them to intervene in the lives of their citizens to a degree that no previous government has ever done, and to a degree which they themselves would probably prefer not to repeat in the future.

In speaking of the Soviets I have consistently referred to *attempted* control, because it is clear that they have not created the "new man" and that they are consciously retreating from many of their earlier ideological dogmas. The supreme example of successful manipulation both of the economic resources and the psychology of a people is Hitler's Germany. The Nazis did not try to revolutionize property relations, and they did not try to eliminate religion or replace traditional economic incentives. They were governing a country characterized by high literacy, a dense communications network, and a traditionally disciplined population. They were diabolically successful in attuning their propaganda both to the immediate grievances and the underlying prejudices of the German people.

Since the Allies did not occupy Germany in 1919, most Germans were never convinced that they had really lost World War I. Since the victorious powers wrote into the peace treaty a humiliating and patently untrue statement placing the total responsibility for the war on Germany, no German ever felt the slightest moral commitment to that treaty. Since Germans even in the heyday of nineteenth-century capitalism had been accustomed to a large measure of state control of the economy, they felt no impulse to oppose the Nazi economic decrees. Since they had been nursed for centuries on mythology about Jewish moneylenders, most Germans were not opposed to the spoliation of the Jews between 1933 and 1939 (as against the later mass murder, over which they had as little control as have any and all peoples over the barbarities committed by their leaders in time of war). Once the Nazis had broken the Socialist and Communist opposition they did not have to coerce the German nation to anything like the extent that Stalin had to coerce the masses in Russia. Their Jew baiting, sporadic anti-Christian propaganda, tight currency control, press censorship, and their purge of German intellectual and artistic life did not arouse any such massive opposition as did the collectivization of agriculture in Russia.

The regimes of Hitler and Stalin have, for different reasons and among different people, raised the specter of overwhelming governmental power. Everyone is conscious today of the fact that a Stalin could deport and execute his own people by the tens of thousands and that a Hitler could make the German people an unresisting instrument of world conquest and genocide. But these are only the most dramatic instances of the question which can fruitfully be studied in connection with all societies: the extent to which governments or social elites control the lives of their citizens or subjects.

A sixth question I ask myself is how a given people view their own history, and how foreigners view that history. The English tend to view their role in European history as the consistent defense of religious liberty and national sovereignties against the pretensions of Habsburg or Bourbon or Hohenzollern empires. To the Irish, however, they are the oppressor who tried doggedly over centuries to extirpate the national religion. And to many Europeans England's foreign policy seemed designed simply to keep Europe sufficiently divided so that British power would be the decisive factor in any major European contest. The Spanish conquistadors saw the hand of God in their rapid victories and assumed that in bringing Christianity to America they had earned the right to any material and human spoils on which they could lay their hands. To the Indians they were incomprehensibly powerful demons who destroyed everything they touched and could be propitiated only by immense quantities of gold and silver bullion. Nineteenth-century Russia was, for the Orthodox, Holy Mother Russia, undefiled by the materialistic corruption of the West. To the Western European countries she was a backward, superstitious giant, and to the Poles she was the national oppressor against whom the smaller people had to fight a constant battle for survival. Examples of this sort could be multiplied at will, and no one can understand history without being aware of how differently the same past can be interpreted by observers who start from different memories and assumptions.

The above questions all have to do with broad interpretation and perspective. It is equally important, however, to study key personalities and leadership groups in as much specific detail as possible. In the largest perspectives, personalities and ideologies may not appear so significant. In ten thousand years of human history the invention of the plow, or the use of the wheel, or the development of accurate clocks is indeed more significant than any individual or national role. Even in shorter perspectives this will often be the case. The United States would surely have become a great industrial nation in the late nineteenth century regardless of who became President or what religion was professed by whom. Twentieth-century Russia would also have entered the industrial era, with or without Joseph Stalin.

But the more one focuses on a short series of events the more he will find himself dealing with individual character and choices. In addition, the more complex the broad pressures and conflicts, the more crucial will be the role of individuals. It is often said that one must not try to study history in terms of "might have beens." However, one can also deceive himself with a false sense of inevitability if he does not ask whether at critical moments events might not have taken a different course in the hands of different people. I believe that United States history would have been very different if George Washington, instead of being a completely honorable and civilian-minded statesman, had had the ambitions of a Napoleon. In the latter case we might have inaugurated a tradition of maximum centralization and military dictatorship. I believe that in the 1930s Germany would surely have denounced the Versailles Treaty and rearmed and that she might quite possibly have made war on her neighbors, but I cannot conceive the genocide without the personalities of Hitler and his immediate entourage. I believe Russia would have industrialized in the twentieth century regardless of her form of government. However, I cannot conceive the speed of that industrialization, and its accomplishment virtually without foreign aid, except as a result of the program and discipline of the Communist party, taken together with the driving, dogged leadership of Stalin. If one then merely asks himself how different recent European history would have been without Hitler and the SS chiefs, and without Stalin and the Communist party, he cannot fail to see how enormously important key people and groups can be. Meaningful history must always be the history of persons, not simply the interplay of "objective factors."

The historian, then, will be constantly searching to understand the working relationships among the broad forces and ideals in a given society. He will need to understand the motives and the role of key people and groups. He will have to deal with events in roughly chronological sequence and will need to synthesize broad characteristics and concrete details into a comprehensible narrative. In doing this he will have to select a relatively small proportion of the available facts; he will have to decide on the tone to adopt in speaking of different phenomena, and the weight to give each factor within the total "mix."

This means that the most important single characteristic of a historian, without which all his technical skill will be worthless, is intellectual honesty. It is perfectly possible to construct a factually correct work of history, displaying incontestable erudition and complete with bibliography and footnotes, which will nevertheless give an extremely misleading impression of the events described. For the major nations since the invention of printing, the data is rich enough so that a historian with fixed prejudices or political aims can almost always find the evidence he needs to confirm his previous beliefs. The literature of highly controversial subjects such as the Reformation or the French Revolution shows that Catholics and Protestants, Royalists and Jacobins, can produce equally accurate but misleading, or simply *uncomprehending,* versions of the same events. At the other end of the scale, the data are so incomplete that historians can plausibly attribute particular cruelty or particular military efficiency to the Babylonians or the Assyrians or the Hittites, without anyone knowing enough to give a convincing final answer.

It is impossible for the historian to come anywhere near fulfilling the witness's oath to tell "the whole truth," and it will be extremely difficult for him, in constructing a narrative, to tell absolutely "nothing but the truth," though he can closely approach the latter ideal. He cannot tell the whole truth either because the amount of data is so overwhelming, as in contemporary history, or because it is so spotty, as for most of ancient history. He cannot tell nothing but the truth because in selecting data and putting it into narrative form he must make all kinds of decisions which in the last analysis are based on unprovable hunches as to significance and motive. There are two things he can do: he can demand of himself the most equitable, unbiased selection of which he is capable in dealing with a mass of detailed evidence, or he can indicate to the reader, by way of a preface or in the web of the narrative itself, his methods of selection and his ideological and emotional commitments. In the end it is a matter of intellectual honesty, which must be as habitual as his literacy, his taking notes, or his typing a draft.

One further point I would like to emphasize under the rubric of intellectual baggage is the importance of personal experience. Assuming a broad general interest in human conduct and the intellectual stimulus of wondering how the past may illuminate the present, there is still the question of the extent to which a person can understand experiences through which he has not lived. When I went to Spain in 1960 my direct preparation for the writing of *The Spanish Republic and the Civil War* consisted of my graduate studies plus the reading of the voluminous book and pamphlet literature available in the Harvard University Library and the Library of Congress. I did not come of Spanish ancestry, and I knew personally only a few dozen Spaniards. But many aspects of my personal experience helped me understand what I had read, and then what I heard and saw on my travels.

I am a Jew, and during my high school years I was religious in formal as well as intellectual terms. Later I grew away from all sectarian doctrines, and I believe that my own religious evolution prepared me to understand the heterodox currents in modern Spain. I could only accept a religion which was truly universal in spirit, and so the doctrine of the Chosen People had made me dissatisfied with Judaism. In a similar way the emphasis on the sacraments and on the unique power of the Church to prepare the soul for salvation had alienated men such as Francisco Giner de los Ríos and the many intellectual leaders associated with the Institution Libre de Enseñanza. Some of these men had simply ceased to be practicing Catholics; others had become avowed anticlericals; still others glorified the sixteenth-century Church and asserted that the contemporary Church was an anachronism. I could understand the nuances of all these positions by analogy to things I had thought or heard in connection with Judaism.

Being Jewish may also have helped me understand the uncertainty and the self-consciousness of the Spanish Republicans of both the moderate Right and the moderate Left. Jews, even in a period of maximum toleration, cannot help realizing that they are thought of as "different." The phenomenon is hard to pin down. At a local level it will take the form of objections to having Jews move into a certain area or join a certain club. At a more general level it will be repetition of old myths about money grubbing or dark hints of what the Soviets have dubbed "rootless cosmopolitanism." In any case Jews always live with a definite margin of uncertainty as to how their neighbors really fell about them, and with considerable anxiety as to what forms hostility toward them may take in times of social tension. The Spanish Republicans were always conscious of the fact that their doctrines were imported. They were consistently snubbed by the aristocracy, and their popular support was constantly threatened by anarchist and religious demagogy. They too lived with a definite margin of uncertainty as to the underlying feelings toward them of much of the population.

The history of the Spanish Republic is full of ideological debate. All the varieties of fascism, liberal democracy, and Marxism had their press and their party organization. At home as a boy, and then in college between 1938 and 1942, I had become familiar with the whole gamut of doctrines, applied principally to the United States, Russia, and Germany. But the same knowledge became readily applicable in studying Spain. And as I had held various positions in student government, both in high school and in college, these experiences helped me understand cabinet factions and inner party debates.

In the army as an enlisted man and aircraft mechanic and later as a cartographer, I had lived for four years on intimate terms with a variety of skilled factory and white-collar workers. This experience aided me to interpret the demands and attitudes of the elite of the Spanish industrial working class. Similarly, my career as a teacher and part-time musician enabled me to understand the educational program, and in particular the *misiones pedagógicas* sent out into the countryside in 1933 and 1934 with plays, concerts, cheaply printed books, and pharmaceutical supplies. I had played in the Vermont State Symphony Orchestra and knew how it felt to perform the classics in a rural high school auditorium for an eager audience which otherwise heard nothing but the jukebox.

Perhaps more important for central problems of interpretation were some of my political experiences of the 1950s. Before the late Julius and Ethel Rosenberg, convicted of atomic espionage, were executed, I asked a number of friends and acquaintances to sign a clemency petition. I may have been right or wrong in thinking that the evidence did not remotely justify the death penalty in time of peace. What surprised me, and what I reflected on for many years, was the violence with which many apparently reasonable and liberal people refused even to consider the petition. People who had seen lifetime professional spies politely exchanged after a few months in jail wildly demanded the blood of two rank amateurs who had been convicted principally on the testimony of Mrs. Rosenberg's embittered brother, in a trial replete with political passion. I remember one friend in particular who was literally unable to eat his dinner after I had shown him the petition.

Seven years later, in 1960, just before leaving for Spain, I sold my house in Natick, Massachusetts, to a Negro engineer. There were threats of blocking the mortgage and breaking the windows. The unprintable names, the stories about rape in taxicabs, and the accusations that I was making a few thousand dollars under the table go without saying. At a neighborhood meeting in my house I related the buyer's professional position, his family and religious ideals, all of which would have made them proud to welcome him if they could have forgotten his color. Only two out of sixteen neighbors would shake hands with me after that meeting. Most of the families on the block were Catholic, and so was my buyer. I called the priest to ask his informal aid, but he insisted in a frightened voice that this was not a religious matter and that therefore he should not intervene in any way.

Several months after the move the Negro engineer and his family were not only accepted but very popular. The happy ending does credit to the willingness of people to change their minds in the light of experience. But I felt that I had learned in the flesh, not just by reading about other people's experiences, how people can go berserk when their silent prejudices are suddenly aroused. The Rosenberg petition incident and the sale of my house prepared me to understand the violence of royalist, anticlerical, anti-Masonic, and anticommunist prejudices in Spain and the almost palpable feelings of class hatred, from above and from below.

Although I had had many experiences analogous to events I was studying in Spain, I was aware that my personal past could not help me understand many things I would need to take account of. I had had no experience remotely comparable to that of an aviator or a hereditary aristocrat. I had never known continued hunger or what it means to be illiterate. I felt that a final indispensable portion of my intellectual baggage must be simply to have an attitude as alert and as open as possible to all kinds of human experience. I had done my reading; I knew what questions to ask, and I had some basis for judging the accuracy and the honesty of what people might say to me. The real task now would be to know the living country, and the living people.

3

Introduction to the Right in Madrid

"Welcome to Madrid," said Sr. F., speaking in English, and offering a hearty handshake. He added, with a slight chuckle, "We have all been awaiting your arrival with great curiosity." Sr. F. was one of the Foreign Ministry liaison officers to the Fulbright program. He was a tall, heavy-set but quick-moving individual with a ready, and completely noncommittal, smile. He went on to say that he was an old-fashioned liberal, that he had been to the United States several times, that he found us a very sympathetic but terribly naïve people. He spoke rapidly, and for several minutes I did little more than nod my indications of agreement, understanding, or doubt. He could understand, he said, why liberals like me were so sympathetic to the Republic. The men of the Republic had been well intentioned. They had tried to govern Spain as if it had been England or Belgium, but they failed. They did not understand Spain. They were Anglophiles. They bought their suits from English tailors (he chuckled again), and they agreed with the foreigners who think that the bullfight is a vestige of barbarism. Incidentally, he added parenthetically, and at the same time shifted his discourse to Spanish, the bullfights had to be canceled in Santander this year. Not enough customers. Football, not bullfighting, is the great national sport in Spain now. Without the tourists there would be no more *corridas* . . . He then asked me about our hotel accommodations, which I assured him were fine indeed, and brought his monologue back to the Republic.

"We know why the Republic failed. It simply wasn't suited to the Spanish people. Nobody here is interested any more. In many ways we are ahead of the West. Communism, the Cold War, we know all about it from our war, which finished communism here. You should have brought the Russians to heel ten years ago while you still had an atomic monopoly. The trouble with democracies is that they cannot act decisively to defend themselves. Spain is America's best friend in Europe. You could learn much from us."

"I have come here to learn," I said. "I know very well that documents alone cannot give you the pulse of a people's feeling. I hope the time has come for frank discussion of the past, and certainly it is my aim to write as unbiased a history as I can."

Sr. F. nodded and smiled encouragingly as I spoke. "You will have free access to everything. Mind you," he went on, lowering his voice confidentially, "it would be very difficult for Spanish professors to see everything. The entire Red press has been preserved in the municipal newspaper archives, and you will have a card permitting you to read whatever you like."

He went on to describe in some detail the meetings of the binational commission which had selected this first group of students and professors to come to Spain under the Fulbright exchange program. He said that very powerful objections had been raised against me. The committee of course had my published articles in front of them. The ones on Joaquín Costa were fine. Costa was one of the Generation of 1898 that he, Sr. F., most admired himself. Costa had, he added, been a precursor of the Franco regime in his recommendations on land reform, reforestation, and irrigation. But my article on the Azaña regime in the *American Historical Review* showed how partisan I was, and my study of anarchism—well, he understood why American liberals were attracted to the anarchists, and some of the anarchists were *simpático,* personally, but I was dangerously naïve. Not that this bothered people excessively. But several members had objected vehemently to awarding me, the author of the Azaña article, a faculty research fellowship. Sr. F. gave me to understand that his voice had been very important in arguing that my scholarly credentials entitled me to the award, and that the committee ought to have faith that once I was here I would correct my mistakes of perspective.

The tone of confidential revelation irritated me. It was perfectly possible that some such discussion had occurred. I felt intuitively, however, that Sr. F. would not have been the sort of person to speak in favor of risks. But then, I may have been unjust in so reacting. Officials in any country, and especially in a dictatorship, learn to look and sound noncommittal, but this is no reason to conclude that they never act out of conviction. Still, why should he have told me this story right away? Was it to establish a feeling of collusion, thereby presumably making me readier to accept his guidance? Or did he want to let me know that he was among the minority of regime officials who really did welcome the plan of a foreign scholar to investigate freely the controversial and myth-laden history of the Spanish Republic and the Civil War?

"You have referred to me several times as being naïve," I said. "Whatever my shortcomings, I hope I will justify your action in helping me to get the fellowship. Could we talk a little about the war ourselves, now?"

He nodded eagerly, while also indicating that unfortunately he had another appointment in a few minutes. "But I am at your disposition for the few minutes!"

"I would be interested in your analysis of who supported the military rising and who opposed it in July 1936."

Again he spoke rapidly, saying that the question was a very difficult one, that the situation all over the country had been very confused, that many people did not choose sides at all, they simply went along with the dominant current. But he chose one point to emphasize: that the poorer parts of the country had supported the generals. "You speak of a military rising, and you Americans don't like to see the military in politics. Very well, the military led the rising. We have different traditions, and someone has to lead. But this was not a plot of the rich oligarchy, as you think. I happen to know the country around Ávila. The well-to-do valley farmers were Republican, the hill people joined the Nationalist rising."

He paused to see whether I had understood his point. I said I did not find such a statement surprising. In the Puritan revolution Parliament had been strongest in the developing cities and in the prosperous southern agricultural counties. Church and king had been strongest in the less economically developed western and northern counties. Similarly in the French Revolution, Royalist support had been strongest in Brittany.

Sr. F. appeared to be delighted by my analogies. "Yes," he said, "and do you know why the militia shot so many people in the first days?"

"Not just the militia," I objected, but he went on without stopping to argue the point.

"Because our revolution in 1936 included all the revolutionary impulses which in England and France had been played out centuries ago. That's what people don't understand when they talk about Spanish violence. They forget their own history."

"I could not agree with you more," I replied. "Believe me, I don't try to explain the war by the psychology of bullfights or the opera *Carmen*. We still have lynchings in the United States. I haven't come here with any sense of superiority about how Americans act when their passions are aroused."

"Good," he laughed, getting up and sweeping a few letters into his desk drawer. "I must leave now. But come back soon, and let me introduce you to some of the intellectuals you should know, people who can help you with your research. But be careful," he chuckled, "Spanish intellectuals *cambian de chaqueta,* change their jackets easily. Some of our professors are ex-Communists or Socialists. Some of our top Falangist chiefs are ex-anarchists. Some of them are secret Communists. Be careful."

He rushed off, excusing himself with a cordial handshake. That very evening, quite by accident, I ran into him at a reception in the American Embassy, and his cordiality seemed much more spontaneous than at our first meeting.

"Let me introduce you to one of our most intelligent young diplomats," he said, guiding me across the room by the arm. "An *hombre ponderado,* a reflective man who doesn't talk as quickly as I do." He brought me to a halt before a handsome, quietly confident-looking man of about forty. The diplomat was deeply sunburned, and he related, addressing himself to Sr. F. rather than to me, that he had just returned from two fine weeks of tennis and yachting in San Sebastián. It was clear from his appearance that he had a natural tendency to become paunchy, a tendency favored by the consumption of rich food and checked by athletics. His expression as he turned toward me was at once interested and disabused.

Sr. F. had been telling him that we had discussed the general lineup in the Civil War that morning, and that he had seized the opportunity to put me in immediate contact with a man who had fought in the Nationalist army throughout the war. The diplomat nodded and, without awaiting any question from me, began in measured tones to summarize his thoughts on the war. His manner was both fluent and fatigued, as though he were rehearsing an oft-told tale. His family had been summering in France when the war broke out. He had come home to Vitoria, where he was scheduled to complete his secondary schooling. But, he said, everyone was intoxicated with war fever, no one could study, and boys were constantly trying to run away and join the army.

"We were all crazy in those days," he said, in a tone which conveyed an almost pathetic feeling of nostalgia. Evidently nothing since had touched him in a way remotely comparable to his initial enthusiasm for the war. He recalled several impetuous attacks, with their needless casualties. The thought of death had been something entirely remote, abstract. He and his comrades had been carried along on a wave of religious fervor, he said. They had not known who the various generals were, nor what sort of regime was to follow the victory. They were fighting to defend the Church and the national unity of Spain, and nothing else mattered. I asked him how, retrospectively, in the light of what he now knew, he would justify what was after all a military rebellion against a legitimate and internationally recognized government.

"To be legitimate," he replied slowly, "a government must have control of the streets and must be responsive to public opinion. The Republic was made by the Marañons and the Ortegas, by well-intentioned middle-class intellectuals. But the Republic was never supported by more than the intellectual middle class. They lost control of the situation in a few weeks—to be precise, at the time of the burning of the convents on May 10. The Republicans could not keep order because their actions, especially their attacks on the Church, were not in accordance with the wishes of the Spanish people. Then, of course, October 1934 was the death knell of the Republic. Asturian miners and the Catalan separatists rose in arms against the government, which had proudly proclaimed in its constitution that Spain was a republic of workers of all categories. After that there was no legitimacy. In 1936 any general would have succeeded. All Spain was waiting for someone to end the farce."

From the way in which he said "any general" I got the distinct impression that he was no admirer of the Caudillo. I asked him whether he was a royalist, but he apparently interpreted my question as a request to meet a royalist, since he replied that he believed the royalist leader Sr. A. was here this evening, and he would be glad to introduce me. A few minutes later I found myself seated in a quiet corner next to the very polished, direct, and open monarchist leader, Sr. A.

In this instance too my interlocutor took the initiative in expounding his general position without any preliminary conversation. Beyond a shadow of a doubt, he said, the monarchy was the natural and only form of *convivencia,* of ability to live together, suitable to the passionate and highly individualistic Spanish people. The monarchists had won the elections of April 1931, and the Republic had been installed by street rioters who had prevented the votes from ever being counted in their entirety. I knew as I listened what an extreme distortion of the facts this was. It was true that the counting of the votes had never been completed, and it is true that hundreds of boss-ridden villages automatically turned in monarchist majorities in the municipal elections of 1931. However, King Alfonso XIII, yielding to the pressure of both his intimate advisers and the army chiefs, had recognized in the April elections a plebiscite against himself. He had left the country, urging his followers to accept the new regime for the time being, and the monarchist press during the first months of the Republic had acknowledged the absence of monarchical sentiment. However, I had not come to argue, but to listen to a man whose judgments and perspective I knew in advance would be very different from mine.

The monarchists, he continued, knew from the beginning that the Republic would not be viable. Unfortunately the masses were confused, and the *flojos,* the wishy-washy ones, turned to Gil Robles, who told them that their traditional interests and religion could be accommodated to various kinds of political structure. He proclaimed himself an *accidentalista,* said Sr. A. sarcastically, meaning that forms of government were merely transitory. "But the monarchy in Spain has been the only satisfactory form of government for more than a thousand years, hence no accident."

The Spanish people, he asserted, lost several years through following Gil Robles, but after the criminal Leftist uprising in October 1934 they began to see in Calvo Sotelo the only possible civilian leader who could bring about the Restoration. The military were rudderless, José Antonio Primo de Rivera was *chico,* a nice boy, but only Calvo Sotelo was capable of intelligent political action. "We monarchists organized the rising of July 1936, not the generals, and not the Falange. I was one of fifty couriers working under Calvo Sotelo to coordinate the action of different garrisons. Mola was the only general active in the conspiracy. Franco resisted till almost the end."

"How is it," I asked, "that Franco became the uncontested Caudillo as early as October 1936?"

"Franco was chosen for his prestige within the army. Mola had been a police chief, and many people considered him foxy rather than heroic. Franco was a soldier's soldier. But notice, Franco was chosen for a very carefully defined and limited role, as head of the armed forces and temporary military government. He usurped the title *Jefe del Estado,* head of state."

"Then Franco's government is no more legitimate in your eyes than was the Republic?"

He nodded decisively, and offered to send me full documentation, which he was circulating privately in mimeographed form, documentation proving that Franco had, without the slightest authorization from the rest of the Burgos junta, simply undertaken to refer to himself as *Jefe del Estado.* I found the point interesting but also rather academic as of the year 1960, when our conversation was taking place. Again, rather than argue over a technicality, I wanted to understand his feelings and also his hopes for the future.

"You said earlier that the Spanish people lost valuable years in following the lead of Gil Robles. Do you think they would be ready now, if given the opportunity to express themselves freely, to welcome a restoration, and if so, in the person of whom?"

"I am confident that they would. The revolutionary ideas of the 1930s were the result of momentary passions, not of lasting convictions."

"And is the sentiment for Don Juan, or for his son Juan Carlos, or for the Carlist pretender?"

He dismissed the Carlists as of no numerical importance, but evaded the question of Don Juan versus Juan Carlos by saying simply that the person of the monarch did not matter, the age-old institution mattered.

"But how," I persisted, "do you know the people want a king? Would you advocate a plebiscite?"

"We are not authoritarians," he replied. "That is the big difference between us and the dictatorship. But neither do we believe in *sufragio inorgánico,* in inorganic universal suffrage. Voting is very deceptive. There aren't more than a half million people in Spain who have information, articulate ideas, intimate convictions about politics. Monarchism is a profound underlying sentiment, not a temporary program which you put to a vote." He could tell from my expression that I was not convinced, and he felt dissatisfied with his own exposition.

"Let's not talk about votes. There has never been an election in Spain which clearly demonstrated the people's will. On the contrary, elections in Spain have only caused confusion. Let me give you an example of what I mean when I refer to monarchist sentiment. Last spring one of the princesses, who had been traveling strictly incognito, was recognized in a box at a soccer match. The whole grandstand rose to salute her."

"Could not that be a matter of courtesy more than of political sentiment?" I asked. "Suppose, for example, a universally respected figure like the late Julián Besteiro were to appear suddenly in the stadium. Would not the grandstand rise to salute him?"

"*Los suyos,* his kind," replied my interlocutor. I caught my breath at the tone of his voice. Never had I heard such scorn, such sneering contempt and hatred focused on the pronunciation of two normally neutral words. That one phrase, *los suyos,* expressed perfectly the elitist, terrible, and hopeless because totally unconscious contempt of the traditional Spanish monarchists for the vast majority of mankind. All the talk of *convivencia,* of a form of government consubstantial with the Spanish people for a thousand years, however sincere, was fundamentally a rationalization of their ignorance of and contempt for their fellow Spaniards. Sr. A. was the chief representative in Spain of several West German industrial firms. I wondered how many German and American businessmen received from him their "inside dope" on Spanish politics. The vivid memory of his words made it easier for me later to understand why there are so many Leftists in Spain who, for all that they have suffered, prefer the now attenuated dictatorship of Franco to the thought of a monarchical regime.

The two men with whom I had conversed at some length during the reception, and the others whom I met briefly, were all representatives of the aristocracy or the upper business and financial circles. I was therefore happy the following day to meet several conservatives of more modest social position. Señorita R., a museum curator, was a matronly woman of perhaps fifty, painfully eager to please Americans but also sincere and warmly maternal in feeling. She was extremely helpful to me and to a number of the other Fulbright students concerning practical details of life in Madrid. I did not ask her whether she was a member of the Falange, but she introduced me to a number of Falange personalities and I am sure that her political sympathies were strongly Falangist.

She had lived in Madrid throughout the war, sharing a small apartment with her mother in the barrio de Salamanca, the predominantly middle-class and well-to-do portion of the city. At the end of October 1936, when the armies of Generals Mola and Franco were converging rapidly on Madrid, the high command announced over the radio that they would not shell the Salamanca district. Mola spoke of four military columns and of a "fifth column" within Madrid which would shortly capture the capital. The military assumed, quite correctly, that the largest proportion of their sympathizers lived in or near the designated area. They hoped at that time to take the city without a prolonged struggle, and they naturally preferred not to destroy the homes of their sympathizers. The Republican militia, retreating pell-mell before the better-armed and better-trained Nationalist troops, did indeed seem incapable of any concerted resistance when the fighting took place in open country. But on the outskirts of the city, with buildings to use as fortresses and with an aroused population bringing food and supplies to the front lines, resistance suddenly stiffened. At the same time, on November 7 the first shock troops of the International Brigades stopped the Nationalist advance in the University City.

From November 7, 1936, until the final Republican surrender on April 1, 1939, Madrid was under constant siege. The Nationalists did not shell the Salamanca district. Thousands of people like Señorita R. suffered, as did the whole of Madrid, from food shortages, lack of heat, and, during the early months of the war, the risk of assassination, but at least they were relatively safe from bombardment and their electricity and telephones remained in working order. Lentils were the principal form of nourishment, and the hot plate was the only source of heat. Señorita R. had belonged to Socorro Azul, a group of about five hundred women of Nationalist convictions organized in cells for mutual aid in obtaining food and medical supplies for families of like sympathies. She described how, before going to anyone's apartment, she would telephone. If the reply was: "Yes, we're all home, do come and see us," she would know that the police were there or were expected. If the reply was: "We'd love to see you, but nobody will be home," she took this as a sign to come immediately.

Señorita R. had spent a number of summers in England. She spoke fluent English and had many contacts with English and American charitable societies. As a result of these contacts she received numerous requests to tutor foreign journalists in Spanish. She spoke with unconcealed bitterness about the blindness of her pupils. They had come to see the heroic pueblo resisting fascism. From their hotel rooms, well stocked with alcohol, coffee, and packaged cookies which were utterly unobtainable for a Madrileño, they gloried in a front-line view of the hard fighting in the University City. "All they could think about was resistance to fascism. Not one of them would come with me in the early morning to see a body lying in the street. They didn't want to know the truth about the Leftist assassinations. It would have spoiled their feeling of being on the side of the angels."

Without her having said so directly, I knew that she was challenging me to be willing to see the truth and not to write another liberal paean to the pure cause of Spanish democracy. I did not say all that was on my mind either, but in fact I sympathized strongly with her remarks about the journalists. In reading Hemingway, Vincent Sheehan, and Herbert Matthews I had often felt that, however unintentionally, they sounded like the excited and privileged spectators of other people's suffering. I said only that any war involves enormous suffering for innocent people, that in almost any war, and most certainly in the Spanish Civil War, there were many men of noble convictions on both sides, and that I hoped anything I eventually wrote would reflect this truth.

Señorita R. gave me letters of introduction to three important Falangist intellectuals. Two of them met me in a cafe. They were voluble, hospitable, affable, but obviously had no intention of discussing seriously either the war or the current situation. Most of the conversation consisted of an exchange of anecdotes between them concerning various Falange personalities. Occasionally, with great solemnity, one or the other would turn to me and say, practically in the same words each time, as though carefully indoctrinating a not very bright child: "To understand our war, just imagine that your Civil War had been won by the South instead of the North." They would pause, approve each other's profundity, and return to their anecdotes.

Señorita R. gave me letters of introduction to three important Falangist intellectuals. Two of them met me in a cafe. They were voluble, hospitable, affable, but obviously had no intention of discussing seriously either the war or the current situation. Most of the conversation consisted of an exchange of anecdotes between them concerning various Falange personalities. Occasionally, with great solemnity, one or the other would turn to me and say, practically in the same words each time, as though carefully indoctrinating a not very bright child: "To understand our war, just imagine that your civil war had been won by the South instead of the North." They would pause, approve each other's profundity, and return to their anecdotes.

Señor V., an important columnist and radio commentator, was a much more serious man, the first, and one of the few really convinced, ideological supporter of the regime that I was to meet. He had been a student of philosophy in the late 1920s, under the *dictadura blanda,* the mild dictatorship, of General Miguel Primo de Rivera. He had idolized Professors Ortega y Gasset (Spain's leading philosopher and above all a great prose stylist) and Eugenio D'Ors (art historian of aristocratic and traditionalist predilections). He had been active in student politics, had known and liked his fellow student José Antonio

Primo de Rivera, and had been an ardent member of the Falange from the time of its founding in the autumn of 1933.

Señor V. received me warmly in an apartment furnished almost entirely, and very handsomely, in Spanish Renaissance style. On the beautifully sculptured walnut desk in the middle of his large living room stood framed, autographed pictures of Ortega y Gasset and José Antonio Primo de Rivera. He spoke rhapsodically about both men, emphasizing that they had been the strongest influences in his life. While I admired the furniture and several excellent Velásquez reproductions hanging on the wall, he prepared two concentrated cups of Nescafé, set out a bottle of Carlos III brandy and two Venetian brandy glasses, and offered to discuss fully and frankly any aspects of recent Spanish history that I wished to hear about.

We began with the Republic, which, he said, in 1931 undoubtedly represented not just the will but the accumulated hopes of the Spanish people. However, the Republic had made two capital errors from which it never recovered: it had "stood by while gangs of kids had burned the churches on May 10" and it had refused to accept Gil Robles and Catholic Action members as loyal citizens of the Republic. I asked whether he had belonged to Catholic Action. He replied no, that he had been a member of Ledesma Ramiro's small fascist party and then of the Falange, both of which were secular in orientation, but that he had always been a practicing Catholic, that he had known many Catholic youth leaders, and that he was convinced that the Left had been totally mistaken in accusing Gil Robles and Catholic Action of wanting to replace the Republic with a fascist regime.

"May I interrupt at this point to ask you what you mean by a republic? It is my impression that President Alcalá-Zamora, himself a Catholic conservative, refused to appoint Gil Robles as Prime Minister because Robles would never commit himself to the maintenance of parliamentary democratic rule. As for your own position, you were a partisan of Ledesma Ramiro and then of José Antonio. Did not both these men sneer at parliaments and elections? Did they not both point to the example of Mussolini? What did such men understand by a republic?"

Sr. V. could hardly wait for me to complete my question.

"Spain needed a national revolution, a thoroughgoing revolution. Everything the socialists and the anarchists had been saying about social injustice, inequality, the scandal of rich landlords taking the bread of the poor—on all those criticisms, *de acuerdo,* agreed, one hundred percent. But we needed a *national* revolution, not a Marxist or a Masonic revolution. The King was *mezquino,* a petty man without an ounce of heroism in his soul, without dignity, without any feeling for Spanish traditions. Spain needed a *cirujano de hierro,* an iron surgeon, in the great phrase of D. Joaquín Costa, a man like Ataturk or Mussolini."

He digressed for a moment to tell me that just after the Nationalist victory, in the spring of 1939, he had gone to Rome with a Falange delegation and had been received by Mussolini. He described in a tone of awed enthusiasm Mussolini's tremendous office with its marble floor and its balcony from which the Duce could address his people massed in the square below. "Mussolini was a great man. He was beginning to rebuild Italy in the traditions of Rome and the Renaissance. The Concordat with the Church, the draining of the Pontine marshes, the extension of wheat cultivation, these were just a beginning. He talked to us as the father and guiding spirit of the Italian people, who had achieved their political unity only in 1870 and who needed to be given discipline and national aims worthy of their heroic past. It's too bad that he got mixed up with Hitler. The Nazis were pagans and racists, very different from Mussolini, different from us too.

"To come back to Spain: that was what we, the youth, hoped for, an iron surgeon. Gil Robles was pudgy, completely unheroic, a parliamentary debater, not a leader of men." He pointed to his autographed photo of José Antonio. "Do you see him there with his shirt sleeves rolled back over the elbow? A little detail, but symbolic. We students in the late Twenties felt impatient with all that was petty and anachronistic in

Spain. We wanted to roll up our sleeves and sweep the board clean. Well, in the years 1931 to 1936 we had little choice. It was either government by tired bourgeois like Lerroux and Gil Robles, or government by *invertidos* like Azaña."

"Just a minute," I interrupted, "how do you know that Azaña was a homosexual?"

"By his fat womanish hands, his lack of courage during the Civil War, his face like a toad's. And he married late, much later than a real man would marry." It occurred to me that Sr. V. constantly related fatness with unsympathetic character. He himself was very thin and nervous, with long fingers that were constantly in motion. These were clearly bachelor's quarters in which he was receiving me, and from the shrill hero worship he had lavished successively on Ortega, José Antonio, and Mussolini, I had wondered fleetingly, before his mention of Azaña, whether he was homosexual.

"I certainly cannot accept what you say without some substantial evidence," I said. "Appearances can be very deceiving."

"No, no, Azaña was an *invertido.* It is a tragedy, because he was an able man, but to govern in Spain one must be *muy macho,* very virile."

"And the Caudillo," I asked, "is he *muy macho*?"

Sr. V. laughed, and his voice became much quieter than before. "Franco is different, cold as ice. In the army he always said '*ni misa ni mujeres,*' neither Mass nor women. A very cold man."

I did not pursue the subject of sexual character in relation to political conduct, not because I thought it trivial but because there is so little evidence and so much prejudice to contend with. Suffice it to add that in all countries I have found fascists obsessed with questions of virility and homosexuality. I remarked that I had been struck also by his reference to the Masonic character of the Republic. I told him that I was well acquainted with the works of Eduardo Comín Colomer, for whom the entire Republic was nothing but a Masonic plot. I added that I also realized how, at the time of the French Revolution and in the Latin American independence movements, the Masons had played an important political role. I could therefore understand, historically, why the Church and the partisans of the Old Regime in Catholic lands should have bitter memories of the Masons. "But," I concluded, "Comín Colomer writes as though without the Masons there never would have been a revolution in 1931. Isn't that a gross exaggeration?"

"The Masons are not just a fraternal organization. They are an anti-Catholic international."

"Perhaps so, but they did not create all the problems which you yourself say called for a national revolution. Doesn't it discredit your own interpretation of history so to exaggerate their power? Comín Colomer's stuff reads like McCarthyite witch-hunt material in the United States."

To my surprise, he readily agreed that there had been too much emphasis on the Masons in Nationalist versions of recent Spanish history. "But still, the Masons were like a foreign body in the Spanish bloodstream. Take Portela Valladares, the centrist Prime Minister who dissolved the Cortes in 1935 and gave us the catastrophe of the Popular Front election. Tall, blond, square face, cold expression—he looked like an Englishman, like Ramsay McDonald. He was not *afecto de las cosas españolas,* not fond of Spanish things. The Masons looked to England always, and they were the political agents of England in Spain."

I replied that his feeling struck me as resembling that of many Englishmen toward the Jesuits, whose order has been traditionally feared as a secret international and as the tool of the national enemy, Spain.

"*Exacto.*"

I had felt from the start of our conversation that Sr. V. was being absolutely candid with me. I hoped that he might express himself just as candidly concerning the present as the past, and I asked him directly how far, in his opinion, the national revolution had been carried out. His face fell. He looked like a man who has just been reminded of the death of a beloved relative.

"The *movimiento* of July 1936 was absolutely necessary

to prevent Spain from falling into the hands of Soviet Russia. We needed Franco for that victory, and he also deserves the gratitude of all Spaniards for keeping us out of the Second World War. But the problems of Spain remain entire."

"And the future?"

"I do not know, but I will tell you, and you may be surprised to hear this, a man I admire, and that many Falangists admire, is Tito. We are not reactionaries and we are not antisocialist. The trouble with communism is its atheism and its international domination by Russia, not its economic or political principles. Stalin and Mao are right when they call Tito a fascist, because he is making a national revolution. He has not let his country become the tool or the slavish imitator of Soviet Russia. That is what fascism means to me: social justice within the national framework. We have the national framework, and the *movimiento* has been able to protect Spain from the worst materialist excesses of the West. But we have not yet had our national revolution."

In taking leave of Sr. V. I was conscious immediately of the great value of this interview. I suspected that there were very few veterans of the original Falange who retained, twenty-five years later, anything like his loyalty to the original ideal, and my later experience bore out this anticipation. For a liberal-to-left democrat of American education it was essential to have talked frankly and amicably with an authentic fascist. I could see what he meant, in a Spanish context, by an authoritarian republic. Likewise, though he did not refer to the Austrian regime of Engelbert Dollfuss or the Polish rule of General Pilsudski, I could align his thinking with that of Catholic fascism in the interwar period. His hero worship of José Antonio and of Mussolini struck me as adolescent, with likely homosexual overtones, but as frank and loyal. Similarly, though we did not talk much about art, I sensed both his knowledge of and deep attachment to the Spanish artistic heritage, and was not surprised some months later to see him lecturing to a group of university students at the special Velásquez exhibition in Madrid. His emphasis on Masonry and homosexuality in connection with the history of the Republic was distorted to the point of being ridiculous, but it was important for someone of my background to know that an intelligent and thinking man could truly hold such views. Sr. V. was a columnist. I followed his column fairly regularly in the months after I had met him, and think it appropriate to close this chapter with a paragraph from one of his weekly articles, a paragraph which expresses concentratedly his ideological preoccupations.

> Yes, we must have the courage to recognize the fact: the "free world" is not, in reality, a Christian world. It contains, without a doubt, many fine Christians, such as there are in Poland and in the other countries of Marxist obedience. But the "climate" which the press, radio, and cinema creates under the secret dictatorship of the Masonic International is in no sense Christian. . . . Western man is being converted little by little into an automation, a petty and sordid being, exclusively preoccupied by money, convenience, and pleasure. All are infected by the capitalist disease: they flee from poverty, from service without payment, from sacrifice for ideals, from the sense of life as sacred and heroic. When in this "free world," materialistic to its marrow, they hurl invectives at "Soviet materialism," it would be a matter of laughter were it not cause to weep. And only the thought that above all human madness stands Divine Providence prevents us from becoming desperate.

4

Introduction to the Left

My initial conversation with Sr. F. led within forty-eight hours to a number of other highly informative conversations with personalities of the Right. I had not had any idea what to expect and had been fully prepared for a cautious, evasive, or even hostile reception. I was therefore immensely pleased by the frankness with which a number of people discussed controversial questions with me. Later I was to realize that in these first meetings, and doubtless also in many later interviews with Spanish conservatives, I benefited from my position as a Fulbright scholar and American professor. Those who knew my published work were anxious to influence me. From their point of view my left-of-center liberalism looked like something close to communism. They knew that I was writing a book about the Republic and the Civil War, and they hoped that if I was at all open-minded I would see the Nationalist cause with some sympathy. And as a matter of pride and dignity they were anxious to prove to an American liberal that he could work freely in Spanish archives and talk freely with individual Spaniards, that Spain was truly part of the "free world" and not a reactionary dictatorship.

Those conservatives who did not know my work almost always assumed my conservatism. After all, the United States was Spain's military and political ally despite the disfavor with which most European democratic governments looked upon Franco's Spain. The United States also had a Republican President at this time, in 1960. They reasoned that no Spanish professor would have received a government fellowship unless his attitude toward the regime was correct, and thus by analogy they assumed that I must be a Republican, or at the very least that I was generally favorable to the policies of the Eisenhower government. My conservative personal appearance, which had been a standing joke between my wife and me for years, probably contributed to the impression.

The problem of communicating with the Left was quite different. In the first place it was risky for anyone with a Leftist past to discuss politics with a foreigner. People were no longer being imprisoned or tortured in large numbers in 1960, but hundreds of thousands of veterans of the Republican army were still living on parole, were obliged regularly to report their doings to the police, and were frequently checked on by police spies. No one who had spent the early 1940s in a damp cell or in a prison labor gang was going to risk lightly his still provisional liberty in order to discuss the Civil War with a foreign professor. In addition, many such men, perhaps the majority of them, looked upon the United States with deep resentment and mistrust. They felt, rightly or wrongly, that the Franco dictatorship would have long since disappeared if not for American support.

My experience as a student in Toulouse now became invaluable to me in a way that I could not have foreseen while studying for my doctorate. The city of Toulouse contained a large community of Spanish Republican exiles, and Elizabeth and I had met their children in the corridors of the Faculty of Letters. In the course of the year we had formed friendships which, a decade later, enabled me to receive indispensable letters of introduction. In particular, the late Gabriel Pradal, municipal architect of Madrid in 1936 and in the 1950s editor of *El Socialista* in Toulouse, was responsible for my later meeting the Socialist chief Indalecio Prieto, the Basque Nationalist leader and Republican Minister of Justice Manuel de Irujo, and many a less famous but very helpful witness to the events about which I was writing.

Also as students in 1950 and 1951 my wife and I had attended social functions of the Jeunesse Progressiste. Most of the members of this youth organization were Communists or fellow travelers. They were also the students with the strongest sense of social responsibility and the broadest cultural interests. They were delighted to meet two Americans who obviously did not share the anticommunist obsessions or the "American century" complex which they had found in their earlier contacts with our compatriots. We shared their criticism of the militarist, imperialist, and racist characteristics that were so unhappily evident in American foreign policy. At the same time we did not hesitate to say that we found their faith in the purity of Soviet intentions rather naïve. In the course of friendly arguments with the Jeunesse Progressiste we met our then fellow student, now one of the world's leading García Lorca authorities, Marie Laffranque. After we had become close friends, and were in fact traveling in Italy together, she told us that she had been curious about us from the moment of our arrival in Toulouse but that she had not wanted to meet us until after she heard us discussing civil rights in a way that showed that we were completely antiracist.

As a by-product of such friendships my wife and I came to know, and to be able to share without awkwardness, a standard of living which was indeed very modest relative to what we had previously known as Americans. We became accustomed to rooms furnished only with straight-backed wooden chairs, to twenty-watt bulbs in unshaded ceiling lamps as the only source of light in a living room, to normal indoor temperatures of sixty-five rather than seventy-two degrees, to weekly or biweekly showers in a public bath house, and to pension rooms without hot water. To begin with, this had largely been a matter of "when in Rome, do as the Romans do." But we gradually came to realize that our living on a scale comparable to that of the French and Spanish-exile students was a substantial factor in our being able to establish spontaneous, unself-conscious communication with them. Ten years later in Spain the Toulouse experience made me a potential equal and friend to people who otherwise could not have thought of me except as a representative of "filthy rich" America.

In the same briefcase flap with my Fulbright credentials I had a letter of introduction to the science editor of one of the important Madrid publishing houses. D. Umberto received me immediately, but having a number of details to attend to, hoped that I would find interesting the several technical publications which he put before me. I was more interested in watching him, however, than in reading about the prospects of the Spanish automobile industry. He was a man of medium height but could not have weighed more than a hundred and twenty pounds. His expression reminded me of intellectually eager, sallow-complexioned night-school students whom I had taught years before. His nose and jawbone looked as though at any moment they might break through the taut skin. His black eyes danced behind metal-rimmed spectacles and were strikingly liquid by comparison with his dry cheeks and thin lips. He spoke fluently to his colleagues in a quiet, well-modulated voice, yet his jaw muscles were in constant nervous motion, as though in fact he experienced difficulty in bringing out his words. His posture, both sitting and standing, was erect, almost military, and the rigidity exaggerated the frailty of his chest and the narrowness of his shoulders. I felt suddenly ashamed of my good health and of the random luck to be an American professor, able to write a book that I wanted to write and enjoying the necessary fellowship support to do so.

After D. Umberto had locked his desk and ceremoniously shaken hands with his associates, we walked halfway across Madrid to his favorite cafe, and here our real conversation began. Although I told him I was interested primarily in his personal testimony, he spoke first about books. Marx and Engels on the Revolution of 1868, he said, were indispensable for understanding the Spanish Republic of the 1930s: that everything they had written about the timidity of the middle class and the weakness of the parliamentary parties applied to 1931–6 as fully as to 1868–73. He also highly recommended the memoirs of the Italian Socialist leader Pietro Nenni. He, Umberto, had fought at the Somosierra in July 1936 and could vouch for the accuracy of Nenni's account in both its military and political details. I ought also, he continued, to read everything of Joaquín Arraras and Comín Colomer, two of the most prolific right-wing historians of the Civil War. Their voices were shrill, and they distorted many things, but they also reported facts not available elsewhere. For much the same reason I ought to read *ABC* for the entire Republican period. It was a thoroughly reactionary paper, but it had the money to pay Spain's best writers for feature articles and its editors were intelligent and literate.

Only after I had obediently taken note of his bibliographical suggestions did he gradually move toward his own experience. He had been a student at the Madrid faculty in 1936 and had volunteered, along with all his friends, at the moment of the military rising. After fighting in the Sierras north of Madrid he had gone to officer training school on the Mediterranean coast and then returned in January 1937 to the Jarama front, south of the capital. He had served there till the end of the war, in March 1939, and then had spent some eight months in a prison labor battalion. Throughout his account, which I had no need to interrupt with questions, he emphasized that his had been a quiet front and that he was telling me only of things which he knew at first hand.

In January 1937 they spent their time digging trenches in the hard, windswept Jarama Valley. That, and close order drill, he said with a smile, were the only available occupations. A few men had pistols, but the only real armament consisted of the *lanzabombas,* primitive grenade catapults which were made in numerous small Madrid metal shops and delivered to the front by bicycle or taxi. It was therefore very lucky that the Nationalists had not attacked in that sector until February. In the meantime several anarchist battalions had arrived to replace the Madrid militiamen whom D. Umberto had found on his arrival as a newly commissioned officer. The anarchists were well armed with recent Czech and World War I German machine guns which they had confiscated at the Pyrennean border posts. Many hours daily during the second half of January were devoted to the delicate task of getting the anarchists to make their arms available to the army.

He described the anarchists as alternately distrustful and

childishly dependent. It was necessary first to convince their leaders, and the best means to this end was to remind them constantly that their national chiefs had taken portfolios in the Largo Caballero government, thereby acknowledging the necessity of active political cooperation among all the elements of the Popular Front. Also, though the anarchists were not people to make up their minds on practical grounds, it was a fact that they had very little ammunition. The only machine gun bullets available were Russian. Soviet technicians had arrived to rebuild the Czech and German guns so that they could fire Russian ammunition. Whether or not the anarchists were inwardly ready to accept a unified war government, they had to turn over their guns to be rebuilt by the Soviet specialists.

At this point I interrupted to ask him his opinion of the degree of Soviet influence in the Republican zone. It was tremendous, he replied, not only because the tanks, planes, and bullets were Russian but because people felt deeply grateful to the Soviet Union as the only major power which would lift a finger for the Republic. But he urged me not to be sidetracked by all the polemics about communism. The key leaders were Socialists, and the key party was the Socialist party. The evolution of the most active groups, the industrial workers and the students, could be traced in the varying fortunes of Prieto, Caballero, and Negrín. In the first days of the Republic, Prieto had been especially popular with the railroad workers, miners, and steelworkers of northern Spain. They had expected nationalization and utopian wage raises, but when as a minister Prieto had resisted these demands, he had lost standing with the workers. The mass of the party were counting on Largo Caballero in 1936: because he was more proletarian than Prieto, because he had adopted a revolutionary program, and because he was the only leader of national standing whom the anarchists would trust. Then in early 1937 Caballero proved to be a poor administrator and embroiled himself with the Russians just when their help was most crucial and their "public image" most favorable. So the party had turned to Negrín, who could get along with the Russians and who could reassure the middle classes and the peasants who were reacting against the revolutionary behavior of the Left Socialists and anarchists.

"In 1938," he concluded his exposition, "the image of Negrín completely effaced those of Prieto and Largo Caballero. His peace proposals were called Negrín's thirteen points, the main course in our one daily meal consisted of 'lentils of Negrín,' and all of us in the army were 'sons of Negrín.' This evolution is the key to wartime politics."

The objectivity of D. Umberto's manner and language was such that I could not be sure where his sympathies lay. On grounds of efficacy and persistence I suspected that he would lean toward Negrín. But except for a bit of light sarcasm in regard to the anarchists he avoided personal judgments. Nor did I know how much actual fighting he had done. He was certainly not a man to exaggerate either his own role or his knowledge.

After a short pause he had a question for me. He said that in February 1939 morale was still high among the troops on the Madrid front, and that one reason for this was a constantly bruited report that a shipment of American aircraft engines was about to be unloaded at Valencia. Did I have any information on this point? I could only reply that it sounded to me like the sort of rumor which seems plausible and which people seize on in desperate circumstances, but that I had never read of American arms arriving in 1939 and I doubted very much whether any had been shipped from the United States after the revision of the Neutrality Act in 1937. D. Umberto acknowledged that U.S. sympathy had always stopped short of military aid to the Republic. But, since Winston Churchill had changed his mind and called for support of the Republic at the time of the Battle of the Ebro, and since Henry L. Stimson had publicly stated in January 1939 that U.S. policy had been mistaken, he thought it possible that aircraft engines might have been shipped at the last minute, and he urged me to look further into the question.

The subject of possible American aid brought us to the question of the attitude of the Western powers toward the

Republic, and the consequences of that attitude. D. Umberto thought the democratic powers had acted foolishly in terms of their own interests, that Hitler could never have launched World War II if the fascists had not been permitted to conquer Spain. He said all this without noticeable emotional feeling. The facts were the facts. He was not distributing praise and blame. But I, seeing the absence of any egotism or taste for petty anecdotes, wanted to have his testimony on whatever controversial matters he would consider himself qualified to comment on. I therefore asked him about the incidence of Leftist terrorism in Madrid.

The topic was obviously both familiar and unpleasant to him. His throat muscles worked nervously for several moments before he answered. The worst months, he said, had been August to November 1936. The principal classes of victims had been *esquiroles,* strikebreakers, and owners of small businesses. He specified small businesses on the grounds that most of the murders were committed from motives of personal vengeance, and that in this sense the boss of a small shop was more vulnerable than the distant entrepreneur in a factory. There were also instances, which he thought were common enough, in which priests had been murdered because they had identified themselves completely with anti-Republican and anti-Left forces.

Having acknowledged the terrorism of the extreme Left, he insisted on the necessary corrective to the many "objective" discussions of Civil War terror which made no distinction between the two sides and which concluded by saying, in effect, a plague on both your houses. He laid great stress on two points: that the government had constantly broadcast instructions over the radio, warning people not to open their doors at night to unknown callers and to report all threats of violence to the municipal police; and that the government had unofficially encouraged foreign embassies to rent extra buildings and had not only permitted but actively aided many known rightist personalities either to take refuge in the embassies or to leave Spain altogether.

He himself had once called the police to help him prevent

a group of anarchists from breaking into an Augustinian *colegio*. After dissuading the anarchists, the police had arrested D. Umberto, with his full consent, and imprisoned him for several weeks to protect him from any attempt on his life by those whom he had frustrated at the entrance to the *colegio*. Many innocent people had died during those months because the government could not discipline the primitive revolutionaries, but many had also been saved by a little energy and courage at the critical moment. Anyone wanting to judge fairly the whole question of terror should remember, he insisted, that the terror was conducted officially in the provinces under military rule, that no one had been permitted to seek refuge in the consulates of Seville or Vigo, and that when Franco entered Madrid there was no question of permitting Leftists to seek refuge in the embassies which had housed thousands of Rightists for over two years.

I asked D. Umberto whether he felt that the Spanish regime as of 1960 was a regime resting on terror. "Not for those who are under forty and who are apolitical," he replied quickly. "And not for women. Even during the worst periods they did not harrass the families of imprisoned men. But for anyone who fought in the Republican army and has not specifically repudiated his past, the danger is permanent." He went on to say that even if full political freedom were to be restored tomorrow, he would wait several years before taking any public stand lest the change be merely temporary, just long enough for the government to identify its enemies. He added that we were sitting at this particular table because he could trust our waiter not to report what he had heard, that he would never have had such a conversation in his office or at another cafe.

The next afternoon, using another of my letters of introduction from the Toulouse community, I met a very different sort of "internal exile." D. Julián had been a professional officer. He came of a small landowning family in the Córdoba district, had been a young admirer and then a personal friend and political supporter of Niceto Alcalá-Zamora, the first president of the Republic. Like his political chief, D. Julián was

Catholic, Andalusian, and petit-bourgeois. He had been a technical aide to Azaña when the latter was Minister of War, and he was proud of his part in designing the army reform laws of 1931 and 1932. He was one of the few men who were elected to all three of the Republican Cortes, a success which can be attributed in part to his known moderation and in part to his membership in the landed gentry of a conservative rural conscription.

Like many Republicans of parliamentary loyalty but conservative beliefs, D. Julián had opposed the Popular Front majority which impeached President Alcalá-Zamora in April 1936. Three months later, at the outbreak of the Civil War, he felt unable to support the Popular Front government but was also unalterably opposed to military government. He escaped from Spain on an Argentine cruiser and worked as a baker in Buenos Aires until 1946. He was currently engaged in the construction business in Madrid. He did not go into detail about his present economic position, but from the horror with which he spoke of his days as a baker, and from the comfortable furnishings of his apartment, I assumed that Francoist friends from prewar days must have helped him re-establish himself after his return to Spain.

D. Julián was a portly man with bushy eyebrows, a loquacious, meridional temperament, and very strong convictions. He had a small spitz who listened to the conversation, barked at me whenever his master became excited, did not obey D. Julián's summons to be quiet, but was very friendly to me as soon as I scratched his head. According to D. Julián, the capital error of the Republic had been its failure to apply a radical land reform. In 1932, when General Sanjurjo had attempted a *pronunciamiento,* the landed nobility had been heavily implicated. The Cortes had hastily voted the confiscation of their estates, but had failed to carry it through. D. Julián thought that Fidel Castro had learned from the Spanish error, and he spoke with firm approval of the Cuban land reform being carried out in 1960. When I expressed mild surprise that a Catholic conservative follower of Alcalá-Zamora should speak in such terms he replied quite simply that experience had made him much more radical today than he had been in the 1931–6 era.

D. Julián was the first of a number of Spaniards I was to meet who had become more radical rather than, as one usually assumes, more conservative with age. In 1931–6 he had been a Catholic conservative Republican. In 1960 he remained, in his manner, dress, religion, and social habits, much the same Andalusian conservative that he had been during the time of the Republic. But in political conviction he had moved consciously to the Left. I was immediately curious to ask him for his interpretation of the most crucial single crisis in the five-year history of the Republic: the Asturian revolution of October 1934.

But before moving to that question I must summarize for the reader the political background of the crisis. The Spanish Republic had been governed from April 1931 to October 1933 by a coalition of Left Republicans and Socialists; and from October 1933 to September 1934 by the Center-Right coalition, which had won the fall elections in 1933. Throughout this three-and-one-half-year period the anarchists, the monarchists, much of the professional officer corps, and the Church hierarchy had each, for reasons of their own, never accepted the legitimacy of the new regime. In Spanish political jargon of the preceding half-century the word "republic" had often been used as a joking synonym for general chaos. It was therefore of the highest importance that the Republic of 1931 prove itself capable of governing in an orderly, constitutional manner. The success of that Republic would depend squarely on the support of the urban and rural middle class (both Catholic and non-Catholic), the socialist workers, and the proponents of regional autonomy in Catalonia and the Basque country.

In September 1934 a serious parliamentary crisis within the Center-Right majority arose over a combination of issues including land reform, educational policy, police repression of strikes, and regional autonomy. The logical candidate for Prime Minister at this time was undoubtedly José María Gil Robles, leader of the CEDA, the Catholic bloc which was the largest single unit within the governing coalition. However,

President Alcalá-Zamora and the entire Left, both Republican and Socialist, completely distrusted Gil Robles because he had employed fascist slogans and propaganda techniques and had refused ever to affirm his loyalty to the Republic as such, even though he insisted that he would use only legal means to gain power and govern. Caught between his fear that Gil Robles might lead Spain to fascism and his obligation to let the parliamentary majority govern, the President refused the Prime Ministership to the CEDA chief but offered his party three posts in the new cabinet. The Socialists and the Catalan autonomists believed that any CEDA participation in the executive branch would lead inevitably to fascism. Conscious of the way in which Mussolini, Hitler, and the Austrian dictator Dollfuss had all come to power "legally," they called for a general strike to prevent the formation of a government that would include the Catholic bloc.

The general strike failed, but the Asturian miners fought the police, and then the Moors and the Foreign Legion, for almost three weeks, creating for the Left a heroic legend comparable to that of the Paris Commune and for the Right a hysterical fear of "Red" revolution. The government's repression of the Left, affecting thousands of individuals who had taken no part in either the strikes or the fighting, virtually created the Popular Front which won the elections of February 1936—the last elections before the Civil War. The October Revolution then had indeed been the most important single crisis in the history of the Republic. From my reading I knew that all historians, both Right and Left, had recognized it as the harbinger of the Civil War. I was conversing with a man who had sat in all three Cortes and had been a personal friend of the then President of the Republic. Never in my life had I felt more eager to ask a direct question.

"In view of what you have just said about General Sanjurjo and Fidel Castro, I wonder whether you would approve, in retrospect, the revolt of the Asturian miners in October 1934?"

D. Julián leaned forward to emphasize his reply. "It would have been totally unnecessary if the government had carried through a real land reform in 1932. However, I am sure also that Alcalá-Zamora would, under any circumstances, have refused to hand power to Gil Robles. He believed that behind Gil Robles were the monarchists and the fascists, whatever Robles might protest to the contrary. I think the President was right."

"Then you agree with the Left that the rising was justified as a means of preventing fascism in Spain?"

"Not entirely. The President had to permit the CEDA to enter the government, since they were the largest bloc in the Cortes. His idea was to recognize the rights of the CEDA within a democratic framework, but to refuse power to Gil Robles as an individual. In October the Left were convinced that if the CEDA entered the government at all, the result would be fascism. I think they misjudged the President, but I can understand their fear. I cannot condemn the rising, which, like all Spanish Leftist revolutions, was much less bloody and cruel than the Rightest repression which followed."

"But didn't that rising by the Left give the militarists a perfect excuse, in advance, for their own overthrow of the Republic in 1936?"

D. Julián looked at me scornfully. "Those gentlemen never needed an excuse. Did they not join Sanjurjo in his *pronunciamiento,* long before there was any threat of revolution from the Left? No, only the fascists would use October 1934 as a justification for the military rebellion of July 1936. October 1934 should have warned the government to move more rapidly with social reforms that were a century overdue."

"Is that what you thought at the time?" I persisted.

"Yes and no. I knew the pathetic land hunger of the peasants in Andalusia, but I was still concerned with legality, more than I am now. When people are desperate, you have to act, even if there will be some mistakes and injustices. That's why I admire Castro."

D. Julián then launched into a tirade against American policy in Spain. The Franco dictatorship was the most *espantoso dictadura,* the most frightful dictatorship, in modern history. Stalin had at least done something for his country in the way of education, medical care, and industrialization. Hitler had lasted only twelve years. But Franco had already held absolute power for more than twenty years, with no end in sight. His lies about the past and his anticommunist mythology had brainwashed a whole generation. He kept the peace by a combination of corruption, American aid, and the memory of his having murdered over a million Spaniards. How could the Americans go on supporting him?

I felt, as I was to feel many times during my months in Spain, that American policy could not be defended positively on either political or moral grounds, but also that complete uncertainty as to what might replace the Franco dictatorship was an important factor in that policy. D. Julián agreed that after twenty years of dictatorship the Spanish people were unfit for an immediate transition to full democracy. When I asked him whether he would prefer a monarchy or a transitional dictatorship, he ruled out the monarchy immediately, and from his remarks about other prominent generals it seemed clear that he looked upon Franco as a lesser evil, despite all that he had just said about the worst dictatorship in modern history. This ambiguous feeling toward Franco was to reappear in many other conversations, and I gradually concluded that one of Franco's great strengths was surely the fear of his opponents that a new dictator might be worse.

D. Julián told me that Sr. P., a major opposition leader, was coming to tea the next afternoon. Would I like to meet him? I readily agreed, and at our meeting the following day, as soon as courtesy permitted me to do so, I asked D. Julián, in the presence of this leader, how he justified the figure of 1.5 to 2 million deaths by white terror, a figure which he had repeatedly used in our first conversation. D. Julián expounded the basis of his reasoning without the slightest hesitation. Franquist sources, he began, generally claim a round total of 300,000 people killed by red terror. He himself had been threatened in August 1936; he knew that dozens of other Cortes deputies had likewise been threatened; and that the large cities, Madrid, Barcelona, and Valencia, had lived through a virtual reign of terror during the first three to four months of the Civil War.

He therefore believed that this apparently incredible figure might be approximately correct.

He was equally certain, on the basis of his own postwar inquiries, that the white terror had produced five to ten times as many victims as the red terror. Through his family connections and associations with both military and parliamentary colleagues in the provinces of Córdoba and Seville, he had concluded that 32,000 had been shot in the former area and 47,000 in the latter. His figures, village by village, came, he said, from priests and notaries who had lived in the same towns before and after the war. Many priests had been moved by the fate of Republican veterans known to them personally and had felt remorseful because of the complete identification of the Church with the Franquist cause. The priests were anxious to preserve the names of assassinated Republican parishioners, especially as every church carried a plaque memorializing those who had died fighting in the Franquist armies. From local testimony he also knew that in many villages the so-called reds had killed a few landlords and civil guards and perhaps a hated priest, and that in the same villages the advancing Nationalist army had shot dozens of men on the grounds that the Popular Front militia were not an army entitled to the laws of war but a rabble of traitors to be shot out of hand.

As I listened to my host's passionate summary of his own researches I knew that he could not possibly be correct in absolute terms. I had made no specific study yet of terror and reprisal data, but I knew that the 1940 census, taken in conjunction with careful demographic projections based on peacetime birth and death rates, indicated that the total war deaths from all causes would lie somewhere between 600,000 and 800,000. It was therefore equally impossible that 300,000 had died by red terror or that 1.5 to 2 million had died by white terror. However, at the time of our conversation, I did not feel capable of arguing with D. Julián about numbers, and in any case the basis of his belief and the qualitative nature of the two forms of terror were more important to me than the absolute figures.

While D. Julián was developing his claims I had watched the opposition leader. Sr. P. was a tall man with a sallow complexion and large, melancholy eyes which peered out intensely through thick glasses. One could easily tell that he was the sort of man who would much prefer the library or the laboratory to politics. He had been very attentive and polite during the first minutes of conversation, but had done little more than nod affirmatively from time to time during our host's explanation of his conclusions concerning the white terror. I now asked him whether he agreed with D. Julián's evaluation.

Sr. P. did not mention numbers in his reply, but he stated slowly, quietly, and with unmistakable affirmation, that D. Julián's calculations might very well be correct. For Sr. P. these large figures were credible because of the intensity of class hatred in 1936—class hatred plus the Spanish attitude toward death "as an incident in a continuum," and the well-known Spanish reluctance to condemn murder, as against great opposition to the exaction of the death penalty by the state.

"What do you mean," I asked, "by a reluctance to condemn murder?"

"Just that," he smiled sadly, and I could feel him sizing me up as one of those innocent, blue-eyed Anglo-Saxons. "Whatever is done out of passion will be pardoned, or at least understood, by Spaniards. We admire martyrs, irrespective of the cause for which they die. Those who kill priests may very well, at bottom, be more certain of their immortal souls than are their victims. Spaniards also understand, regardless of their political convictions, the delirious bloodlust of the Carlist and Falangist youth during the war. What they do not understand, what in their hearts they despise, is the cold, methodical way in which, weeks or months after the fighting, the Nationalist authorities could shoot men for the simple crime of having fought on the other side."

"Do you believe also that the Nationalists killed five to ten times as many people as the Popular Front?"

"They had five to ten times as many enemies." He paused and stared at me with a smile that was at once dejected and tender. "The generals figured that perhaps ten percent of all Spaniards would have to be killed in order to purify Spain for the remaining ninety percent. That would mean close to three million people. I am not of the opinion that that many died. I am saying that the gentlemen who rule over us today were prepared, if necessary, to kill that many people. The first provinces which they conquered, Andalusia, Galicia, and Asturias, were heavily Republican. They were in a hurry to reach Madrid, and they sensed the hostility around them. They would send a firing squad into each village and ask their partisans: Who is to be shot? Just like that. Well, it could be anybody with a trade-union card, anybody who took a drink in the workers' casino, anybody who had spoken disrespectfully of the Church or the army. That would be a great, great many people."

Again, as with D. Julián, I did not think there would be any point in pressing the question of absolute numbers. The qualitative judgment of both men was crystal clear. In the months to come I was to discuss the same question with dozens of businessmen, officers on active duty, and civil servants, the great majority of whom had fought on the Nationalist side. I was to be astounded at the way in which practically all of them took it for granted that Nationalist reprisals had been numerically far greater than Leftist assassinations. Eventually I tried, in writing *The Spanish Republic and the Civil War,* to make sense of the conflicting statistics and oral testimonies.

Without repeating the detail of that study I will say that I came to the provisional conclusion, based on the evidence available as of 1962, that the Nationalists had indeed purged their enemies in the proportion of more than ten for one. Both revolutionary and counter-revolutionary terror during the French Revolution had been far less destructive. The scale of mass murder was roughly comparable with that carried out by the French army in repressing the Paris Commune of 1871. It could also be compared, both qualitatively and quantitatively, with what we know of the Turkish massacre of the Armenians in World War I, the communal slaughter between Hindus and Muslims in 1947, and the wholesale massacre of the Left following the Indonesian military coup in 1964. On the other hand, the Spanish Nationalist purge totals were substantially smaller than the Nazi genocide of the Jews and the Stalinist executions of the 1930s and 1940s.

I was initially shocked and skeptical at what I heard from so many partisans of both Right and Left. Like most inhabitants of a prosperous, free society, I could not really visualize political executions except as very rare occurrences connected with wartime treason and espionage. It was only by repeated reference to other known events such as those mentioned above that I could gradually accustom my mind to the scale of the white terror. The difference between me and my Spanish interlocutors was that they were by no means the inhabitants of a prosperous, free society. On the contrary, they had lived for upward of twenty years with the full consciousness that men in the middle of the twentieth century were capable of massacring their brothers for a variety of totally irrational religious and ideological motives. The overwhelming first impression of my meetings with older Leftists inside Spain was the sense of long-repressed emotion and a desperate conviction that nobody outside the country understood what they had lived through and how they had suffered not only from the past events, but from the massive propaganda which had distorted the whole meaning of their struggle.

5

A Peripatetic Scholar

Madrid is a glorious city in which to walk: rich in broad avenues and parks, varied in architecture, bracing in climate. It is not one of Spain's oldest cities. There was a town here in medieval times, but the real development of the city dates from the early sixteenth century, and Madrid became the capital of Spain only in 1561, by the decision of Philip II, who chose it for two principal reasons: its proximity to the exact geographical center of the Iberian peninsula and its isolation in the middle of a windswept plain. The character of the city as a royal residence and the open, sparsely inhabited country in which it is located are responsible for the ample dimensions of the thoroughfares, public buildings, and parks. In the center of the old city, near the Plaza Mayor, there are wine cellars, dungeons, narrow alleys and stairways, artisan shops dating from the sixteenth century.

Throughout Madrid there are churches and palaces built in a succession of handsome styles: austere Spanish Renaissance, seventeenth-century Baroque with ornate, Italian-influenced exterior decoration; eighteenth-century rococo and neoclassic. In the older wealthy sections such as the Salamanca district one sees stately nineteenth-century apartments like those of the Clichy district in Paris; and in the newer well-to-do areas close to the University City one sees every type of mid-twentieth-century apartment building, with colored cement façades, large windows with fiberglass drapes, and elegant balconies. It is a hilly city, and from numerous high points one can see the majestic profile of the Guadarrama mountains off to the northwest, the mountains which form the background in Velázquez's many equestrian portraits of Habsburg princes. The air is dry and biting, the city often windy. Bright sunlight and constantly shifting cloud patterns give a subtly differing hue to the brick and cement buildings from day to day. As of 1960 automobile traffic was still light, at least by American standards, and industry had not developed to the point of creating the current unhappy smog problem. Madrid was, and hopefully it will remain despite industrialization, a beautiful city in which to walk.

My first excursions started from a base of operations which had been truly well selected for us by the Fulbright Commission. The Hotel Carmen was comfortable without being luxurious. It did not have uniformed porters or a travel bureau and gift shop in the lobby. The clerks and the chambermaids were friendly without being obsequious. The rooms were reasonably clean, the food reasonably well cooked, the water pressure reasonably adequate if there were not too many people trying to wash on the floor below, and the "hot" water reasonably warm in the morning and evening when reasonable people were wishing for hot water. There was an elevator which could ascend with three people and their suitcases at a dignified pace, and which was in working order a reasonable proportion of the time. There was a marble staircase surrounding the elevator cage, at the bottom of which stood a patient old porter whose job it was to teach the Americans by gesture that the elevator was not to be used for coming down. *Hombre,* no reasonable human being needs to come *down* by elevator!

During the two-week orientation period in late September most of the Fulbright scholars spent their mornings at lecture sessions intended to introduce them to Spanish life and culture. I and one or two other professors who had previously studied in Spain were excused. I used my mornings to arrange for the various entry cards I would need for libraries and archives, and I walked everywhere in order to get the feel of the city. Around 1:30 we all gathered at the sunlit cafe tables in front of our hotel and exchanged news of the morning's experiences.

The students were half-amused, half-annoyed at the obviously canned version of Spanish politics being fed to them: Franco as the "sentinal of the West" (subtitle of his official biography); Spain as the nation which had fought "international communism" while the corrupt Western powers were cooperating with Stalin; Spain as an "organic democracy" whose government was more truly representative than any parliamentary government.

The students all knew that I was writing a history of Spain in the 1930s. I did not want to spoil the agreeable atmosphere of my first official contacts, and so I answered leading questions as briefly and inoffensively as I could without perjuring myself. I agreed that the Franco government had been more consistently anticommunist than the Western governments, so from a certain point of view it was understandable that the present Spanish regime should consider itself politically in advance of those other governments. I likewise allowed that parliamentary democracy was not necessarily fully representative and that it might not be the best form of government for all countries. However, I added, I could not myself apply the term "democracy," with any adjective, to a government which held large numbers of political prisoners and which censored the daily press. After such discussions, Professor Kossoff of Brown University, who had come to Spain to prepare a definitive edition of the sixteenth-century poet Herrera, would delight in introducing me to new acquaintances with the following formula: "I'd like you to meet my friend Professor Jackson, who is making his last trip to Spain."

When the orientation period came to an end and most of my companions were leaving for other cities, I did not want to be stranded at the Carmen. Also, I wanted to save as much money as possible, and in view of the experience as a student ten years earlier in France, I knew I could manage on a standard of living considerably more modest than that which Americans were, so to speak, expected to expect. The inner city was full of small pensions. Typically they would occupy a couple of upper stories in an apartment or business building and would have ten to twenty rooms plus a dining room and one or two baths. There were lots of rooms available, but most of them were furnished as doubles, and the walls were very thin, so the real task was to find quiet and privacy. I must have looked into two dozen pensions in the course of a few days' hunting. Unfortunately, those which offered the most in the way of privacy and general cleanliness repelled me by their atmosphere. They were run by pinch-lipped, bourgeois ladies whom I did not want to have to see at three meals daily.

I finally settled in a very unbourgeois establishment entitled the Las Vegas, in the Calle de Gravina. The location was ideal. Within ten minutes I could walk to the Biblioteca Nacional, the Prado Museum, the Gran Via, or the Puerta del Sol. The rooms were neither very clean nor very quiet, but just as Sancho Panza had always dreamed of ruling an island, I had always dreamed of having a balcony. Since they could offer me a single room with a balcony overlooking the street, I decided for that reason alone to move in.

At the Las Vegas the company was interesting, the food was tolerable, and the service was awful. The steady inhabitants were medical students and theater people, and there was a floating population of traveling salesmen and priests. There was a star guest, a woman jai-alai champion, who spent about one week a month there. I usually ate with the medical students, who asked friendly, intelligent questions about the American standard of living, about Spanish-American relations, the military agreements, and American economic aid, but who were careful to avoid Spanish domestic politics. The theater people lived in their own world. They came late to all meals. The faces of the women were frequently masked in cold cream. They complained about the food and often did no more than nibble their main course. They were well disposed toward the foreign professor who played the flute and would sometimes join me if there were no empty tables. They would greet me rapidly and floridly, all talking at once and expecting no reply. They would make no effort to include me in the subsequent conversation. I liked the absence of hypocrisy and found it relaxing just to listen to them talking about the roles which were of course unworthy of them, the draftiness of the stage, the impossible lighting, the stupidity of the managers, and their weariness from lack of sleep. Occasionally they included me in a misery-loves-company complaint about the absence of hot water or engaged in friendly kidding about my apparently unfailing good appetite.

My closest association was with the clerk, who also, in the absence of the owner, doubled as a kind of general manager. He was tall, nervous, intelligent, and dyspeptic. Growing up in Burgos in 1936, he had seen bodies sprawled across the highways during the first months of the Civil War. In 1945 he had gone to Sweden, worked as an electrician's apprentice, married, left his wife under circumstances about which he was not precise, and had returned to Spain in 1959. He spoke disparagingly of everything Spanish. The government was not only dictatorial, but stupid, inevitably, since it was run by military men. The press was so dull that people were forgetting how to read and write Castilian. The officials of the Falangist unions were a bunch of *granujos* (his favorite printable epithet, literally, "pimple"). They collected the equivalent of six months' social security payments from the chambermaids, he said, as a bribe for getting them jobs. Nobody was honest because nobody was paid enough to live on. Spanish industry was backward not only because one had to be an imbecile with *enchufe,* "pull," to get a management job, but because the workers were not sufficiently literate to read the directions on machinery plates. I believe that he spoke this way partly because he felt that through such criticisms he would appear "enlightened" to an American and partly because he had lived in Scandinavia. Any intelligent man who had experienced the high educational standards, the efficient workmanship, and the honest social services of the Scandinavian world would feel desperate when comparing Sweden with Spain. I was a convenient escape valve for his feelings of shame concerning his own country: feelings which were spontaneous and specific, directed against ignorance, fraud, and stupidity rather than against the ideology of the regime.

The heating system in the Las Vegas did not extend to

my room, a fact which I had not noticed on the warm day in early October when I had moved in. When I pointed this out to the clerk he offered to put another comforter on the bed. I replied that that would be fine, but also that I had long searched for a single room because I was planning to do a lot of writing and that I had to have some sort of heat during the day. He said he would take up the question with the owner. Nothing happened for about a week, but then he suddenly appeared, gesturing triumphantly, ready to install *two* heaters. One of them was a standard metal radiator which had been wired for electric heating. We lugged it over to the sink together, filled it with water, and plugged it in. It took about twenty minutes to attain the first sensation of warmth, and close to two hours to reach the point at which one could feel heat radiating from it. The second heater was a portable radiant coil which I could place next to my work table and direct on me like a sun lamp. The clerk was tremendously proud of his performance, and I thanked him profusely. He went into a long description of his negotiations with the boss, much of which I did not understand, but two things were clear: in return for not having my rent raised, I must be absolutely sure to turn off both heaters whenever I left the room. I accepted that condition with pleasure.

In the ensuing weeks I was able to do him a return favor. One of the jobs for which the *sereno,* the night watchman, was paid extra was to light the hot-water furnace each morning. Approximately once a week he would either forget or lay the fire so poorly that it would die out a few minutes after he had left the building. Nobody in the Las Vegas rose before eight thirty except me. When I noticed that there was no lukewarm water (the adjective "hot" would be misleading in the best circumstances) I would descend to the cellar and light the fire. After doing this for about a month, I pointed out to my friend that the operation of the warm-water system was extremely wasteful of coal, which from his many complaints I knew to be expensive. The heater had no asbestos cover, so it served more to take the chill off the cellar than to warm the water. In addition, the water pipes did not run through the furnace which served the radiators. I explained that if they made this one change in the path taken by the pipes they could save a good deal of coal and probably have much warmer water. I also murmured something to the effect that a boiler without an asbestos cover could create a fire hazard.

He was much excited by both pieces of information and wanted to know whether I had had training as an engineer. No, I laughed, I had merely inhabited coal-heated New England farmhouses in which, as a matter of course, the boilers were lined with asbestos and the hot-water pipes passed through the central-heating furnace. He clapped his hands against his thighs and whistled—another example of how much better foreigners did things! He was enthusiastic to make the improvements right away and was sure that the owner would authorize them, especially since they would save money in the long run. Actually, nothing was done to the furnaces, and neither of us ever mentioned the matter again. However, he must have gotten after the *sereno,* because I did not in the future have to light the hot-water stove personally.

During my months at the Las Vegas I flourished on a thoroughly Spanish work-and-meal schedule. From nine to one thirty I spent a long morning in the municipal newspaper archives, going through the daily press for the years 1931 to 1939; back for dinner at two, followed by a nap; then from about four until midnight, a varied schedule of interviews, letterwriting, long walks, museum or theater visits—punctuated somewhere along the way by a half-hour of flute playing—and supper. The newspaper reading and the flute were the most constant elements. The former was necessary to my study, but with the exception of *El Sol,* a high-quality journal fully comparable in value to papers like the *Manchester Guardian* and *Le Monde,* the press made rather dreary, tendentious reading. The flute gave me esthetic and humorous pleasure, which I appreciated all the more by contrast with the uninspiring work of the morning.

The afternoon and evening meetings often combined work with friendship. Early in October I met the brilliant sociologist Juan Linz, who was as peripatetic as I. Juan was the son of a German father and a Spanish mother. His earliest years had been spent in Weimar Germany. He had gone to high school in Salamanca, the native city to which his widowed mother had returned shortly after the start of the Civil War. Several years after the war he had gone to the United States as a graduate student. In 1960 he was dividing his time between Madrid and Columbia University and was making pioneer studies of the Spanish professional and business classes in modern times.

From Juan I learned to distrust the easy and oft-repeated generalizations about Spain as a country dominated by a heridi-tary aristocracy. He had amassed a tremendous quantity of data concerning the social origins of both the civilian and military elite. These data showed that the proportion of career military officers coming from the nobility in nineteenth- and twentieth-century Spain was smaller than the same category of officers for France or Prussia before 1914; that the majority of corporation and bank directors in twentieth-century Spain came from modest economic and social backgrounds; and that the executive posts in the civil service and in the judiciary were awarded on the basis of *oposiciones,* competitive examinations open to all candidates without regard to social origin. Clearly then, Spain of the last forty years, the Spain of Primo de Rivera, of the Republic, and of Francisco Franco, had not been ruled by a closed aristocracy. The same data showed that the business and banking elites had been intimately connected with the regime during the Primo de Rivera and Franco eras, whereas under the Republic intellectuals and doctors had held top responsibilities, but the civil service and business elites had not been close to the government.

Juan had none of the penchant for secrecy which afflicts so many scholars. He was enthusiastic about his discoveries and wanted them to contribute to the work of others. He loved to demonstrate, argue, persuade. Speaking generally, he was of the moderate Right as I was of the moderate Left. He criticized the various Center and Left Republican parties for their anticlericalism, and he regarded the Catalan regionalists either as romantics, in the pejorative sense, or as wreckers of national unity. He insisted that when the Socialists and the Catalan Left had taken part in the revolution of October 1934 they had forfeited all right to consider themselves the champions of Republican legality. He defended ardently the efforts of Gil Robles to form a parliamentary Right which could represent the interests of the Church and the rural middle class within a republic which had swung much further to the Left than had the true balance of Spanish public opinion in the period 1931–3. Juan considered that October 1934 had destroyed the Republic because the President, Alcalá-Zamora, had refused to name as Prime Minister the man who in fact was the majority leader in the Cortes, i.e., Gil Robles, and because the Socialist and Catalan minorities had resorted to violence against the very regime which they had created three years earlier.

Through Juan I met Gil Robles himself, as well as several Roblista deputies of the Cortes. Most important, however, were Juan's generosity and intellectual companionship. When one works for years on a particular limited subject he cannot help wondering intermittently whether that subject is really worth all the time he is putting into it and whether anyone else will find it as significant as he does. Juan dug voting maps and political clippings from provincial newspapers out of trunks. He lent me annual economic and military reports which were absolutely not to be found either in libraries or second-hand bookstores. Walking back and forth at midnight between the Nuevos Ministerios and the Plaza de Alonso Martínz, after we had already debated for hours in his apartment, he urged me to understand the problems of conservative farmers in Castile and the Levant, the resentments of an army humiliated by the Azaña reforms, the fears of a clergy whose school system the government was threatening to destroy, and above all the efforts of the CEDA, the Catholic bloc in the Cortes, to satisfy the demands of these disgruntled groups within the legal framework of the Republican constitution. My own interpretation of the critical year 1934 remained fundamentally sympathetic to the Left, but to the extent that I learned to comprehend, and do justice to, the motives of the parliamentary Right, I owe much of that comprehension to the long peripatetic discussions with Juan.

I have repeated brief meetings and valuable discussions with several older men who had been notables of the Republic. Most cherished in personal memory are those with the late General Vicente Rojo, who had organized the popular defense of Madrid in November 1936 and who had been the chief of staff of the Republican armies at Teruel and in the Battle of the Ebro. General Rojo had none of the chest-thumping, eternally adolescent character of the typical military man. Before the Civil War he had been one of the army's intellectuals, always assigned to responsible teaching or staff planning posts. He came of a profoundly conservative family and had himself steered clear of politics. In July 1936 he had taken the side of the Republic out of loyalty to his oath to serve the legitimate government of Spain, and out of belief in the importance of civilian supremacy.

In my personal experience of him he was a slow-spoken, melancholy, deeply reflective man. These qualities may well have been magnified by the loss of the war and by his twenty years spent in exile, but from earlier photographs I have the impression that he must always have been of a reflective and mildly melancholy temperament. We met several times, at two- or three-week intervals, for coffee. These conversations helped me make the necessary allowances in reading Nationalist military histories of the Civil War. In general, the problem of handling Spanish sources was very different for the Republican period and for the war. During the Republic there had been a free press, with vigorous debate and constant publication of information relevant to all public activities of the time. During the war, of course, both sides had censored the press, and everything published in Spain for the twenty years since the war represented purely and simply the victors' version. In battle after battle, according to the official histories, the Republicans had had more men and guns but had suffered two or three times more casualties than the Nationalists, because the latter possessed a worthier cause, greater discipline, and greater physical courage.

General Rojo pointed out that the Republican armies had repeatedly shown tremendous courage and discipline when on the defensive, but he admitted ruefully that they had never had the training or the equipment for a sustained offensive. With regard to casualties he flatly contested the official versions of the Jarama and Ebro battles, explaining that when the Nationalists had been attacking across hard flat ground at the Jarama or against entrenched positions in the olive groves on the slopes near the Ebro, they would undoubtedly have suffered more casualties than the defending troops. He answered simply and gravely my technical questions, but the subject which clearly aroused his enthusiasm was the defense of Madrid. He kept coming back to the "miracle" of November 5–9, 1936: how several hundred loyal officers had organized the defense of the western approaches to the city, how the women had brought food and medical supplies to the front lines, how the populace as a whole had obeyed orders broadcast on the radio the moment they had been decided on in General Miaja's headquarters. His feelings as a patriot were deeply involved, since he asserted that even the best foreign accounts, such as Robert Colodny's masterful *The Struggle for Madrid,* had exaggerated the role of the International Brigades. He told me that he was completing a book on the subject, which would be published after his death.

I found it very enlightening, not just about the Civil War but about the psychology of an honorable professional officer, to listen to General Rojo on the subject of the civilian leaders of the Republic. He did not speak ill of Largo Caballero as a man, but clearly he believed that the Prime Minister of a war government must understand military affairs and must be capable of firm administrative decisions—two qualifications which Caballero lacked. On the other hand he honored Caballero for his defense of General Asensio, whom Rojo himself did not like personally, and for his consistent efforts not to have pre-Civil War jealousies and ideological differences interfere with the building of the Republican army. He had found Indalecio Prieto excellent to work under because of his rapid comprehension and his amazing memory for detail.

But he had admired Juan Negrín above all the other personalities of the Republican camp. Partly this was a matter of culture. General Rojo himself always appeared in a Homburg hat and carried a cane. He was proud to have been a staff officer and to have a daughter who translated English with professional skill. He admired in Negrín the professor, the doctor, the man who was equally at home in several European cultures. He admired even more the man of physical endurance and courage, who could work for eighteen hours in the office and then visit the front lines under fire, and whose sons were also at the front, not abroad on diplomatic missions.

Negrín had more than once confided to him that he felt more kinship with the best elements in the Franco zone than with many members of the Popular Front government. General Rojo saw in him the nonparty statesman-patriot. He waved aside the accusations against Negrín as a budding dictator. In order first to win the war, then to reconcile those who had fought on the other side, and then to rebuild a shattered economy, Spain would need a leader who could command the loyalties of patriots of all political colorings and whose international standing would assure the country of economic and diplomatic aid from the Western powers. In 1938 Negrín was the only such leader available in Spain, and for General Rojo other consideration seemed very minor by comparison. He had thus worked enthusiastically under Negrín until the fall of Catalonia, i.e., until the military situation of the Republic had become hopeless. Rojo's further evidence of Negrín's patriotism was his advocacy, in contrast to the vast majority of Republican and socialist exiles, of Marshall Plan aid for Spain and the stipulation in his will that the Soviet receipts for the Bank of Spain gold be returned to the Franco government.

By no means all my contacts and conversations had to do directly with my work. Toulouse friendships had also brought me into touch with young intellectuals more concerned with the future of Spain than with its past. Lonely as I felt for my own family, I was particularly happy to be able to come and go freely in the home of Bernardo, a young architect and furniture designer. Coffee was always available on Sunday afternoon, and if Bernardo himself occasionally had to spend part of the afternoon at the drafting table, he simply went about his business and neither I nor other guests would need to ask ourselves whether we had dropped in at the wrong moment.

Bernardo and his friends despised the dictatorship and were at the same time uncomfortably aware of their own relatively privileged position in contemporary Spain. One of them, the son of a local notable in Zamora, constantly told stories about ugly methods used to keep local agricultural labor on starvation wages. He himself was living on a dole from his father. Bernardo, as an architect, and another of the company who worked in film production talked angrily of the need for *enchufe,* "pull" with the Falange if one was to have an opportunity to exercise his profession. One had constantly to flatter venal officials and tip janitors and night watchmen who doubled as police spies. One could be a "pure" and refuse all such compromises with the system—at the price of remaining totally isolated in a society which needed new initiative and enthusiasm in every direction.

Spiritually all these people were in revolt, but they were completely uncertain as to what could or should be done. Brought up entirely on Francoist versions of recent history, they believed that the Republic, however well intentioned, had been a total failure in practice. They regarded me with mingled sympathy and skepticism when I stated that in the given circumstances—world depression, the rise of fascism, anarchist and monarchist agitation—the Republicans and Socialists had made an intelligent, vigorous start on many of the accumulated problems facing Spain. Like many Spaniards of the past century, they idealized the pueblo. I might argue that frequent strikes, anticlerical demonstrations, and occasional lynchings of a landlord had gone far to discredit the potentially most constructive Spanish government since the time of Charles III in the eighteenth century. For them the oppressed but wonderfully talented and expressive pueblo could do no wrong. Their imagery was more esthetic than political. The pueblo meant flamenco, whose mood is both more impassioned and more sober than the popular dance music of the West. The pueblo produced a great poet like Miguel Hernández, the stages of whose life represented for them a modern Calvary: a Catholic upbringing rejected because of the gulf between ideal and behavior on the part of the Church; self-education while working as a shepherd; poetic themes and images drawn from the life of the peasants; wartime commitment to the Communist party as the most effective champion against fascism; death from tuberculosis contracted in prison.

Looking toward the outside world, they admired both the Soviet Union and Cuba, but warily. The Soviets had built an industrial state without depending on foreign capital and had maintained civilian supremacy in government. But they suspected that in any one-party state the evils of *enchufe* would be much the same as in Spain. As for Fidel Castro, they wondered whether he was an "infantile Leftist." Curiously enough, traits which they admired in the pueblo they distrusted in a political leader. They hated United States foreign policy for its consistent support of reactionary dictatorships all over the globe. However, like almost all Europeans in my experience, they made a clear distinction between national cultures and foreign policies and did not let their emotions about the latter disfigure their appreciation of the former. For Bernardo, everything new and vital in architecture received its greatest opportunities in the United States, even if the ideas and the architects often came from other countries. All of them were jazz fans and took great pleasure in introducing this old-fashioned historian, with his knowledge of the classics and his ignorance of jazz, to the glories of Dixieland, Louis Armstrong, Art Tatum, the Dave Brubeck Quartet, and many others.

The most enjoyable aspect of these conversations was the complete absence of pose or self-consciousness. This trait was particularly evident with regard to sex. One afternoon we had been talking about *Yerma,* the Lorca play concerning a woman who is obsessed with the desire to have a child but whose husband prefers not to have another mouth to feed. Someone suggested that if birth-control information were universally available people would not become so obsessed with questions of whether and when to have children. I remarked, in my ignorance, that naturally in Spain only the crudest methods would be available. Not at all, several people hastened to correct me. There followed a detailed, clear, completely unembarrassed and nonprurient account of the means available in every Spanish pharmacy, the reasons why the Church permitted same, and the ways in which one could best broach the subject with male and female pharmacists. It is true that there is a steadily increasing flow of objective information on birth control in all literate societies today, but I have never elsewhere participated in so natural a discussion including men and women, married and unmarried. Some months later, when I read Richard Wright's *Pagan Spain* I noticed that he had been struck by precisely the same naturalness of attitude.

The easy frankness extended to money also, a subject which in middle-class America is second only to sex for self-conscious overtones. Often we would meet, not in Bernardo's apartment, but in a cafe near Cuatro Caminos, chosen for its working-class neighborhood and its heroic Civil War memories. Dutch treat was understood, with the exception that anyone had the right to offer Bernardo's four-year-old daughter one of those garish, saccharin mint drinks which Spanish children adore. Usually I took the trolley home or walked, but one bitter cold afternoon Bernardo decided to take the family home in a taxi and invited me to join them.

On the way, I asked him to let me pay.

"No, no, Gabriel. I took the taxi for my family. We are going to pick up my mother on the way, and your coming makes no difference at all."

"Well," I said, "I have been such a frequent guest in your house. One doesn't calculate such things, but it would give me pleasure to cover this if you will allow me."

Bernardo maintained silence for a minute, then spoke of other things. I waited for our arrival at his home to see what would happen. As the taxi pulled to a stop he turned to me with a quiet smile: *"De acuerdo,* Gabriel," "agreed," and I paid.

Altogether I worked uninterruptedly for four months in Madrid. The newspapers of the Republican era and the many interviews with political personalities of that period formed the core of my research. A settled feeling of purpose helped me maintain a regular schedule, but spiritually I do not think I could have survived without the circle of Bernardo and his friends. It was not primarily a question of living alone. It is rather that the dictatorship was bathed in an atmosphere of hypocrisy, to which the victims had perforce become accustomed but which contsantly depressed me. The daily papers, the radio and TV, the newsreels—all the sources of public information were deformed by half-truths and innuendoes more difficult to cope with than outright lies. I tried to maintain perspective by reading *Le Monde*. But once or twice a week *Le Monde* would not reach Spanish newsstands—precisely on the days when something significant was reported from Spain. After reading *ABC* and *Ya* I would feel an almost physical need to cleanse my mind of the pervading atmosphere of falsehood. That was why it meant so much to be able to talk frankly, objectively, truthfully, about any subject, political or nonpolitical, with people who for years had been struggling gallantly and good-humoredly to withstand that atmosphere of falsehood.

6

The Virgin of Pilar

On December 20 I bid fond, temporary farewells to the librarians at the Hemeroteca and to my table companions at the Las Vegas. In the late afternoon I was to meet my family, who were making the twenty-four-hour train journey from Paris. Meanwhile, I would open my first, least expected, and luckiest Christmas present—a three-bedroom apartment lent to me by Fulbright art students with whom I had talked music and Spanish history at the Hotel Carmen in October. They had left Madrid for a few weeks' skiing. I had enjoyed their hospitality several times and had played music there occasionally. They had always asked after my family, and before their departure had assured me how much pleasure it would give them to think of us having Christmas in their otherwise empty flat. I spent an hour getting the coal furnace started and then walked through slush and now flurries to the North Station, only to learn that the train would be about seven hours late.

The girls were bone-weary at their midnight arrival, and both had heavy colds which lasted throughout the ten-day visit; but the apartment was warm, they each had a room to themselves (in contrast with the Paris apartment, consisting of two rooms without a door truly separating the living room from the bedroom), and we all appreciated each other as never before. I was startled by the way my daughters recognized main landmarks in Madrid, a city they were seeing for the first time. Twice a week during the fall I had sent each of them a picture postcard. They had studied those pictures so carefully that when we passed the Prado, the Cibeles, the Telephone Building, the Puerta del Sol, they were telling me where we were!

Kate, our older daughter, whose eighth birthday fell on December 27, seemed especially moved by the reunion. On Christmas and the day after we knew that she was very busy with some private project for which she had requested Scotch tape and writing paper. At lunch time on the twenty-seventh, we found a conically shaped paper container between our places at the table. Upon opening it we first came upon two pairs of blue grapes, each with a bit of red ribbon around the stem, one pair for each of us. Then there were two short quizzes, of the sort given in French schools. Under teacher Kate's direction we filled in the blanks, and she informed us gravely that we had each received a perfect score, "twenty over twenty." Then we unrolled a short scroll which contained a message of thanks for the listed Christmas presents, and a drawing of a little girl who has just gotten a scooter (the birthday present which she would receive upon the return to Paris). The scroll ended with separate statements in capital letters that she loved each of us. Rachel, our six-year-old, had known nothing of Kate's preparations and had followed the ceremony in silence. She now commanded us to close our eyes. She then peeled a tangarine, placing two sections each on the "I love you" statements. In telling us to open our eyes she kissed us and informed us that she loved us too.

After ten days of late sleeping and unhurried sightseeing, we all left Madrid together. I was on my way to Saragossa and other cities for a series of interviews, and my wife and daughters were returning to Paris. I could accompany them as far as Miranda de Ebro, at which rail junction I would transfer from the Madrid-Irún line to the Bilbao-Saragossa-Barcelona line. Our parting was marked by an incident which upset me for hours and has left one of those painfully vivid memories which repeatedly thrust themselves into one's consciousness in the most varied circumstances. Everyone had been cheerful and apparently relaxed when we embraced and kissed one another before I stepped off the train. Since the train remained in Miranda for about ten minutes, I stood on the platform under the window of the girls' compartment. There was something of an awkward, anticlimactic feeling in unexpectedly finding ourselves with several minutes of which we could not take real advantage. My wife and I knew from experience that we were not very good at small talk, but for the girls it may have been more disconcerting than for us.

As the train began very slowly to move out, I walked along beside it, then began trotting, thinking—if one can apply the word "think" to a purely spontaneous reaction in a novel situation—that it would be fun to wave at the receding train from the end of the platform. But suddenly I saw an absolutely anguished expression on Kate's face and heard her shrieking, "Don't, daddy, don't." I stopped short. My eyes were blinded by tears. I felt that I had been a wretched buffoon and could not bear to look toward the train again. My wife wrote later that Kate had cried for an hour. Meanwhile, wandering aimlessly in the streets of Miranda (my own train did not depart until the following morning) I remembered the many little instances over the years which had shown that Kate tended always to be upset whenever I looked ridiculous. Her reactions have frequently inhibited my sense of humor, for better or worse, but rarely in my entire life have I felt that a gesture had been so misplaced, and so helplessly irretrievable.

From Miranda to Saragossa the Ebro River follows a winding course, now cutting through narrow gorges, now forming great oxbows, then passing through hilly vine country, and gradually broadening as it approaches the flat, semidesert country close to the Aragonese capital. The railroad track follows the river. It had been raining heavily for several days, and although the weather had now cleared, the track was under water at frequent intervals, and we proceeded at speeds varying between fifteen and thirty miles an hour. The landscape was beautiful, and the perspective shifted constantly because of the grades and curves. The gentler hillsides facing the sun were covered with vines, as they have been through thousands of years of Celt-Iberian, Roman, Visigothic, Arab, and Christian cultivation. On the upper craggy slopes stood evenly planted young fir trees, the result of the reforestation program of the Franco government, and from time to time we passed small dams and hydroelectric plants completed in the 1950s. Silently surveying these evidences of millennial human endeavor were the majestic ruins of Romanesque churches and of twelfth- to fourteenth-century chateaux. In the eleventh century, from the heights above the river, Navarrese and Aragonese warriors had observed the prosperous Arab agriculture on the valley floor. In the twelfth century they conquered these valleys, gave generous terms to the Muslim farmers and serfs who remained to cultivate the land for their new rulers, and steadily extended their small but vigorous kingdoms through a combination of intermarriage, legal claims, and sporadic warfare.

While watching the landscape, I was also reading intermittently an anthology of medieval romances. The Spanish romances are short narrative poems embroidering favorite incidents from larger epics or legends. They are realistic, dramatic, egalitarian, swift-moving, and conversational in style. Originally the work of professional poets in the small, relatively unsophisticated courts of the medieval Christian kings, they were spontaneously revised over several centuries of oral transmission. They reflect rather haphazardly the facts of history, but quite accurately, by virtue of their popular character and collective composition, the sentiments of the "man in the street." While the train crawled through several inches of water as we circled beneath the church of San Vicente de la Sonsierra, founded in 1137 by a son-in-law of the Cid, I was reading a seventy-line romance entitled *La Campana de Huesca.*

The hero of the tale was the monk-king of twelfth-century Aragon, Ramiro II. According to the poem, Ramiro was much troubled by the fact that his nobles laughed at the notion of being ruled by a former monk. Ramiro sent a messenger to seek advice from the abbot of his old monastery. The abbot said nothing to the messenger but led him into the garden, carefully sharpened a pair of pruning shears, and lopped off the top branches of a number of trees. The disconcerted messenger reported the strange, silent behavior of the abbot, whose meaning was perfectly clear to his royal master. King Ramiro called a Cortes at Huesca, in order, as he put it, to ring solemn bells which would resound throughout Spain. The assembled nobles laughed. All were arrested. Fifteen of those who mocked most loudly were beheaded, and the rest were pardoned. Through this example the monk-king became feared and—the tone of the poem implies without directly stating—respected.

The historic Ramiro, as against the Ramiro of the legend, did not behead any of his nobles so far as we know. He was indeed a monk and had become king involuntarily, but for important political cause which he himself well appreciated. His brother Alfonso the Battler had died without heir in 1134 and had willed his newly expanded kingdom to several crusading military orders. The Aragonese nobility, desperate to maintain their possessions, demanded that the younger brother, the monk Ramiro, repudiate Alfonso's testament and mount the throne. Ramiro not only left the monastery. He married, sired a daughter, Petronila, who was married in infancy to the Count Ramon Berenguer IV of Barcelona, and passed the royal authority peacefully, during his own lifetime, to his son-in-law. The descendants of Ramon Berenguer and Petronila were the rulers of the prosperous medieval kingdom of Aragon-Catalonia.

This particular romance obviously deviates far from the historic truth. But the man in the street, whose taste shaped the poem during two to three centuries of oral transmission, created the legendary Ramiro. Popular opinion evidently supposed that a monk-king would have difficulty establishing his authority, that once on the throne he would feel a passion to command and to be obeyed, and that summary executions, ordered and carried out publicly, would be the surest means to make himself feared and respected. The tone of the poem indicates neither approval nor disapproval of the supposed incident, but rather conveys the feeling that, as a famous television journalist puts it at the end of his daily report, "And that's the way it is," circa 1150 or 1250. Nor could I help reflecting that in the summer of 1936 the Insurgent military authorities over half of Spain and the anarchist fanatics in Madrid, Barcelona, and several dozen villages had all carried out their private "Campana de Huesca," killing with little apparent hatred and no remorse, in order to make their authority feared. And that General Francisco Franco, the slow-to-decide but politically skillful chieftain of a military rebellion, had sanctioned as many summary executions as he felt were necessary to establish his authority over an unwilling, but hardly mocking, population. Unfortunately, he had acted more like the legendary than the historic Ramiro. He and his supporters would also claim what is implied in that medieval romance: that only by such methods can an unexpected, ad hoc regime establish its authority.

My first visit in Saragossa was to a medieval historian, a moderate supporter of the regime but primarily a painstaking scholar and a man of peace. Through his extensive family connections he would be able to give me confidential introductions to people of very differing class backgrounds and political affiliations. I could easily sense that he did not wish to discuss the Civil War with me himself and that he was not sure either of the viewpoints or willingness to talk of the persons to whom he was sending me. Probably he had not discussed controversial ideas or emotionally charged memories with them any more than he was doing with me. So far as my work was concerned, he wanted to be helpful, but to avoid any involvement.

At the same time, sitting before the fire as we drank tea, and speaking in a very low voice so that even his children in another part of the large living room would not hear him, he opened his heart on two significant points. Some men can express more feeling in a few oblique comments than in a long specific account, and he was such a man. He told me that as a civilian he had performed very important functions during the war, which he could document accurately and which he had for years wished to put in book form. But, he said, it would be extremely difficult to write honestly in Spain today, and even more difficult to publish an honest book. As long as he could not be sure of saying exactly what was true and exactly what he had felt, he preferred not to publish. He also said that the war had taught him to value human beings rather than ideologies or parties. In the beginning he had frankly thought only of surviving, of accommodating himself to the military regime which he was sure would eventually be established, and of doing his work as a scholar. He had made whatever gestures he had found necessary to achieve this end. But, living in Madrid throughout the war, he had been affected both by the decency of some of his political enemies, in this case the anarchists, and later by the pitilessness and the mediocrity of those whose triumph he had awaited. Musingly, as if talking more to himself than to me, he kept returning to the thought that in April 1939 Franco had been unable to believe that the war was over, that the Republican soldiers had been more than ready to lay down their arms, that the population were aching for a gesture of reconciliation on the part of the victor. The Generalissimo had seen only enemies to be punished and to be controlled permanently by fear.

The next morning at ten o'clock I met Sr. E., a bank president who had been described to me in Madrid as one of the most powerful individuals in Spain, a constant hunting companion of the Caudillo and his host whenever Franco visited Aragon. Sr. E. received me without delay, and without ceremony. He was short, fat, jolly, and decisive in his movements and in his speech. We sat facing each other in a committee room whose upholstered chairs somehow looked familiar to me, and I suddenly realized that the fabric and color were precisely those of the first-class compartments of the Spanish State Railways. Sr. E. began by remarking that none of his statements was for attribution, and I assured him that that was a well-understood condition of most of my interviews.

"I never recognize from newspaper accounts things I have seen myself," he chuckled.

"I am not a journalist," I replied. "I am writing about things which happened twenty-five years ago, and I have the time necessary to compare different oral and documentary versions of the same events."

He nodded approvingly, and after a short conversation about the relatively self-sufficient nature of the economy of the Saragossa area, I asked him his opinion of the wheat import program of the Republic in 1932.

"Marcelino Domingo was much attacked by the conservative press at the time," I said, "on the grounds that payment in gold for these imports weakened further a peseta which was already sinking in value."

"It was a great coup for the minister and his friends," said Sr. E., shifting in his seat and smiling. "Domingo made millions on it."

I was almost too startled to reply, but taking the same light tone as my interloctor, I said: "In Madrid the CEDA people laugh at the mention of Domingo because he was so ignorant of real economic conditions in the wheat country. And I know for a fact that he died without a cent."

"The wheat import was just a speculative venture. I remember it very well," said the banker decisively. "Economically it was nonsense, but Domingo made millions."

I realized that there would be no point in pursuing this topic. The modalities of the 1932 wheat import program may have been wise or clumsy from a technical point of view, but there was no question about the honesty of the motive: to stop the steady rise in the price of bread. To the extent that any speculation was involved, it was the speculation of large wheat growers hoarding their harvest for a further rise in price. The cynical thought occurred to me that Sr. E. was perhaps judging Marcelino Domingo by his own motives. If he had been connected with the ministry he *would* have made millions, and perhaps he had made millions in the several expensive, if not heavily publicized, food import programs of the 1950s. I turned from the Republic to the war.

"For July 18," I said, "the Saragossa picture is not at all clear to me. The exciting events were occurring in other cities, but I have read very little concerning Saragossa. Could you tell me about the first days of the *movimiento* here?"

"Everything was confused," he began, throwing his arms high over his head. "The rich people ran off to Pamplona, the syndicalists headed for Barcelona, and the municipal government handed the workers arms, but only fearfully and in small quantities. The Reds could have won if they had had any kind of leadership. I remember watching them from the roof of this building on the afternoon of the eighteenth. They were just milling around in the Plaza de Independencia shouting antimilitary slogans, nothing more. That night, at 1 A.M., General Cabanellas declared martial law—with some younger officers holding a pistol to his back." He paused for effect, leaned toward me and grinned, then made a palms-out gesture and shrugged his shoulders. "Within a few weeks the city was the arms production center of the Nationalists," he continued proudly, "and we remained that until after the capture of Bilbao."

"Thus Saragossa was spared the kind of street fighting that took place in Madrid and Barcelona?"

Sr. E. nodded affirmatively, rose and walked quickly to the window. Pushing the drapes aside, he pointed toward the Cathedral. "It was a miracle of the Virgin of Pilar. The Reds could easily have taken the city that first day. It was a miracle; there is no logical explanation."

"And the city became an arms production center, you say." He nodded vigorously. "And was there no trouble with the workers?"

"Oh, they shot a few leaders. The military showed the workers that they would not have any nonsense."

"I understand too that they shot the civil governor, a man who had enjoyed a high reputation for justice and for cooling off hotheads during the spring of 1936."

"Yes," he acknowledged sadly. "Franco was very angry, and removed the colonel who was responsible. He died a few months later, in prison, I think." The banker's eyes took on a faraway, almost enraptured expression. "It was a *castigo de Dios,* a punishment of God."

"I have been told," I said respectfully, "that you are very close to the Caudillo. He certainly maintains a completely unemotional countenance in public."

"He is shy," said Sr. E. "Besides, to govern in Spain it is best to appear dignified and cold. Our people like it that way."

"You have been most generous with your time," I said, "and I do not wish to abuse the privilege of your granting me this interview, but may I ask you: the Caudillo has just made a trip through Andalusia—does he really know the misery of the peasants there?"

"I've talked about it with him many times," replied my host, again relaxed and cheerful. "Here in the Ebro Valley property is reasonably distributed, and we have fine irrigation works. The peasants here are prosperous and content. The Caudillo knows that Andalusia needs a land reform, but he can't do anything about it. The peasants in Andalusia are ignorant and lazy, *mala gente,* bad people, Africans. And they have no Virgin of Pilar. The Caudillo cannot change that."

With this explanation of General Franco's helpless knowledge of the land reform problem, offered confidentially by a powerful banker who knew him well, I took leave of Sr. E. and went to call upon the retired rector of the University of Saragossa, D. Miguel Sancho Izquierdo.

Professor Sancho Izquierdo lived very simply in a third-floor walk up apartment in the center of the medieval quarter of the city. He and his kindly looking wife, who, exceptionally for a Spanish household, stayed with us throughout the conversation, reminded me of a pair of comfortable elderly cats. The walls were lined with books from floor to ceiling, and on his desk the professor had a large autographed photo of General Franco. He was a historian of law and had spent his entire life in or near Saragossa. He had heard the day before that I was coming, and he had put out on the desk several out-of-print publications which he was sure would help me write my book and which he would gladly lend me for the days I would spend in Saragossa. These publications were speeches and manifestoes of the Partido Social, a Catholic party of the 1920s which had been inspired by the Sturzo movement in Italy and which in turn became a precedent for the CEDA of Gil Robles under the Republic.

D. Miguel was a very kindly man, constantly thoughtful of my physical comfort in the barely heated living room and extremely happy to be able to talk about recent Spanish history with a foreigner who knew something about it. I could not bring myself to interrupt his monologue. He told anecdotes about all the personalities whose speeches he was lending me. He explained in loving detail their doctrinal disputes and their soul-searching debates about whether, and how far, to cooperate with the Primo de Rivera dictatorship. None of the persons or incidents he discussed had really exercised wide influence. He had a weakness which is all too common among intellectuals in politics: the exaggerated emphasis on doctrinal exegesis coupled with ignorance of the real political forces in presence. Listening to Professor Sancho explain the problems of Spain between 1920 and 1940 one would never have known the importance of landless peasants, revolutionary factory and mine workers, ambitious and disssatisfied army officers.

But one important thing I did learn from listening to him: that moderate Catholics with a social conscience, like himself, had had doubts about cooperating with fascists which were closely analogous to the doubts of Left liberals and socialists about cooperating with communists. Under Primo, and then much more acutely after the October 1934 Asturian revolt, the hardest political-moral question for the moderate Right, as for the moderate Left, was how far it might be necessary to accept undemocratic means to achieve a democratic end. I got the impression also, though he did not say this directly, that he supported Franco because his regime had preserved social peace since 1939, and that the simple absence of violence in Spanish political life after the 1930s was an enormous virtue to be credited to the dictatorship regardless of its many specific shortcomings.

Eventually I was able to ask him about the first days of the Civil War in Saragossa. Like the banker, he described a reluctant, partial arms distribution by the municipal government, followed by quick military control of the city once martial law had been announced.

"We old ones," he said proudly, "formed Acción Ciudadana, Civic Action, to help the authorities maintain order. We patrolled the streets at night during the first weeks. Fortunately I never had to shoot anybody. I would describe the city as having been quiet, but tense, until August 3. That was the night of the Miracle of Pilar. The Reds carried out an air raid, and several bombs dropped close to the Cathedral. But they did not explode. That night somehow broke the tension in the atmosphere. The entire city, even our Reds, were indignant at the bombing and grateful to the Virgin. The people donated a million pesetas, largely in gold rings and ornaments, for medical supplies, and also to continue the restoration of the Cathedral façade, work on which had been interrupted by the outbreak of the war."

"Why do you think," I asked, "that the Left were so uncertain of themselves on July 18?"

"We were a city of a quarter million, and there were less than one thousand votes difference between the Right and the Left in February. Also, General Cabanellas was popular, as most generals were not. He was a liberal, a Mason, a man with a Santa Claus beard. I remember how, at the anniversary parade for the Republic on April 14, 1936, the women of the working class pelted him with flowers and the workers included his name among their 'vivas.'"

"Well," I said, "Saragossa certainly seems to have been lucky in the moments of worst social tension. For instance, according to my information, no churches were burned here in May 1931."

He nodded gravely and sweetly. "The Virgin of Pilar protected us, as I hope and trust she always will." We talked for a few minutes about mutual acquaintances at the university. Sensing my desire to be on my way, he made one more careful check of his library to be sure that he had given me all his materials relevant to the Partido Social. Then, standing at the top of the stairs, he and his wife waved and wished me repeated farewells as I descended the circular staircase.

By now I was very curious to see the Virgin of Pilar, and happily the businessman with whom I had lunch, and who related to me a number of illuminating experiences with anarchist labor delegates in the 1930s, offered to show me Saragossa's patron saint. The church which houses the Virgin stands near the Ebro, in the middle of an immense plaza which enables one to view the building from several perspectives. It struck me as an imposing, monumental edifice, but hardly as a beautiful one. The chapel of the Virgin herself seemed to be all marble, silver, incense, incredibly ornate sculpture, and rich drapery. In the center, on a silver dais, rested the sober, unsentimental fourteenth-century plaster image. My host, visibly excited, told me that the Virgin's costume was changed daily. He lit a candle for himself, and I, embarrassed by my inability to be moved by the chapel, eagerly accepted his offer to light one for me too.

Afterward we visited the rich collection of jewels in the sacristy. Fortunately his enthusiasm was so great that he needed no confirming expressions from me. I kept wondering how much of my negative reaction was esthetic, a revulsion against the display of so much ornament and wealth; how much it was moral objection to the amassing of unproductive wealth in a country where there was so much desperate poverty; and how much it was religious, dating from my boyhood memories of the Old Testament prohibition against graven images. As a facet of my work I was glad to have seen the Pilar in the company of a man for whom she was a worker of contemporary miracles. I could witness his sentiments but could not in any way enter into them.

Toward five o'clock, after having taken notes on Professor Sancho's books, I went to see another lifelong resident of Saragossa. Sr. K. was a typesetter and a Socialist of the moderate, Prieto wing of the party. From his initial reaction I knew that my introduction through the medievalist created suspicion rather than trust. Hiding his eyes beneath his green printer's shade, he suggested that I write out my questions, leave them with him, and pick up the answers the following day. I took the risk of replying bluntly that only a dialogue was meaningful to me, that doubtless I could mimeograph a questionnaire and send it to dozens of people concerning whose personalities I would have no impression whatsoever, but that I did not think the procedure would have much value in helping me understand the emotional context of events about which I had already read thousands of pages.

The risk paid off. He shoved back his chair, turned and looked directly at me for the first time, and asked me to explain in detail how I had become concerned with the Spanish Civil War. In my reply I deliberately included several of my current political convictions, notably opposition to atomic testing by all powers and provisional sympathy for the two-year-old Castro regime in Cuba. Sr. K. was pleased with what he heard, and invited me to pose whatever questions I wished.

"I have twice heard today," I began, "that the Virgin of Pilar prevented the burning of any churches in Saragossa in May 1931."

Abruptly he swung his chair back to the desk, thereby placing the green shade again between my eyes and his tightly contained profile. "Who told you that?" he asked suspiciously.

"A bank president and a retired professor."

He smiled momentarily, without, however, looking at me. Then, in a deliberate monotone, he said: "In May 1931 the anarchists were conducting a general strike against the newly installed bourgeois republic. The small, but active, Republican and Socialist youth organizations had been mobilized to prevent violence of any kind: violence by the police against the strikers, or violence by the anarchists against the authorities. Thus, before May 10, we were on the alert, knowing that any outbreaks would be used by the Rightist press to discredit the Republic. We were patrolling the streets from the first moment that radio reports carried the news of church burnings in Madrid. That is why churches were not burned in Saragossa." He paused and again smiled fleetingly. "Perhaps one might say that the Virgin had warned us of danger."

"I have the impression so far that there was relatively little fighting in Saragossa after July 18, that the military dictatorship established itself without much trouble."

"That is correct."

"Why?"

Sr. K. smiled wearily. "No leadership, and very little armament. Those of us who were militant and who believed in organization—you must always remember that the anarchists were the strongest element numerically among the workers—had been bending every effort for five months, from the time of the Popular Front victory, to prevent violence of any kind. In the twenty-four hours between the first news of the rising and the imposition of martial law we simply weren't able to change our signals. I was arrested at home, and so were most of the others."

"Then how is it that the war lasted for two and a half years, against such odds?"

He swung around again and looked at me as though I was an idiot. "Because the Republican army fought like hell!" he exploded, and we both laughed. He went on rapidly, for the first time speaking unguardedly. "Why, *hombre,* I was in a prison labor battalion near here in the spring of 1938. We watched the Nationalist equipment rolling up toward the Segre river front: tanks by the dozen, we counted them like kids counting freight cars; GM trucks, good solid American trucks; and out on the airfield, pursuit planes and bombers lined up wing to wing. We watched it all sadly. We hadn't seen a Republican plane for over a year. We didn't see how the war could last, and the officers around the camp boasted that it would all be over in a few weeks. But the war went on for another year, and without the Munich Pact it would have gone on still longer."

He pulled a bottle of anis out of the lower drawer of his desk, and together we drank to the health of the Spanish Republican army and the soon-to-be-inaugurated Kennedy regime. A moment later Sr. K. was again concerned about the possible indiscretion of his conversation with me. I assured him that his name would never appear in anything I wrote, and that I would not ever—in accordance with his explicit request —send him a copy of my book through the mail. He had spent twelve years in prison, and literally hundreds of his friends and acquaintances had been shot. He had not discussed the war with any foreigners, and he hoped he would never have to regret having spoken freely to me.

It was dark, windy, and cold when I left Sr. K. to make my last visit of the day. I had the name of a monarchist landlord who had lived under the regime of *comunismo libertario* in 1937. I had been assured that he would be glad to talk to me, but I had been unable to reach him by phone. Finally I had decided simply to ring his doorbell, a procedure which is not discourteous in Spain, since telephones are not nearly so common as in the United States or northern Europe.

At first there was no answer to the doorbell, and I had almost given up on Sr. G. when the door was slowly opened by a pleasant-looking man of about sixty who was wearing slippers and an old sweater and who had not shaved for two or three days. It was Sr. G. himself. The tempo of life being much slower in his world than in mine, he did not act as though he was admitting someone who had been standing long before the gate. We ushered me into a completely unheated, barely lit stone hallway. Among the austere furnishings were two complete suits of armor and a large collection of lances and muskets. Without a word, he led the way past these displays. I followed him up two narrow flights of wooden stairs, at the top of which we entered a study furnished with straight-backed wooden chairs. The walls and floor here were also of stone. Sitting in the room were two friends, whom Sr. G. did not bother to introduce, but the atmosphere was immediately cordial and relaxed, so that their presence did not in any way inhibit my conversation with the host.

At the outbreak of the war Sr. G. had been leading a quiet life on his family farm in the province of Huesca. The anarchists had immediately established libertarian communism in the village and its surroundings. Sr. G. was well known and liked in the village, where his family had been local gentry for many generations. Theirs was not, however, a large or imposing estate, and the G. family were on informal, neighborly terms with the local peasants, some of whom owned their own land and some of whom rented land from Sr. G. The local committee had come out one afternoon to inform him that money had been abolished in the village, that the harvest would be collectivized, and that his house—other than the room in which he himself lived—was being requisitioned as a hospital for soldiers wounded on the Huesca front.

A few weeks later he was taken to Monegros, the headquarters of the most important anarchist chieftain in Aragon, Buenaventura Durruti. Durruti, who was later to be killed mysteriously at the Madrid front and to receive a state funeral in Barcelona, conducted the questioning. Sr. G. said that he had naturally been somewhat intimidated by the long ride and by the freedom with which the anarchist guards tossed around loaded pistols and strings of hand grenades. However, he said, Durruti, although gruff in manner, had quickly inspired his confidence. He had been invited to begin by making a statement about himself. He had replied that he was a monarchist and a Catholic, and Durruti had interrupted to say that they didn't care about his beliefs, that they were concerned with acts. Four witnesses from his village were then brought in, and they were asked to identify him and to describe his relations with the local peasantry. The gist of their testimony was that Sr. G. had always been a decent man, that his rents were reasonable and that he readily granted moratoria in difficult years, that he had once used his car to rush one of the village children to the hospital, and so forth. Sr. G. was then asked if he would cooperate willingly with the collective regime in his village, and upon his replying affirmatively, the interrogation was over and he and his guards returned to the village.

I asked him how long the regime of libertarian communism had lasted, and whether it had worked.

"The economic life of the village was not greatly upset," he said, after a moment's reflection. "The committee of Saragossan anarchists and local peasants worked fairly well together. The collectivized harvest was sold for cash in Lerida and Barcelona. The committee controlled the money, using it to buy seed, gasoline, and a tractor, of which they were very proud. They gave me money once for a trip to Barcelona when I was trying to get my family from Madrid. The peasants were used to cooperating on the harvest and sharing granaries and tools. Their daily life was not greatly changed."

Sr. G. looked to his friends for confirmation, and they added anecdotes of their own concerning the anarchist rule in rural Aragon. Meanwhile, everyone crowded around the small electric heater which stood on the floor between our chairs. Inevitably our knees bumped, and the three Spaniards joshed each other about who was pushing whom.

Our host turned to me with a dignified preparatory gesture. "Shall I tell you the profound definition of Spanish liberty given by one of my professors?" he asked. *"Sentarse en una silla y media*—to sit down in a chair and a half." We all laughed, and crowded in a little closer.

"The regime lasted almost exactly one year," he said, returning to the theme of our conversation. "The peasants accepted it but did not like it. They would have much preferred a distribution of the land, not a collectivization, and they distrusted the committee's accounts. They asked me to keep separate records for them, against the day when a cash economy would be restored."

"I assume that these changes were not made without violence," I inquired. "How many people were killed or imprisoned?"

"In the first few weeks of the war the anarchists must have shot between fifteen and twenty people in the district. Many others were interrogated, like me, and later lived on a sort of parole. But there were no prisoners. They shot the people they judged to be their irreconcilable enemies, and really tried to work with everyone else by persuasion. They were naïve people, primitive but not evil. In the summer of 1937 the authority of the Barcelona Generalitat was restored. The land was returned to its owners and the money economy was restored. The anarchist authorities were already pretty demoralized before they were removed. No one was shot at this time. In the spring of 1938, when the Nationalists overran the area, lots of people were shot."

"Have you any idea how many?" I asked.

He shrugged his shoulders and ran his hand pensively over his stubble beard. "Who knows how many? Many more than the anarchists had killed, many many more." He turned to his friends. "There were very few able-bodied men in the village after 1939, am I right?" They nodded, muttering phrases about the *matanza terrible,* the terrible slaughter, and the *locura de venganza,* the vengeful insanity of the victors.

As if to dispel a disagreeable mood, he suddenly offered me a drink, apologizing at the same time for not having done so earlier. But I was extremely tired from almost twelve hours of continuous conversation and note taking, and I felt certain that although Sr. G. was very courteous and friendly, I had in fact interrupted a visit among intimate friends. I therefore declined with thanks. Calmly and slowly he led me back down the narrow stairs and across the museum-like corridor. Opening the gate before saying goodbye, he stood in the blustering cold as though completely unaware of wind or temperature and watched me down the street for several seconds before closing the door.

Crossing the Plaza de España on my way back to the hotel, I caught sight of a newsstand display of the German periodical *Der Stern* with a cover headline reading ARTHUR AND MARILYN TO SEPARATE. I bought a copy and while waiting for supper looked at the candid, serious photos of each and read the statements which they had prepared with the hope of maintaining a dignified respect for each other despite the fact that their marriage was ending in divorce. I had never seen Marilyn Monroe in a movie, and her beauty as reflected in stills did not appeal to me personally as much as that of any number of less famous stars. But like millions of other people, I had been intrigued by the marriage of a leading intellectual with a Hollywood star. Clearly she was herself no intellectual, but she must have had dreams, ambitions, standards different from those of the average Miss America. I imagined her simultaneously appearing before thousands of soldiers with nothing on under her evening gown, and studying to become a skilled, disciplined actress; making millions on cheesecake photos which she tirelessly posed for and edited herself, and settling large sums of money on her mentally alienated mother and on various actors' educational and benefit organizations. During the few years of her marriage to Arthur Miller she must have made a tremendous effort to bridge the gap between a career of Hollywood publicity and sexy photos and the hoped-for career as a serious actress and the wife of a playwright.

By sheer association of the day I thought of her in comparison with the Virgin of Pilar. The little Virgin, with all her jewels, her daily changes of rich costume, and her countless adorers, felt the quiet confidence of those who are sure that God is with them. But Marilyn, like numberless beautiful and semieducated girls, could feel no confidence in anything and had nothing to fall back upon except the temporary, uncertain magic of her sex appeal. I thought about the carefully nurtured American cult of youth and blatant sex appeal —was it not just as credulous, and less attractive, than anything I had heard attributed to the Pilar? At the end of a long day I did not feel that I had the answers for anyone. I felt only overwhelmed by all that is naïve, ridiculous, touching, and credulous about human beings, be they bankers, anarchists, or beauty queens.

7

In Partibus Infidelium

From Saragossa I took the train to Barcelona, Spain's most important industrial city and the capital of the linguistic-cultural region of Catalonia. The Catalans form a compact unit of four to five million people, or roughly one-seventh the population of Spain, grouped in the four north-eastern provinces of Tarragona, Lerida, Barcelona, and Gerona. They are somewhat isolated geographically from Aragon by the semidesert of Monegros, north of the Ebro, and by the rude Sierra de Maestrazgo south of the river. This isolation, however, is no greater than that which separates other population centers between which there is no such linguistic difference as that between Catalonia and the Castilian-speaking provinces. Whatever contrasts one remarks between Catalonia and the rest of Spain, and whatever significance one attributes to these contrasts, must therefore be seen as the result of history, not geography.

Any historian of Spain must be aware of the smoldering tensions between "Catalonia Infelix" and the central government in Madrid. But I had deliberately tried not to crystallize, solely on the basis of reading, any tentative hypotheses concerning those tensions. I intended to discuss the Catalan question with the people I would be meeting, but I was not going to ask leading questions that would encourage outpourings of nationalist sentiment. I hoped to be receptive to the Catalan context rather than to place the Catalan "problem" in the foreground. Actually, many of my conversations had no more direct relevance to Catalonia than if they had been conducted in Madrid or Seville.

Through the good offices of a Spanish lawyer whom I had known previously, I had the opportunity of a detailed interview with D. Miguel Maura, an outstanding conservative Republican of the 1930s who was now living in what he himself characterized as the semi-exile of Barcelona. Maura was the son of the distinguished conservative Prime Minister under the monarchy, D. Antonio Maura, and it was clear from much that he said that his personal relations with the social and professional elite of Spain had been bitterly affected by his career as a Republican. Like Franklin Roosevelt, he was accused of being a traitor to his class, but unlike Roosevelt, he was incapable of joking about the accusation. Laic and Left Republicans had not greatly trusted him in office either: because he was intensely Catholic, because he was the son of Antonio Maura, and because he either lacked, or scorned, the average politician's talent for avoiding the statement of uncomfortable truths. Numerically his following had never been important. There were very few people in Spain who combined his aristocratic background and manner with Republican convictions. But he had played a major role in the provisional government of 1931, and on several occasions between 1931 and 1936 he had been an all too accurate Cassandra as well as a respected intellectual opponent and consultant for Left Republican and Socialist leaders.

Maura had been Minister of the Interior from April to October 1931. He had therefore been responsible for the maintenance of public order and for police behavior during the first strikes of the Republican era and the church burnings of May 10. He had resigned in October as a protest against the passage of Article 26 of the Constitution, which officially separated Church and State. He had, however, in contrast to most conservative Catholics, maintained a strong, publicly affirmed loyalty to the Republic while disagreeing with its religious policies.

What struck me most forcibly in his discussion of the church burnings was his absolute conviction that most of the fires were set by provacateurs, professional labor spies or scabs whose aim was to discredit the new government. This conviction seemed to be based on the nature of the telephone calls reaching the ministry during those days: gleeful, threatening, sometimes obscenely phrased calls stating that such and such a church would be burned next. More often than not, nothing happened to the churches so named. He also mentioned, though without stressing the point, that both verbal and physical attacks on the Church were a traditional form of antigovernment protest on the part of *sinvergüenzas,* shameless ones.

"This was no spontaneous or passionate social protest on the part of any mass organization. Once the cabinet had given me permission to use the Civil Guard, on May 12, the country was quiet the next day."

I asked him why, if it had been so easy to restore order after the twelfth, the police had been so ineffective on the eleventh and twelfth.

"The police waited for orders. It was the government's fault. My colleagues refused for almost forty-eight hours to let me issue the necessary orders. That was the terrible error."

"But I have seen pictures of police and firemen just standing around while the fires burned."

"Only a few people set fires, but lots of people enjoy watching them burn. The average policeman will do what he's told if he gets orders."

Obviously we were operating on different wavelengths, perhaps attributable to the differing reflexes of a man used to Anglo-Saxon self-government and a man used to paternal government. I kept wondering why the police did not stop arson the moment it began, and he kept blaming the central government for not issuing specific orders.

We talked also of July 18, 1936, of the first reactions of the Madrid government to the news of the military rising, and of political responsibilities for the outbreak of the Civil War. On the latter point he spoke most bitterly and vehemently of Gil Robles. If the leader of the CEDA had, at any time in the year 1935 between the Asturian revolt and the Popular Front election, declared firmly and unambiguously his loyalty to the

Republic, there need not have been a war. According to Maura, President Alcalá-Zamora had wanted in late 1935 to form a coalition cabinet under Maura, to group all tendencies from the Catholic conservative Republicans to the parliamentary Socialists. Gil Robles, wishing to see the Cortes dissolved and confident that he would sweep the ensuing elections, refused, and thus the President was forced to turn to Portela and have him preside over the elections which produced the Popular Front victory of February 1936.

"But," I asked, after his tirade, "how could the President offer power to you rather than to the leader of the Cortes majority? Isn't it perfectly understandable that Gil Robles should refuse?"

"According to the Constitution the President had the right to name the Prime Minister, and he had the *duty* to protect the Republic from a cunning politician who refused to say whether or not he accepted the Republic as the legitimate form of government in Spain."

As in the discussion of police conduct, I was struck by the paternalistic element in his thought. I tried several times to make my point about the rights of the leader of the majority, but my interlocutor found nothing requiring justification in the refusal of the president of a democratic republic to appoint the majority leader as prime minister, nor in his effort to appoint instead the leader of a very small party, which party also represented the right wing rather than the center of a proposed coalition. Maura clearly thought of himself, in the 1935 context, as having been "above parties." So he may have been, and so may the President have thought of him, but he seemed, sitting opposite me in his law office, to be unaware of the "rules of the game" in a parliamentary democracy.

On the morning of July 18 itself, he said, the recently elected President Azaña had telephoned to ask his advice in the face of imminent civil war. Throughout the spring the government, composed entirely of middle-class Republicans, had been unable to control effectively either its fascist and militarist enemies or its Left Socialist and anarchist supporters. A wave of assassinations from both sides had culminated on

July 12 in the deaths of the Leftist lieutenant José Castillo and the prestigious monarchist leader José Calvo Sotelo. On the evening of July 17 army officers in Morocco had launched a *pronunciamiento* against the Republican government, and it was in the light of this situation that President Azaña had telephoned Maura on the morning of the eighteenth.

Maura's opinions were already on record. Exactly one month earlier, in *El Sol,* he had called for a "republican dictatorship" which should simultaneously restore order by use of the Civil Guard, proceed rapidly with agrarian reform, and revise those constitutional clauses which were hostile to the Church and those which prevented the President from acting strongly in national emergencies. Azaña wanted to know whether Maura would be willing to preside over a cabinet representing all tendencies from the conservative Catholic Republicans to the moderate Socialists. According to Maura, his own response was positive, and in the course of a few hours Azaña had also received the consent of Prieto and the laic Republican leaders Sánchez Román and Martínez Barrio. But Largo Caballero, leader of the Left Socialists, had refused, saying that such a cabinet would mean civil war, i.e., that the workers would resist such a government as a forerunner of fascism. The President had then tried, unsuccessfully, to form a cabinet under Martínez Barrio. Finally, on July 20, José Giral was able to form a Republican cabinet with Left Socialist and Communist backing because he was willing—as Maura and Martínez Barrio had not been—to arm the workers. By this time the *pronunciamiento* had become a civil war.

Since this was Maura's version of the July 18 crisis, and it was a version consistent with everything I had read, I wanted to know why he held Gil Robles rather than Largo Caballero responsible for the outbreak of the Civil War. His reply was passionate, and imprecise. The gist of it was a judgment of character. He had known Caballero as a cabinet colleague and had found him an honorable man, always frank in his views and without demagogic, dictatorial ambitions. Gil Robles, on the other hand, he found weak, evasive, and demagogic. In later months I was to hear similar favorable judgments of

Caballero from Martínez Barrio and from the Basque Minister of Justice, Manuel Irujo, and these judgments strongly influenced my own interpretation of Largo Caballero as a wartime prime minister. Also, thinking of the interpretation of the entire Civil War, I was impressed by the fact that for Maura the only significant forces in July had been the Catholics, the Socialists, and the army. He barely mentioned the Falange, the Communists, and the anarchists, and only in terms of minor troublemaking, not of cohesive power. We went on to discuss military and diplomatic developments during the war, but these he had known only at second hand, and much that he said was very melodramatic and unreliable. This did not invalidate his testimony on events in which he had participated, and about which I was able to check with other individuals and with printed sources. But this long, impassioned conversation was one of many in which I saw clearly that in putting together the history of the war I would have to distinguish very carefully between the "primary" and "secondary" portions of my interview materials.

My Barcelona conversations dealt as much with the present as with the past. This was due in part to the fact that I was meeting a number of people who had been children at the time of the Civil War, but I believe it was also due to the atmosphere of Barcelona itself, a booming industrial city in which all the people I talked to, old and young, seemed to be free of the painful inferiority complex and the combination of nostalgia and nausea toward the past which pervaded the atmosphere in all the other provincial capitals and which was common, though not pervasive, in Madrid. Typical of such experiences was my meeting with Father Casimir Martí, a young Catalan priest who had studied under and later collaborated with the magnificent Catalan historian Jaume Vicens Vives. My specific reason for seeking out Father Martí was to discuss with him the detailed studies he had made of industrial strikes throughout Spain during the years 1931–36. Since he offered immediately to lend me his unpublished notes as well as the tables which were about to be published in the Catalan magazine *Serra d'Or,* and since he was curious to hear about

French and American politics, most of our conversation dealt with the present.

Father Martí, who was really much too boyish to be thought of as a "father," was a left-wing Christian Democrat. While technically not a worker-priest, he clearly had familiarized himself with the living conditions of the Barcelona working class. He was Catalan in culture and sentiment but truly catholic, in the etymological as well as religious sense, in his sympathies. When he talked of Murcians and gypsies there was no trace of the racism that colored many Catalan remarks about the immigrant industrial workers. Where education and social improvements were concerned he made no exclusions on grounds of politics. Thus he evidently worked with anarchists and communists when their objectives coincided with his. He refused to be frightened by either bogeyman, property confiscation or anticlerical agitation. Concerning the former he saw that the Spanish regime intervened in the economy as much as did many a socialist regime, but not in the interests of social justice. As for the latter, he held the reactionary past of the Church to be largely responsible for popular anticlericalism. The proper answer to anticlericalism would be to prove in action that the Church belonged to the people and not to a wealthy minority.

Since Father Martí was so knowledgeable about the living conditions of Spanish workers, I took advantage of the opportunity to ask him to compare, if he could, the situations of the 1930s and the present. Broadly speaking, he said, literacy and notions of elementary hygiene were more widespread in 1960 than in 1935, although, he hastened to add, they were still far from being universal. Movies, bicycles, and mass-produced clothes had certainly added a welcome variety to life. At the same time, food had become more expensive, if only because Spain's population had risen by two or three million since 1935, whereas agricultural production in 1960 had barely recovered to the 1935 level. The economic squeeze was clear from the fact that, if they could, most workers held more than one job. Young workers were glad to have a bicycle now and to be able to think in terms of a motorcycle or a small car for the future. Older workers often complained to him that thirty years ago they had had time to read or play *bola* (an outdoor form of bowling) but that now they arrived home completely exhausted. Having read many sociological studies of industrialization, Father Martí knew that the early stages of economic progress, whether under capitalist or communist auspices, always exert strong pressures on both the pocketbooks and the energies of the workers. Thus he was cautiously optimistic about Spain's economic future. The real problem with which he was concerned was to achieve a society which could be governed more by consent and less by force than the present one. For this reason he wanted the Church to do everything in its power to improve both the economic and the educational opportunities of the working class. Quite aside from the value of the information he gave me, I felt exhilarated by his openness and his constant concern with the possibilities of a better future rather than with the painful memories of the past.

I received a similar feeling of pleasure and hopefulness from a very different sort of visit. One of the most impressive short personal memoirs I had read was a book entitled *Tribunales Rojos* by Gabriel Avilés, a lawyer who had defended political prisoners in the Barcelona courts during the Civil War. The book had appeared in 1939, when the term *rojos* had been the universal pejorative for everything connected with the Republican regime. But the book itself was clearly the work of a conscientious, humane, courageous man. I had hoped to meet him personally. As it turned out, he had died several years earlier, but I did meet his married daughter (also a lawyer), her husband, and an aunt who had been very close to her father. They told me that as a young man Sr. Avilés had been a Socialist; that during the Civil War multiple inefficiencies and injustices on the part of the Popular Front had made him more conservative; but that in his last years he had again been a Socialist. He was not a Catalan. He had been a professor of law in Madrid, had brought his Catalan wife to Barcelona to have her baby—my hostess—and had been caught here by the outbreak of the war. María Avilés and her aunt both confirmed to me in detail what I had inferred from the book, that Sr. Avilés, discouraged by the violence of Spanish politics, had concentrated all his intelligence and energy on the protection of political defendants regardless of their party. He had been a friend of the president of the Catalan regional government, Luis Companys. Under circumstances of Communist terror in 1938 and Nationalist terror in 1939 he had proceeded at no small risk to his personal safety. He had been able to survive through a fortunate combination of factors. Being little known in Barcelona, he had no political enemies seeking to settle scores with him. The Companys government and the central government of Juan Negrín had both approved of his efforts and those of a number of other lawyers to restore peacetime safeguards in the courts. After the Nationalists had occupied the city there were many conservative voices testifying to his courage in dealing with revolutionary tribunals.

The aunt, who was clearly a woman of strong opinions, took a considerable part in the conversation, warming up especially when she realized that I intended to write a book not only about the Civil War but about the Republic. She was particularly anxious to set the record straight on two points concerning which the Franco government had, in her opinion, deliberately and constantly lied: the conditions of Catholic worship under the Republic and the political-personal character of Luis Companys. She had been a practicing Catholic throughout her life and as far as she was concerned, regular worship and the observance of Holy Week in Barcelona had been perfectly normal. In her opinion the dictatorship had taken occasional anticlerical propaganda meetings and magnified them into a problem of so-called persecution and disorder. Disorders and murders had indeed occurred in reaction to the military rising of July 18, but not before that. Catholic secondary schools had also continued to function normally until the start of the Civil War. The Cortes in 1933 had passed a law which demanded, among other things, the closing of Catholic private schools, but the elections of November 1933 had produced a conservative majority and the schools had remained open.

With regard to Companys, she inveighed against the many Francoist references to him as a *rojo-separatista.* The *rojo* half of the epithet was unworthy of discussion. As for separatist tendencies, the Catalan autonomy movement had always had an extremist, i.e., separatist, wing. Companys, however, had always enjoyed, and deserved, the confidence of Madrid. I told her that just two days previously Miguel Maura had recalled to me how, as Minister of the Interior in 1931, he had depended on Companys to outmaneuver the separatist hotheads during the first days of the Republic.

"Yes," she said, "we would never have had the autonomy statute without Azaña's confidence that D. Luis meant autonomy *within* the Republic, not separatism. But then," she continued, as if anxious not to falsify matters through oversimplification, "he didn't really have control of the situation on October 6, nor during the first days of the Civil War. You know that he was the lawyer who had defended the anarchists and the tenant farmers, and he had gone to jail in 1917 and in 1923. It's very hard to say 'no' to people with whom you have shared a prison cell."

Besides the accusations of communism and separatism which were standard among conservatives, I had also heard from several former members of the Esquerra, Companys' party, that he had been *mujeriego,* fond of the girls. In fact, one retired civil servant who insisted on his personal sympathy for Companys attributed his famous October 6 declaration of a "Catalan state within the Federal Spanish Republic" to the influence of a young mistress who was a separatist. I wanted to see how this lady, bourgeois and Catholic to her fingertips, would comment on this question.

"You say that he couldn't really control the ardent separatists in October 1934. I have also heard it said, in Esquerra circles, that he was strongly influenced by a girl friend who was a separatist."

"We were all so excited in those October days. I don't know just how he got carried away. We all thought a new era was dawning. We were drunk with the Statute and didn't notice the fact that Madrid had a conservative, anti-Catalan government while we were passing liberal laws in Catalonia. As for D. Luis and the girls: yes, he was separated from his wife, who had never had any sympathy for his politics. Divorce is practically unknown in Spain. So he had a *chica;* that's of no importance to anyone but him."

She paused for a few seconds, but with an expression that indicated that she had more to say and was searching for the right phrases. "They have slandered his memory with these petty personal details. That's because he was a good man, and they shot him, and they know that he was a good man. First of all, he was a lawyer who defended the oppressed. He organized the union of *rabassaires,* the vintners who had always been at the mercy of the landlords. Under the Republic he was the only Catalan political leader who was trusted both by the Madrid Republicans and the majority of Catalans. During the war he was loyal to the Republic, and he also did everything to help priests, and any innocent persons threatened with assassination, to escape to France. After our war the Gestapo sent him back from exile. María's father tried to defend him. Nothing doing. Shot as a *rojo-separatista.*"

María Avilés and her husband listened quietly. I had the impression that while the aunt's words were not new to them as information, such conversations had been infrequent. We talked about the beauty of Barcelona, and they showed me their father's library and a number of attractive landscapes he had painted. Both of them were lawyers, and Sra. Fina Sanglas, to use her married name, was enthusiastic and optimistic about combining marriage with a professional career. For both husband and wife the increasing number of women receiving university education and entering the professions was one of the most important, politically neutral, factors preparing Spain for a better future after the dictatorship. They referred to the regime without emotion, and obviously with the sentiment that it would be temporary. Toward the autonomy movement they seemed to be sympathetic in retrospect, but clearly they identified it with the past rather than the future. Like most Spaniards, they were quite uncertain what regime would succeed the dictatorship, but they did not seem to be preoccupied with it. Education, economic development, personal liberty, mutual respect for differing political and religious convictions—these were the factors upon which the future of Spain as a whole would rest. I was moved to see, and I am sure that such men as Luis Companys and Gabriel Avilés would have been moved to see, the persistence of fine ideals under difficult conditions, the appreciation of the past without sterile bitterness, the devotion of talent and energy to the preparation of a better future.

During some ten days in Barcelona I had many short, valuable meetings with lawyers, businessmen, and bank officers, most of whom had lived in the city during the 1930s and a few of whom represented the postwar generation. Through an accumulation of details, most of which were not terribly precise or weighty in themselves, I nevertheless came to be aware of how much the life of the city was affected by consciousness of the Catalan question. An intimate friend of the late Cardinal Vidal y Barraquer of Tarragona very clearly attributed the cardinal's broad intellectual interests and his provisionally friendly attitude toward the Republic to his being Catalan. A lawyer who had been about twenty years old in 1939, and who was both a practicing Catholic and a Catalan patriot, emphasized that there had been very little looting or destruction of factory equipment on the eve of the Republican collapse in early 1939; and for him the credit went not to "workers" but to "Catalan workers." An otherwise very open-minded businessman insisted to me that as a matter of experience he knew that all the violent anarchists had been immigrants from Murcia and that the best elements among the immigrants learned Catalan at the first opportunity. Any discussion of economic questions would sooner or later reveal Catalan resentment that the proportionately higher taxes paid in Catalonia were spent on the "Madrid bureaucracy." And in any political discussion of the 1930s the names Cambó, Macià, and Companys occurred far more frequently than the names Azaña, Gil Robles, and Largo Caballero.

The city of Barcelona made a very different impression from either Madrid or the other provincial capitals I had visited. The shops in the Gothic quarter were more esthetically arranged and offered a wider variety of merchandise than those of any other Spanish city. I found bookstore clerks ready to consult catalogues or call other bookstores if they did not have what I was looking for. In Madrid, Salamanca, and Saragossa, clerks had just shrugged their shoulders if they could not find the book on their own shelves. In banks and department stores there were not nearly as many employees standing around without any apparent functions to fulfill. The Ramblas flower stalls, the Gaudi and Gaudi-influenced apartment buildings, and the coffee bars all showed, it seemed to me, a kind of fantasy and decorative flair which I had not seen elsewhere in Spain and which reminded me of the most beautiful parts of Paris. Uniquely useful, and esthetically attractive, were the lighted plaques on street corners which enable one at night to know which numbers are found along a given block.

The combination of physical impressions and conversational items provoked me to think more conscientiously than I had been previously inclined about the real and the illusory aspects of the Catalan complex. The most tangible distinction between Catalonia and Castile is that of language. The distinction is not unique, since there are several hundred thousand Basque-speaking peasants, and since there are several Spanish dialects, of which Galician is the most important. But Catalan is the normal family language of over four million people whose territory happens also to constitute the economically most advanced portion of the entire Iberian peninsula. Medieval Catalan literature is comparable in quality to that of Castile or Portugal. In the seventeenth and eighteenth centuries Catalan was almost entirely a spoken language, but for the past century it has again been a flourishing literary language.

History, and historical consciousness, have also been fundamental and undeniable factors of distinction from Castilian Spain. Medieval Catalonia, as an independent principality and then as the dominant partner in the kingdom of Aragon-Catalonia, played a major political and economic role in the Mediterranean. Barcelona was a kind of city-state, comparable to the Italian city-states of the time, with industrial, shipping, banking, and commercial facilities virtually unknown in the rest of Spain. During the same period her forms of land tenure and church organization were closer to those of her French neighbor to the north than to those of her Castilian neighbor to the west. Both in imperial times and in modern Latin American experience, Catalan export industries and Catalan businessmen have played a role far out of proportion to their numbers. The evidence of a thousand years of economic history all points up the fact that Catalonia has always had a much larger middle class and a more developed commercial spirit than Castile. For some historians this is cause for compliment, and for others cause for disdain, but none contest the fact.

From my reading of the Barcelona press and Catalan political literature of the past century, I also knew that the tone and the preoccupations of politically conscious Catalans were different from those of other Spaniards. There was almost no trace of Krausist influence, and practically none of the rhetorical nostalgia for the era of the Catholic kings which figured so prominently in the self-examining literature of Castile between 1890 and 1930. Catalan writers of both the Right and the Left were apt to speak of the peoples of Spain or of the Spains rather than to use the singular forms of those nouns. Relative to the Castilian press there was less Marxism in Catalan political commentary, also less concern with Spain's African ambitions and more concern with foreign trade and with European economic and cultural affairs.

Very significant for the misunderstandings and resentments of the present was the startling difference of attitude toward the Primo de Rivera dictatorship. For Castilians it had been a mild, well-meant form of paternalism. For Catalans it was remembered as a time of national oppression, as the powerful if unsuccessful attempt of a centralizing dictator to eradicate the Catalan language and all forms of distinctive Catalan culture. Thus in 1960 many older people of differing political viewpoints could say to me in Madrid, Seville, Valladolid, and Saragossa that, all things considered, the Primo era had been the best period of their lives and that they felt hopeful that the Franco dictatorship was slowly evolving toward the kind of *dictadura blanda,* mild dictatorship, which had been exercised by Primo from 1923 to 1930. In Barcelona I heard no such fond nostalgia for Primo and no such optimism concerning Franco. Examples of such differing perspectives concerning experiences which they have shared with Castile over the past five centuries could be multiplied at will.

The substantial basis of Catalan national feeling resides then in the possession of a separate language and literature, a separate history until the marriage of Ferdinand and Isabella, and a very different perspective on the shared history of Spain since the unification which occurred at the end of the fifteenth century. To this substantial basis Catalans tend to add all kinds of illusory characteristics, such as their claims that Catalan anarchists are less violent than others, Catalan priests more enlightened, Catalans biologically more musical (because there are more choral societies in Catalonia than in Castile), biologically more intelligent (because per capita income and productivity are higher in Catalonia than in Castile), and so forth.

But the fact that Catalans may make all sorts of unverifiable, quasi-racist distinctions between themselves and Castilians does not diminish the significance of their genuine history and culture. The interesting questions are why they have remained a distinctive people, and how Spanish political life might be better structured to accommodate the existence of so important a national minority. Actually the history of Europe offers many examples of the persistence of compact peasant nationalities where the people involved differ in language or religion, or both, from the larger and more powerful nationalities around them. Czechs, Magyars, Slovaks, Croats, Serbs, Rumanians, and Bulgars have all survived centuries of Turkish, or Austrian, or Russian rule. This phenomenon alone could account for the continuing existence of the Catalans as a compact language area surrounded by the larger Castilian and French nationalities.

In addition, history also indicates that a minority whose intellectual and economic culture is superior to that of the surrounding majority will not assimilate itself with that majority. Under the Roman Empire, Greek communities retained their identity in Italy and in the Near East. From the early Middle Ages through the eighteenth century the German farmers, artisans, and merchants who settled in Transylvania, in Russia, and along the Baltic coast all retained their own language and culture. On the other hand, East Europeans emigrating to France or Germany in the nineteenth century became Frenchmen and Germans, and the much larger numbers of people of all European nationalities emigrating to the United States became Americans. In the former instances a culturally superior minority retained its separate culture; in the latter instances the emigrants gladly assimilated themselves in a society which offered wider economic opportunities than had the "old country."

In the case of Catalonia both major factors are present. There is a compact peasant population speaking a distinctive language, as in the case of the Czechs, the Rumanians, or others. And there is a higher economic and educational standard in relation to the surrounding majority, as in the case of the German communities in Eastern Europe. It should cause no wonder, then, that the Catalans survive as a distinctive national minority regardless of the pressures to which they have been, and are, subjected. It has been one of the great misfortunes of Spanish history that from the Conde-Duque de Olivares in the seventeenth century, through the energetic Bourbon kings of the eighteenth century, to the twentieth-century dictators Primo de Rivera and Franco, the strongest rulers of Spain have attempted, always unsuccessfully, and to the great economic and political detriment of Spain, forcibly to assimilate the people of Catalonia.

My experience in Barcelona, together with these historical reflections, inspired in me also a new respect for the Catalan Statute of Autonomy passed by the Cortes in 1932 during the Prime Ministership of Manual Azaña. In order to protect national sovereignty the statute expressly reserved to the central government the domains of defense, foreign affairs, tariffs and currency, and Church-State relations. It granted to the regional parliament the control of municipal government, local taxes and public services, museums, radio, and cultural organizations of all sorts. There was to be equality of languages in the schools, law courts, and public services, and the University of Barcelona was to be bilingual, and governed by a mixed commission of Castilian and Catalan professors.

Because of the October 1934 revolution and the general repression of 1935, the peacetime career of the Statute was extremely brief, barely two years in all. But during the hectic spring of 1936 Catalonia, under the restored regional government, was noticeably more peaceful and orderly than the rest of Spain. During the Civil War, until the final months when starvation and bombing had broken the morale of the civilian population, Catalonia under the regional government was the political and economic bastion of the Spanish Republic. The Franco government, on the other hand, repealed the entire Statute of Autonomy and has applied to Catalonia the same authoritarian military rule as to the rest of Spain. I have no doubt myself that the 1932 Statute, whatever its shortcomings, provides the only intelligent basis ever offered by a Spanish government for the harmonious, freely accepted incorporation of the Catalan people into a unified Spain. The Statute, like many of the best plans of the Republic, may have been a half-century ahead of its time. The subsequent large-scale industrialization of Spain, and the slow but steady tendency to associate Spain more closely with the prosperous Europe of the Common Market, may make it easier in the future than in the past for Madrid governments to accept a measure of local autonomy for Catalonia.

Actually, the problem of autonomy for national minorities is a general European problem, and one which need not make Spaniards feel unduly self-conscious or victimized. In both Eastern and Western Europe the generally rising economic prosperity since about 1950, and the world revolution of rising expectations on the part of the common man everywhere, have reinforced the historic self-consciousness of linguistic and religious minorities. Yugoslavia has decentralized economic controls in order to conciliate the culturally advanced Croatian minority. Rumania is trying to reconcile rather than forcibly assimilate the Hungarian minority in Transylvania. In Czechoslovakia the economically more advanced Czechs hope simultaneously to raise economic standards and satisfy the linguistic-cultural demands of the Slovaks. Of these situations the Yugoslav is the one one most closely parallel to the Spanish, since the Croats, like the Catalans, constitute a substantial, economically advanced minority whose cooperation, in return for a measure of autonomy, can greatly speed up the development of the entire nation. At the same time, to put matters in full perspective, the tensions between Catalans and Castilians have never, at their worst, been as bitter as the relations between Italians and Germans in the Tyrol or between Flemings and Walloons in Belgium.

It was not solely in Barcelona that I felt myself to be *in partibus infidelium.* I had only the briefest two days to spend in Valencia, but in conversation first with a trio of Falangist journalists, and then separately with several lawyers who had belonged to the Autonomous Valencian Right party of Luis Lucía, I realized that in Valencia as well as Barcelona regional feeling was a substantial element in politics. For the conservatives, the political geneology of Valencian regionalism stretched back to the beginning of the eighteenth century. During the War of the Spanish Succession, Valencia (like Catalonia) had embraced the cause of the Austrian Archduke Charles. When in 1714 the Bourbons were finally confirmed in possession of the Spanish throne, Catalonia and Valencia were punished by the loss of their *fueros,* or traditional rights of self-government. In the nineteenth century Valencian conservatives had been Carlists, out of a combination of Catholic opposition to liberalism and resistance to centralization. Under the Republic they had supported the regional conservative party of Luis Lucía. For the Left, the regional coloration was present but not as specific. The Valencian journalist and novelist Blasco Ibañez had been the great personality in the local development of anticlerical republicanism before 1914. However, in the 1930s Valencian Republicans belonged to the same parties as Castilian Republicans, and the Socialist Party, which was never sympathetic to regional autonomy, was strong in Valencia.

A fair proportion of Valencian farmers and businessmen had turned to the Republic in 1931 out of specific resentment against the Primo dictatorship. In 1925 the Primo government had, at the behest of the Andalusian olive growers, closed down the Valencian factories which produced peanut and vegetable oils. Theoretically the manufacturers were to be compensated. The dictatorship never paid the compensation, but the promise was honored in 1932 under the Republican Minister of Agriculture, Marcelino Domingo. Small citrus farmers too, who resented the dictatorship's policies favoring the large shipping interests, were attracted by the plan of the Azaña government to build a national fleet which would free the growers from absolute dependence on the oligopoly of private shippers.

The man who explained these agricultural economic questions to me in considerable detail was the former Republican mayor of Valencia, a member of Azaña's party in the 1930s. On his desk he had a picture of Harry S Truman, whom in fact he slightly resembled. When I remarked on the photo, he told me that he admired Truman as a self-made man, a real man of the people; as the President who had stood up to Stalin in Greece and Korea, thereby ending the postwar expansion of the Soviet empire in both Europe and Asia; and as the President who had cut down to size the military proconsul General MacArthur.

After our discussion of Valencian economics and Truman-era politics he told me something of his own past. He had begun life as a sailor and dockworker, had earned a law degree in the mid-1920s, and had been one of the militants of Azaña's party, Acción Republicana. As wartime mayor of Valencia he had fallen, by definition, under the sweeping law of political responsibilities which formed the legal basis of the postwar purge by the Franco dictatorship. He had been condemned to death in 1939, but the sentence had been commuted to life imprisonment, and he had spent four years in a labor battalion. Each morning in the prison courtyard, the inmates, almost all of them ex-Republican soldiers, were obliged to sing the Falangist hymn, *Cara al Sol.* Several times a week they were obliged to hear Mass and were told by the priest that they did not deserve to live, that they had been poisoned by their secular education, and that they owed everything now to the grace of General Franco.

My host had escaped after four years, had hidden for two more, and then been officially amnestied in 1946, at which time the government was extremely anxious to gain the goodwill of the democratic powers. Upon his return to Valencia he had been reinstated in his law practice *en el acto,* right away. He was obviously both proud and grateful that his colleagues had so treated him. He was equally proud and happy with his present success. Laying out on his desk the list of tax assessments for all the registered lawyers of Valencia, he showed me that his was the highest assessment.

When he heard that after a few days in Seville I would be going to France and Switzerland he laughed suddenly and said he had to tell me about his first vacation after the war outside Spain. He and his wife had saved for several years to buy a small Seat, and, in company with his sister and brother-in-law, they were off for a vacation in southern France. They were four people of substantial bulk, and they stopped frequently to stretch their legs. When they crossed the French frontier the weather was glorious, and on their first leg-stretching stop the two men sang *Cara al Sol* at the top of their lungs. In the law office of the former Republican mayor of Valencia we now clinked glasses to Harry Truman, and between gales of laughter we sang the Falangist hymn. It was a fitting end to my journey of inquiry *in partibus infidelium.*

8

Passion and Tragedy in Andalusia

It took me a full eighteen hours, from one in the afternoon until seven the next morning, to travel from Valencia to Seville. All Spanish trains in 1961 were slow, but on the main lines, such as those I had just traveled, from Madrid through Saragossa to Barcelona, and then down from Barcelona to Valencia, the coaches were reasonably clean and comfortable. I left Valencia in a third-class carriage dating from 1896. The lining around the window frames was completely threadbare, and one could see the vertical outer slats of the coach quivering as we jolted over the uneven roadbed. The benches were also wood, and the backrests formed an austere ninety-degree angle with the seats. The windows were narrow, and dangerous to open, because the constant expansion and contraction of the frames caused raised windows suddenly to slam shut.

However, a slow train journey enables one to feel the change of environment, both geographical and human. We moved at a leisurely pace, never more than thirty miles an hour, across the flat, mild, intensely cultivated rice fields and citrus orchards of the Valencian *huerta.* We paused for a half-hour outside Játiva, with no visible purpose other than to refill the boiler of the coal-burning locomotive, and then climbed arduously to a height of about two thousand feet. As a result of that long ascent we had left behind a California-like garden and now found ourselves on a dry, windswept, Dakota-like plain. Between the villages the only signs of life were occasional goats feeding on the stubble of wheat fields. At each halt the entire population seemed to be awaiting the train, to sell sweets, oranges, sausage, beer, or water from platform to compartment; to hold out a cap or a tin cup; or simply to stare at two-legged creatures who lived elsewhere than in this particular village.

There was an extraordinary rate of both verbal and commercial exchange, with apparent satisfaction on both sides. As I munched my own *chorizo* sandwich I wondered for the first time about a question which has often intrigued me since: the extent to which the size and longevity of the Spanish empire might have been due to the manner in which Spaniards speak. Most of these people had never left their native village; many were illiterate; and a high proportion of them were missing several teeth, or an eye, or a leg, and would have been physically repulsive if not for their extroverted animation. Their physical ailments, however, did not enfeeble their personalities. They looked directly into the travelers' eyes; they knew before we replied whether we were ready to buy something or not; they were anxious to sell, but also to please. Although their pronunciation and their phrases were as peculiar to me as my accent must have been to them, we understood each other easily, in part because of the animated gestures and eager approach, in part because the spoken Spanish language has very distinct, clearly identifiable sounds (even though local accents are strong) and a very simple sentence structure. As the train passed through these primitive, homely villages, and as we exchanged greetings and bought snacks, it seemed to me that the Spanish language and the Spanish temperament were ideally suited for the quick establishment of human contact, and that something of this character must have been involved in the rapid growth of the empire and the rapid spread of the Spanish language among the Indians from Mexico to Patagonia.

Darkness was falling as we approached Albacete. The occasional buttes threw long, rapidly shifting shadows across the absolutely level plain, and reddish rocks turned blue in the declining light. It was easy to imagine the excitement and fanciful mirages that would be experienced by a Don Quixote, or a highwayman, or a contemporary goatherd in that open, windy, varyingly colored, sparsely inhabited landscape. And I admired profoundly the people who could draw a living from that harsh soil and who could enjoy the spectacle of and the brief contact with the railway voyagers.

It was almost midnight when we reached the rail junction with the Madrid-Seville line at Alcázar San Juan. There being no sign yet of the Seville train, I enjoyed the clear cold air, the star-studded sky, and the opportunity to stretch and walk after ten hours on crowded wooden benches. I was happy to have ridden the slow train, but as I had a full schedule of interviews for the next two days in Seville, I wanted to get some sleep. When the Seville train arrived, I gladly paid the *suplemento* which allowed me to ride first-class, and I had the good luck to find a compartment to myself. But I was unable to sleep for more than about two hours. We were passing through territory which was both beautiful and historic. The moon was not bright, but its light was well diffused, and the coach windows were wide and clean. We were moving slowly, this time because the train was descending through the forested gorge of Despeñaperros, famous for smuggling in recent centuries and for skirmishes between Muslim and Christian armed detachments in the early Middle Ages. Just below Despeñaperros, at Las Navas de Tolosa, the combined armies of Castille, Aragon, and Navarre had broken the power of the Almohads in 1212, thereby opening Andalusia to Chrisian reconquest.

A few miles farther on, we passed Bailén, where in July 1809 the ill-equipped but emotionally exalted troops of General Castaños had forced the surrender of a French army corps; and Andújar, where the train stopped briefly, had been the headquarters of Napoleon's invading army and the site of the formal surrender. From here on the valley widened, and even in the darkness I could see beautifully watered fields, a variety of crops and fruit trees, and handsome villages. Time after time I was to notice the evidence of hard work, careful maintenance, and agricultural productivity where the nature of the soil and the water supply permitted a prosperous agriculture to flourish. And I was to resent, on behalf of the Spaniards, the many generalizations about Spanish laziness by those who had never paid attention to such evidence.

Next we passed through Córdoba, capital of the tenth-century caliphate which was the most economically and intellectually advanced state in the Europe of its time. Finally in the early morning light we reached Seville, most brilliant of the *taifa* kingdoms of the eleventh century, a period in which Muslim Spain, like eighteenth- and nineteenth-century Germany, was divided among competing prosperous small states, each of which took pride in its intense artistic and cultural life. After the *taifa* period, Seville was the Almohad capital from 1146 to 1248; later still it was the favored residence of the Castillian kings through the fourteenth and fifteenth centuries, and during the sixteenth century it was the center of the Indies trade.

My contacts in Seville I owed principally to Professor J., whom I had known briefly, and liked immensely, at an international conference of Latin American historians. Professor J. was the son of a career officer. He had been educated in Catholic secondary schools and in 1936 had volunteered, like thousands of his middle-class contemporaries, to defend the Church against communism. Not until after the war did he have any knowledge of the extent of the Francoist repression, and only in 1948 did he learn of the 1937 encyclical *Mit brennender Sorge,* in which Pope Pius XI had condemned the attitude of the Nazi government toward Christianity. By a slow process of disillusionment through the 1940s he had lost all his original enthusiasm for the *movimiento.* But he was Spanish to the core, in love with the city of Seville, and dependent on the Archive of the Indies for the raw material of the studies in Spanish colonial economic history which were to give him a worldwide reputation among historians of the New World. Over coffee and rolls at my hotel he prepared a list of names and wrote brief messages explaining my mission.

"You can be absolutely frank with everybody," he assured me while puffing rapidly on his cigarette. "These are all serious people, people who have suffered, but men of complete integrity and honesty. If they trust you they will tell you things they have never discussed with Spaniards."

He mused a moment, then wrote one more name, and suddenly grinned at me. "You can try *este señor* also," he said, pronouncing *este señor* with the kind of concentrated sarcasm that enlisted men can lavish on the word "sir." "He is a detective, not a bad sort personally, and we have remained friends since our army days together. Of course he always told me I was a fool to subscribe to English periodicals while in the army—for which, moreover, I was indeed considered 'unreliable'—but he likes Americans, now that the winds have changed, and he can tell you what the jails were like in the forties, and how many political prisoners there still are."

I began my rounds with the police officer, but from the very manner in which he shook hands and read the card, I knew he would say nothing. "So you are a friend of Professor J., an American historian. How interesting . . . Do you like Seville? . . . Be sure to visit the Cathedral . . ." He took me out into the street and very ceremoniously explained how to reach the Cathedral, whose spires were clearly visible from where we stood. "Also the Giralda, *que maravilla!*" and so forth. We parted as rapidly as courtesy would permit, and I went on, through the beautiful barrio de Santa Cruz, to the office of Major Silvio, one of the minority of career officers who had chosen the Republican side.

Major Silvio was a man of large gestures and elaborate courtesies. When I rang the bell he fairly shouted for me to enter. Removing his glasses, slowly folding them and then precisely sliding them into his breast pocket, he watched me silently as I walked from the door, through a small waiting room, into the large office at the far end of which he sat. In one continuous movement he rose, shook hands, took my introductory card, and motioned me to sit down. Evidently he was far-sighted, but having removed his glasses he preferred to hold the card at arm's length. He read it slowly, perhaps two or three times over, now smiling slightly, now clearing his throat. He was a handsome man, with an oval face and florid complexion. One could sense that he was both physically powerful and deeply emotional.

"Hombre, que tragedia era nuestra guerra," he began without looking up at me. "What a tragedy was our war. Do you think you, or any foreigner, can understand it?" He paused, and fixed his dark, intense eyes on me while drawing a long breath. Slowly, still with his eyes fixed on me, he closed the several large account books at which he had been working. "I am just a small businessman now in this Spain of ours, *una, libre, y grande,* but there is one thing you will not see in this office which you will see in every other office in Spain."

"What is that?" I asked, indeed without the least idea of what he might be referring to.

He indicated the four walls of his office in a sweeping circular gesture. "No photo of el Caudillo, no photo of the man who murdered half a million Spaniards and then sold the country to the Americans." Suddenly he rapped his knuckles hard on the table. *"Que me maten,* let them kill me." He leaned forward whispering hoarsely and constantly staring at me, "I have a sense of honor, the oath of an officer, which I kept on July 18, and which they betrayed." He leaned back, momentarily relaxed. "Now what would you like to know?"

I told him that two things interested me in particular, his direct role in the Civil War and his knowledge and experience of the repression. He began by recalling the atmosphere during the spring of 1936. He had belonged to the UMRA, the organization of antifascist officers formed at the end of 1935 to combat the profascist propaganda of the much larger UME, or Union of Spanish Officers. He and dozens of his friends had received anonymous threat letters in May 1936 telling them to leave Spain or expect to be shot. He was positive that these letters came from the UME, that only Rightist fellow officers would have known the names of the antifascist minority and would have used the particular combination of military terms and blackmail which characterized the letters.

"But I did not come into the streets in Madrid on July 18 because of death threats. I came because, like every officer in the Spanish army, I had sworn an oath of allegiance to the legitimate government of Spain, and that government was the government of the Republic, whose President was the Honorable D. Manuel Azaña and whose Prime Minister was the Honorable D. Santiago Casares Quiroga. At the Montaña barracks," he continued, "We defeated the military rebellion. The officers knew it, and followed their surrender by collective suicide."

He then told me in great detail how the people of the city had surrounded the Montaña, how a handful of loyal officers had directed the artillery fire during the brief siege, and how at one moment the besieged had raised the white flag and then fired upon the crowd which surged forward expecting to enter the fort. A controlled but ever-fresh anger characterized his recital.

"Is it not possible," I asked, "that the officer firing into the crowd did not know that the white flag had been raised? Or that the white flag may have been run up without the consent of many of the besieged?"

"It was an act of deliberate slaughter," he replied without the slightest air of doubt. "They were conscious of what they were doing. Later, at the time of surrender, Lieutenant Moreno went in so to hurry General Fanjul out the back way before the mob could tear him to pieces. A group of lieutenants and majors then closeted themselves in an upstairs room and committed suicide. They had broken their oath to the Republic and they had fired on unarmed people who had advanced because of the white flag. It is to their credit that they committed suicide."

He then went on to describe his role in defense of Madrid. He had directed an artillery battery in the Retiro Park which had played a crucial role in slowing the advance of the Nationalist troops in the first days of November 1936, and he spoke with immense enthusiasm of the militiamen who had had no idea of military discipline in July and who had become, in his opinion, expert in the maneuvering, cleaning, and firing of their guns.

Later we turned to the question of repressions. Thousands had been killed for motives of personal vengeance or were victims of a spasm of bloodlust. Others, of whom he was one, had been saved through particular personal circumstances. Major Silvio, during the first weeks of the war in the mountains north of Madrid, had helped the mother of a Francoist aviator to cross the lines from the village where she had been vacationing, and where she might well have become the victim of an antifascist *paseo* if her relationship to the aviator had been known. When Major Silvio came before a court-martial in late 1940, this woman's testimony meant a commutation of the death sentence to life imprisonment. Some years later he was released in one of the mass amnesties for prisoners of war. He told me that while awaiting trial in Seville between February 20 and June 20, 1940, he and his fellow prisoners had counted 457 shootings, of which thirty-two had occurred on one night in March. Among the many individual cases he cited I remember most vividly the story of one Lieutenant Delgado, shot ostensibly for the crime of defacing the altarpiece of a church in Jáen. The lieutenant had tried to explain to his court-martial that he had sent the altarpiece to Madrid precisely to save it from destruction. According to Major Silvio, the said altarpiece had indeed been returned from Madrid years later, long after the execution of the lieutenant. This was one of many highly circumstantial accounts whose truth I could judge only by the character of those telling the stories and the context of feverish hatred in which the war had been fought.

From Major Silvio's office I took a taxi to the suburban orphanage where I was to meet Father Heriberto Morilla Luengas. Father Heriberto was one of the Basque priests who had willingly served the Republic despite the anticlerical excesses which had discredited it in the eyes of many Catholics. In May 1936, with the Popular Front government in office, with increasing outbreaks of violence in the streets, and with civil war being freely predicted by spokesmen of all political tendencies, Father Heriberto had accepted a post as principal of a secondary school in Murcia. He held that post throughout the Civil War, and was afterward one of several dozen Basque priests condemned to death for collaboration with the "Red" government. His sentence, like that of most of his follow priests, was commuted on the intervention of Cardinal Segura. He nevertheless spent some five years in prison. For several months he had shared the cell of the former president of the Constituent Cortes, the moderate Socialist Julián Besteiro, who died of tuberculosis in the Carmona prison on the night of September 30, 1940. I did not expect to discuss Besteiro's political career with Father Heriberto, but rather to learn something of the man himself.

Padre Heriberto received me in what must have been the janitor's house of the eighteenth-century estate, which had been left to the Church as an orphanage some decades earlier. He was an old man, with stooped shoulders and slightly quivering hands, but his eyes were very alert and his movements quick. He poured two glasses of sweet wine, apologized for having spilled a few drops, and raised his glass to drink to the memory of *el dueño de España.* I had never heard that phrase before, in any context, but from the padre's tone, and from the frequent use which he made of the phrase throughout our conversation, I could tell clearly that he meant something like "the spiritual master" or "the saintly shepherd," and indeed he referred to Besteiro even more frequently as *este hombre santo,* "this saintly man." I wanted indeed to know why a priest should think in such terms of a Socialist, but I did not ask questions, feeling instinctively that my host wished to follow his own train of thought, that he would tell me what he would tell me, in his own manner, in his own time.

First we were going to see the orphanage, to which he had devoted himself since his release from prison. Upon leaving his two-room house we made a short turn into a clump of bushes where he pointed out the grave of Besteiro's cat, the latter's only personal possession, he said, which had been left in his care the night D. Julián had died. Thence to a tour of the dormitories, all built within the past five years in the charming, simple, clean stucco of Andalusia, with large bright windows everywhere, flooded with sunlight—but without heating facilities. Each child had a cot, a small shelf at the head of his bed, and one bureau drawer. There were spotless shower stalls and sinks, and over each doorway a small crucifix. I hoped that I did not appear inarticulate in my briefly phrased praises. I was overwhelmed by his tenderness and pride in every stick of furniture, his tales of the wealthy women of Seville who had paid for the dormitories, as the wealthy should, and who tried sometimes to interfere with the methods of instruction, which the wealthy know nothing about. And he laughed, then listened to a half-sentence of my pleasure, then interrupted to say that in his opinion only small crucifixes should be hung, because the symbol of Christ should be always present, but unobtrusive lest the young revolt against a heavy-handed indoctrination.

He described himself as a disciple of Montessori in educational matters. He had insisted on movable tables and chairs, on a swimming pool, on flower beds to be planted and tended by the children. He was proud of the many crayon drawings lining the classroom walls, and asked me, half humorously and half seriously, whether they did not compare favorably with the recent UNESCO exhibit of drawings by children of all nations.

From the dormitories and classrooms we walked to the administrative offices, located in the original eighteenth-century house. The sitting room was filled with ornate, heavy upholstered furniture. Dimly lit, as in so many museums, were two Zurbaráns and a "school of Murillo" canvas. The place of honor was reserved for a seventeenth-century altar, rich in gold and silver ornaments, which had been transferred truckload by truckload over a period of three years from the estate of one of the orphanage's wealthy benefactors. Father Heriberto was proud of the altar and the paintings too, but they were, he said offhandedly, the proper business of the *monjitas,* the little nuns who were very good at keeping things clean and polished.

Also in the original house was a small ward for foundlings. As we walked up the stairs and past the dispensary he explained to me that every week or so a newborn infant would be abandoned on the steps of one or another church in Seville.

We tiptoed into a small, semidark room in which there were three cradles, each covered with gauze. The infants must have been between a week and six weeks of age. Padre Heriberto went to each cradle in turn. Folding back the gauze he would smile quietly as he observed each infant's breathing. Then he picked up each one, so skillfully that not one of them awoke, an accomplishment in which he clearly took great pride. Then he showed me the kitchen where the formulas were prepared. "They can be fed by the *monjitas,*" he said, "but they take the most when I feed them." Again he laughed as he ushered me out of the kitchen.

Just as we left the building we ran into a swarm of five-year-olds. Seeing the padre, they fairly trampled each other in their eagerness to hug and kiss him, and I, by my proximity, received the same enthusiastic treatment. But just as quickly their hugs and kisses were succeeded by shouted demands, *"bonbones, bonbones!"* with imploring hands outstretched. Father Heriberto apologized helplessly. The demands gave way to screams and bitter crying. Then just as suddenly as they had appeared, the children ran off. The good priest was shaken. He stopped to explain to me that when he visited a classroom, perhaps once a week, he always carried a supply of caramels. How could he have been so careless as to be walking in the middle of the school grounds without any caramels in his pockets? It took him several minutes to recover from the sheer anguish of having disappointed the children.

For me the experience had been troubling in a different way. I was struck by how an apparent outpouring of spontaneous affection had turned into an equally spontaneous gust of rage. How completely uninhibited were the reactions of these children! I had been a counselor of five-year-old boys in a summer camp, and I had seen disappointed kindergartners on various occasions, but I had never seen such a quick alteration of intense feelings or such an open reaction of hatred against someone beloved. Father Heriberto seemed to be concerned entirely with his own failing, as he saw it, and not at all with the wild reaction of the children. Images crossed my mind of priests being lynched, of Christ being mocked by those who obviously enjoyed the mocking, and I wondered whether it was only my "northern" sense of restraint which had been shocked, whether the problems of disorder and indiscipline of which Spaniards speak so much begin in such incidents, or whether (hopefully but without much inner conviction) such unrestrained reactions in childhood would produce more emotionally stable, less "repressed" adults.

When we had returned to Father Heriberto's quarters I began by asking him about the conditions of the Basque priests in prison. But he brushed this aside as of no importance. The important thing for an American historian was to know the personality of that *hombre santo,* D. Julián Besteiro. Besteiro, he said, was already in an advanced stage of tuberculosis when he arrived in Carmona. He knew that he would die soon, and seemed psychologically to be perfectly prepared for the eventuality. The warden had offered to let him buy food from outside the prison, but he did not take advantage of this offer. The only point on which he ever made the slightest complaint or showed the slightest bitterness was the refusal of the authorities to allow his wife to visit him. He enjoyed the company of the Basque priests and spoke freely, though quite impersonally —the padre emphasized this point—about a wide range of philosophical and religious questions. I had noticed that my host seemed puzzled by the apparent peaceful acceptance of imminent death by a man who was presumably a materialist and an atheist.

"Did you ever ask him directly about his beliefs?" I asked.

"Once one of the other priests invited him to take communion. He replied that he had always respected the beliefs of Catholics, and that he hoped they would respect his. Naturally no one raised the question again."

"But what do you think yourself?" I persisted.

"I was particularly close to D. Julián," he replied, speaking more slowly than usual, and weighing each word. "I do not say that out of pride. We happened by chance to be assigned to the same cell. For several weeks I had a badly infected finger, and during this time D. Julián daily made my bed.

Later, when he was too weak to leave his own bed except for the needs of nature, I often sat up with him as he slept fitfully. Once, a few weeks before he died, he told me that in a dream he had been saying the credo. 'And what did you do when you woke up?' I asked. He replied, 'I continued.' Nothing more than that."

Father Heriberto offered no interpretation of the incident, emphasizing only that he was reporting the words *textualmente*. "Everyone in Carmona worshiped this saintly man," he concluded. "He died at ten in the evening, the authorities removed his body by eleven in order to avoid demonstrations, and the townspeople were arriving before midnight with flowers."

Father Heriberto accompanied me back to my taxi, which had been waiting for almost two hours during a visit which I had thought in advance might last twenty minutes. He took my arm to guide me around the many mudholes made by the winter rains. A few yards short of the vehicle he stopped and turned to me.

"One time in Carmona a boy, he couldn't have been more than sixteen, was condemned to death for killing two priests in his village. He swore to me that he was innocent, and implored me to get in touch with his village, where they knew he was innocent. I did. Four days after the boy was shot, the two priests appeared in person. Shot, *en el nombre de Cristo,* in the name of Christ, in our poor Spain. Goodbye, Mr. Historian, it was a pleasure to talk with you. Try to understand our poor Spain."

After that wonderful and painful visit I would gladly have spent a few hours by myself, but I had told Major Silvio that I would return to his office before lunch, at which time he would show me the Church of the Macarena. The Macarena, one of the most populous working-class districts of Seville, is also one of the oldest parts of the city. Despite the jumble of modern buildings one can still see Roman and Arab masonry. The name itself is that of an Arab princess, and parts of the original Arab gate are incorporated in the existing Puerta de la Macarena. The church was built in the fourteenth century, and the Romanesque structure includes portions of an earlier minaret. In 1936 the church was partially burned, and in 1947 it was restored and greatly expanded. Most particularly, it became the home of the Virgin of the Macarena, Our Lady of Hope, one of the most passionately beloved of the images carried in the Holy Week processions.

As we walked through the gate and briefly admired the exterior of the nearby church, Major Silvio described with great gusto the competition among local workmen for the honor of carrying the Virgin during Holy Week. "Communist and anarchist workers," he said with a flourish of his cape, "would gladly die in defense of the little Virgin."

There is a small museum attached to the church, and we hurried there first, as it was approaching the lunch hour, when the museum would be closed for three hours. My host guided me rapidly past the various religious ornaments and precious stones to show me the collection of uniforms belonging to famous bullfighters. There were costumes of Joselito, Manolete, and, more evocative for me as a reader of García Lorca, embroidered jackets belonging to Ignacio Sánchez Mejías, the *torero* who had been the friend of many of the liberal poets of the Republican era, and for whom Lorca had composed the magnificent elegy *Llanto por Ignacio Sánchez Mejías.*

Then we entered the church. Major Silvio barely indicated the image of the Virgin, but took me to a large burial plaque—and paused for effect while I read the name. "There you have the real purpose of this newly built church," he whispered sarcastically, "the tomb of our honored savior from communism, our great Captain General, our descendant of the Cid, the Butcher of Seville, D. Gonzalo Queipo de Llano."

Indeed I knew, and thousands of foreigners who were no scholars in the history of the Spanish Civil War knew the name Queipo de Llano, the radio general of 1936 and 1937 who, from his fief in Seville, broadcast nightly threats of rape to the women of the Republic and of murder to their menfolk and who delighted in colorful oaths and tales of pornography. Queipo had, however, been a very able man, and no mere buffoon. His fabled capture of Seville in the first days of the

Civil War had been easy enough, since he had all the serviceable guns and trucks at his command, as well as the fierce, highly trained Moors. But he had shown true political and economic skill in governing Andalusia after the conquest. The radio talks were a form of sport. He enjoyed embarrassing his formal and stodgy chief, General Franco, just as much as he enjoyed frightening his thousands of listeners in the Republican zone. He had warned the "Red" workers of Seville in very plain language to don what he called the *salvavida,* the life jacket of the Falange. Thousands of them had eventually fought in the Francoist armies, and thousands of others had paid for their political affiliations or their armed resistance with their lives.

"What a disaster, what an insult to civilized men in the twentieth century is that tomb," said the major. "What is such a man doing buried in a church? I ask you. Believe me, he never came near a priest before the war."

I replied that I did not doubt his word, but that unhappily the history of the Church was filled with hatred and violence, that one had only to remember the Crusades, the fighting bishops, the promises of heavenly glory for those who died fighting the infidel. "How many of those war captains were any more Christian than the late lamented D. Gonzalo?" I told him I was reminded of the Orozco murals which I used to see each time I visited the Baker Library at Dartmouth College. As the climax to a series of panels showing money-grubbing capitalists, corrupt generals, and professors dissecting dead knowledge, Orozco had created a violent red-yellow image of an angry Christ destroying His own Cross as if to curse the human race for whom His crucifixion had been a futile sacrifice.

The major listened quietly. I could not tell whether he was impressed by my words or disappointed that I did not appear dramatically scandalized by the tomb. "We Spaniards have no shame," he said. "We glorify our executioners. Here we are, standing on the honored grave of a butcher. Under the altar you will find the grave of his second in command, Colonel Francisco Bohorquez. I do not know which of them was worse. Some time we'll ask the Virgin."

After a two-o'clock dinner and a short nap I was able for the first time to enjoy the city itself. I walked to the Guadalquivir River to see the Torre de Oro, the Golden Tower, built in the early thirteenth century by the Arabs, and called golden for the color of its tiles, now a dusty tan. The tower, like most Arab buildings, is very pleasing in its general proportions, and I enjoyed the thought that it had already watched the river for over two hundred and fifty years when Columbus was preparing his first voyage. A few steps farther on I photographed a massive wooden gate, furrowed and cracked by centuries of dry heat and adorned by decorative iron hinges and huge iron bolts. The photograph now hangs on the bathroom wall and enables me in imagination to cross centuries and cultures while I shave.

But I did not linger along the river. Factories, barracks, and shoddily built apartments dominate the skyline, and there is no such prosperous, purposeful shipping activity as makes it a pleasure to stand for hours along the Meuse Canal or in a port such as Amsterdam. I walked along the broad esplanades surrounding the Palace Gardens and the Park of María Luisa, then entered the narrow, winding streets of the Barrio Santa Cruz and wandered slowly past house after house of delicately colored stucco. Handsome iron grillwork set off the windows and narrow balconies, and doors were open in the advancing afternoon. I could see through to sheltered patios and listen to gaily dressed children on the ground level and gaily chattering canaries and parrots on the balconies. Women were vigorously scrubbing the hallway tiles. It is another of the pejorative generalizations one hears about Spain that people there have no idea of cleanliness. No one who has seen the shining tiles in even the poorest working-class vestibules or the dishes and cutlery in even the most modest restaurants would subscribe to such a generalization.

From the Barrio Santa Cruz I went to the Alcázar itself. The main portions of the palace were built in the 1360s during the reign of the Castilian king Peter the Cruel (who was destined to be murdered in hand-to-hand knife combat by his bastard half-brother Henry Trastámara). The work itself was done mostly by Muslim architects and workmen living in Andalusia under Christian rule, the so-called *mudéjars*. There are several lovely patios and reception rooms with the thin columns, the colored tile floors and walls, and the delicately diffused light which are characteristic of Muslim buildings in both Spain and North Africa. Mixed with the arabesque decorations and the carved wainscotings are the blasons of Castile and León. There is an annex built by Charles V, handsome in itself, but entirely lacking the esthetic delicacy of the *mudéjar* rooms; and the upstairs apartments are full of frightful furniture chosen by Isabella II or Alfonso XIII and piously catalogued by the guide.

Having satisfied my curiosity about the interior of the palace I was glad to wander about in the gardens. Here too there is a hodgepodge of different styles, Roman, Moorish, and French classic. But there is also a fundamental tranquility and a sense of physical luxuriance which is disciplined, measured, confident, and ageless. Palms and relatively untended lawns may dominate in one area, orange trees in another, formal flower beds in another. But everywhere there is shade, running water, and an atmosphere of peace and leisure despite the noise of trucks and motorcycles just outside the palace grounds. Here I felt able to recall the morning's conversations without being unnerved or depressed by the recollection. In the back of my mind, like the ground bass in a complex polyphonic structure, I heard the voice of D. Jorge Guillén, reading aloud to his Wellesley class the *Llanto por Ignacio Sánchez Mejías: "A las cinco de la tarde, a las cinco en punto de la tarde . . . con su muerte a cuestas . . ."* "At five o'clock in the afternoon, at precisely five o'clock in the afternoon . . . carrying his death on his shoulders . . ." *A cuestas,* a concentrated, dramatic, untranslatable image of upward toil, a back bent under the weight of a crushing burden. I repeated the lines slowly, in an effort to slacken my heartbeat to the rhythm of the poem and to comprehend in all its succinctness that terrible *con su muerte a cuestas.* In the beautiful, quiet gardens

9

An Intensive Day in Seville

The next morning I went to see the archivist D. Raimundo. Before me sat a tall, thin, stoop-shouldered man with a long, sorrowful, but exalted face of the kind one sees on El Greco canvases. He wore a black suit, shiny with age, and a white shirt with detached collar and French cuffs. He was attentive, dignified, courteous, but also somewhat distracted, and he seemed disinclined to serious conversation. We talked disconnectedly about the training of librarians in the United States, about how microfilm would transform the work of archivists, about the slowness of Spanish trains, and about Spanish meals and meal hours, which he was surprised to hear that I liked. After a few minutes he asked me whether I thought the inauguration of President Kennedy would affect American policy toward Spain. I said I did not think so, and he reacted quickly, expressing both disagreement and disappointment. I apologized for sounding so skeptical at the start of a new era, but asserted that only a very strong and determined President could change the long-established military and State Department preference for quite dictatorships in potentially revolutionary countries, and I did not think Kennedy had either the determination or the strength to make such a change.

A messenger came in with his morning mail at this point. He seemed undecided what to do next, suddenly shoved back his chair, rose and invited me to walk out with him for coffee. Away from official surroundings he was a different man. Guiding me by the arm across the plaza he assured me he would be happy to answer any questions he could about the history of the Republic. When, moments later, we were seated in the booth of an espresso bar, I posed my first question.

"Since you lived here throughout the years 1931 to 1936, and since the present governors of Spain are constantly harping on the 'disorder' of those years as a justification for the Civil War and the dictatorship, I would like to ask you, as I have asked many people, whether in your experience there was a serious problem of public order in Republican Spain."

D. Raimundo smiled. "Seville is the home of the Luca de Tena family, publishers of the royalist newspaper *ABC*. It is also the home of many timorous Catholic ladies. These ladies read *ABC* every morning and talked to the priest every afternoon, thereby convincing themselves morning and afternoon that there was a grave problem of public order in Seville."

"But even from *El Sol,* or *El Liberal,* I have the impression that there was much effervescence in Seville in the early 1930s."

"Short strikes, yes, and a high proportion of them involved the Luca de Tena interests because this family dominated the freight-transfer business on the riverfront. I would estimate that there were perhaps a total of four to five months over the five-year period 1931 to 1936 during which strikes actually interfered with the normal economic life of the city. No more than that. And such strikes really interfered with normal life much less than has police control in the Forties and Fifties. But," he changed the subject abruptly, "Spain wasn't ready for the Republic in 1931, and that is a much longer story. The Republicans and the Socialists—I was a Socialist in those years—had no plans. They were positively surprised by the king's abdication. They were journalists and high school teachers. They didn't know how to give orders, and they could not win the respect of the civil servants, the police, and the army. The game was lost from the beginning."

"What you say sounds very much like what the apologists of the regime say. Of course they tailor their words when talking to an American who they know belongs to the Left.

They say the men of the Republic were *honrado,* well intentioned, in their thoughts, but *pobrecitos,* incapable weaklings when it came to making decisions and controlling their mass following."

"There is an uncomfortable amount of truth in what they say. But I don't want to leave the question at that point. It is so hard to know now what really happened under the Republic. A foreigner like you comes and asks questions we have been asking ourselves for years. But we are all conditioned by twenty years of propaganda. We live on a dosage of half-truths, and it is almost worse than if we could tell ourselves that everything the government press prints is a lie. There were disorders, especially in the spring of 1936. The government was weak, it did lack firm plans. But I can't accept for all that the conclusion that Spain deserves the present dictatorship. We must talk more. I must return to the office now. Will you have dinner with me? And in the meantime I can think a little bit about things you will not have read, but that may help you to understand."

Over a delicious dinner, the expense of which must have been enormous to my proud and kind host, we spoke first of his early years in Seville. D. Raimundo came from a provincial capital in Old Castile. His father had been a pharmacist, and Raimundo, the most talented of six children, had been educated as a scholarship pupil by the Jesuits. He remembered the Jesuits with affection, and remarked that it had been a stupid error for Azaña to expel the order from Spain. On the one hand they had not been so powerful as he thought, and on the other they were easily able to continue both their schools and their business interests under other corporate names. I asked his opinion of the education he had received.

"Very poor," he laughed. "They kept better discipline than in state schools, but otherwise the education was bad. I was half a socialist by the time I graduated. What I first remember about Seville," he went on, "is my surprise that the professors, and middle-class professional people generally, were completely excluded from society social life. At home there was one casino. The rich landlords exercised more than their fair share of control. They were offered a certain semivoluntary deference. But my father, and the notary, and the teachers, and the engineers belonged to the casino, and everyone met there on terms of near equality. Here, nothing of the sort. The wealthy aristocracy have their own social life in their *cortijos,* their rural mansions, hermetically sealed off from the despised middle class of the city. When the civil governors arrived from Madrid under the Republic, they were thoroughly snubbed."

He paused momentarily, and I took the opportunity to ask about the reception of Martínez Barrio, who had been a respected party leader and a Sevillano by birth.

"Exactly the same! An *hombre honradísimo,* self-made in your sense of the word. The aristocracy despised him. He and all the other Republican deputies were completely isolated from the powerful families of Andalusia."

D. Raimundo had not been especially active politically, but he had served on one of the mixed juries, i.e., groups of labor and capital spokesmen who, under the chairmanship of a representative of the Department of Labor, were assigned to arbitrate labor conflicts during the Republic.

"Ironically I owe my life to that jury service. In August 1936, Queipo's military government arrested all Socialists, Masons, and anyone remotely connected with any Leftist organization. We all appeared before the local purge committee. One of the members was a landlord who had known me on one of the mixed juries. He testified that I had tried to be fair, and that I did not always vote with the other 'Reds.' His opinion surely saved my life because many men as innocent as myself were shot in those months. I escaped with arthritis, brought on by living for weeks in damp cells and standing in the overcrowded prison courtyard during the rain. But in the spring of 1937 I was released."

He went on to speak at some length of General Queipo de Llano, who, he said frankly, fascinated him and who undoubtedly had been a charismatic figure for a large fraction of the working class in Seville.

"He had a boyish manner, a sense of humor—and not just gallows humor or pornographic humor. He had a naïve egotism with which poor devils liked to identify themselves. He threatened the landlords and talked a lot about social reform. He was always collecting money for some 'cause.' First it was a fund for the *soldadito,* the dear little soldier who was close to his heart—and whose language he spoke. We never knew what became of that money, which was deducted from everybody's paycheck, but next it was a fund to rebuild the Baleares, the largest Nationalist warship, which had been heavily damaged by the 'Reds.' A little later he was going to establish an agricultural colony for the families of deserving veterans. He bought for a song the estate of one of the very few wealthy Andalusians who had been a Republican. Naturally the latter was in no position to bargain with the representatives of the newly established Patronato Queipo de Llano. Businessmen all contributed, voluntarily of course. Actually he did give farms to a few families, and he did lower some rural rents. It was a little bit of Robin Hood, and a lot of Al Capone."

"Still, I don't see how boyish humor and an occasional favor to a peasant family would win over people who had been ardent anarchists or communists."

"Don't misunderstand me," he replied quickly. "The really militant workers held on to their convictions; moreover, passed them onto the next generation. Under the surface Seville is as Left today as it was in 1936. But most people cannot easily resist a combination of steady propaganda, armed force, and a colorful personality. Another thing: the unions were divided between gangsters and idealists. I saw that in every strike and every election campaign. The gangsters, and a lot of confused poor devils who had expected the revolution ever since April 1931, went over easily to Queipo. The middle-class liberals had no fight in them once he had captured the city. The Moors were cooking their rations and dividing their loot in the city squares. Everyone could remember the editorial line in *ABC* throughout the months leading up to the Popular

Front election: eliminate in every village the handful of troublemakers whom we all know. Queipo did exactly that—interpreting liberally the notion of a handful.

"Recall, as well, that we were alone. It was just a few miles to Gibraltar. A number of Masons escaped, and the English are civilized people who did not turn the refugees over to firing squads, but the British navy was in collusion with the generals from the start, and Britain's historic ally, our neighbor Portugal, was openly aiding Franco and turning refugees back at the frontier."

I hastened to say that I hoped he did not think I was making a moral judgment against people who had tried to adjust themselves to a catastrophic defeat and reign of terror. D. Raimundo waved aside my quasi-apology and continued his analysis.

"The Spaniards as a nation have an inferiority complex. That's what lies behind all the antibourgeois breast beating of both the Right and the Left. We have never developed civilian government, general economic well-being, good schools. So we scorn the English and the French as 'shop keepers' and 'petite bourgeoisie,' and talk instead about our religious agonies, and how 'Africa begins at the Pyrenees.' It was disgusting, during the Second World War, to see how many people here admired the Germans. There was something feminine, masochistic about it, like the love of a weak woman for a man who masters and brutalizes her. The Germans were so strong, so healthy, so efficacious. Our newspapers celebrated the fall of Paris, and later the fall of Manila. Nobody went near the American Consulate until late 1944, the Francoists because they hated the United States, and still do, the rest of us because we couldn't risk going to jail again for a gesture.

"Then, of course, we expected everything of the United States in 1945. Mussolini and Hitler were finished. The little dictator here had his bags packed. But nothing happened, and we have had fifteen years of stagnation since."

"Spain has certainly had bad luck where international conjunctures are concerned," I said. "At the moment of the Reformation, when religious diversity, and eventually toleration, were achieved in northern Europe, Spain by a dynastic accident became the spearhead of the Counter Reformation. And in 1820 she chose to have a liberal revolution just when the Metternich system had fastened reaction on post-Napoleonic Europe, so that in 1823 the 'Hundred Thousand Sons of St. Louis' could cross the Pyrenees and restore the dictatorship of Ferdinand VII."

He gazed at me sadly, and slowly ran his finger around the circumference of his wine glass. *"Mala suerte,* bad luck, and an evil destiny. What next?"

"That's what I want to ask you. Let me be frank too. The United States and its allies missed a perfect opportunity, and made a great mistake by not getting rid of Franco in 1945 along with the other fascist dictators. But right now, in 1961, or any time in the past decade, what could or should they have done? First of all, the Left in any country would be the first to raise the cry against foreign intervention. And if you are going to try to force out one government you have to have some idea what comes next. From reading about the opposition and from meeting some of the leaders, I have no idea, much as I like the men personally, how they would govern Spain. They have no real plans, and they are constantly quarreling among themselves. Suppose the President was to encourage a change. What would the new government be like?"

D. Raimundo did not reply directly to my question, but again spoke reflectively and discursively of the past. "I was a Socialist, as I told you. I would give a lot to see Spain governed the way Norway and Sweden are governed. But— Spain is still a Catholic country. We need both things, socialism and Catholicism. There were many religious vocations among the young here in the Forties and Fifties. A desperate faith if you will, considering the world as it is. Remember that we have been alone, and that the world offers no really admirable model except that of a secular democratic socialism, and this model is not appropriate to our temperament. We are not like Englishmen or Scandinavians.

"In the 1950s I began taking communion again, just occasionally, and by preference in France. Now and then I got to Paris, and would confess with one of the Basque priests in exile. I felt that it was a way of breaking the terrible isolation. Perhaps prosperous people can live without any metaphysical baggage, but not those who suffer. And then it was a way of returning somewhat to my origins. Why should I, so to speak, abandon the Church to the Carlists and the Falangists? My father was Catholic, my teachers were Catholic, good men, good men.

"Later I began to feel it was artificial only to take communion in France. I began to go to the Cathedral, here, right across the square." He smiled. "I had not been inside that building for thirty years. I used to go to listen to Cardinal Segura. You know who he was?"

"Yes, the cardinal who embroiled himself with the Republic right away in the spring of 1931?"

"The same. I knew of him in my boyhood. My father used to laugh about Segura's *disgustos,* his chagrins, with the liberal Archbishop of Valladolid. He had a fanatical following among the women, and as Bishop of Coria he organized admirable charities in one of the most forsaken areas of the peninsula. Alfonso XIII was so impressed that he appointed him Archbishop of Toledo, Primate of Spain, and that is what made the man a fervent royalist. In 1931 he compared the mild fledgling Republic with the 1919 communist governments of Bavaria and Hungary, and proposed to dedicate Spain officially to the Sacred Heart. Even the Vatican was glad to have him out of Spain. He spent the Republican and war years in Rome, then returned to us as Archbishop of Seville.

"Well, he was an authentic man, a good man too, who helped the Basque priests when the rest of the hierarchy would not turn a finger for them. He enjoyed also being the *enfant terrible,* a little bit like our Queipo. He thundered about military corruption and about selling out to the Protestant colossus—your country. It was wonderful to hear him excoriate the government for not distributing land to the peasants and for, in his opinion, coddling the Protestants! His real trouble was paranoia. I will never forget the speech he made on his thirtieth anniversary as a cardinal. The history of Spain since 1931 consisted of his personal war against the Republic, the plots of the Masons, the stupidities and failures of the Franco government, which did not accept his excellent advice."

I must have looked puzzled, for he suddenly broke off his description and chuckled. "Never mind what he said. He was an authentic human being, and there are so few of them in Spanish public life. It was good for my soul to sit in the Cathedral and hear a man who I knew was really saying what he thought. But—to come back to your question, as utopian as it may sound now, Spain needs both socialism and Catholicism. Christian Socialism has a bad name from the Austrian postwar example, the Dollfuss dictatorship, the mixture of anti-Semitism in their party propaganda, and all that. But since the Second World War there are the examples of Belgium, Holland, West Germany; above all, Italy, which was fascist, and which has many of the same problems and characteristics as ourselves. If Italy can achieve parliamentary democracy, with Christian Democratic and Socialist parties sharing power, why cannot we in Spain one day do the same?"

We had been eating, drinking, and talking for two hours. D. Raimundo had to return to his office, and I had other appointments to keep in the afternoon. He insisted on accompanying me back to the hotel.

"You know," I said as we walked along, "I am very suspicious when people talk about national character. But it struck me, when you talked about Queipo, that you didn't express any of the moral indignation that the Anglo-Saxon world felt at his vulgarity and salacious language."

"Hombre," he laughed, stopping in midsentence, "naturally it wasn't one of the things I most admired in the man. But such a little thing. Look across the street from where we are standing. Behind that wall is the courtyard of a Jesuit school. I stood there for five days and nights solid in the winter of 1937. So did a couple of hundred other men who had no room to sit down. It was just one of many little detention centers."

In front of the hotel we shook hands warmly, and he walked rapidly away.

There was barely time for me to put in the most skeletal

note form a summary of my long conversation with D. Raimundo. I planted myself in a wicker armchair in the lobby, wrote down the key phrases and viewpoints as they recurred to me pell-mell. I had found from experience that I could recapture a conversation better by that method of "free association," than by trying to reconstruct it in the same sequence as it had occurred. Then I went upstairs to throw a little cold water on my face, read over what Professor J. had told me about each of the next group of people I was to meet, and consult the city map for the route to the office of the lawyer D. Francisco.

Our meeting took place in the small waiting room of D. Francisco's office. Sitting stiffly in a leather armchair, with his cane in his right hand, was Colonel C., an elegant man in a pinstripe suit and with a thin, carefully clipped mustache. He might have been sixty. Professor J. had told me that the colonel had suffered a stroke some months earlier. He inclined his head toward me and smiled, but neither shook hands nor rose. Across the narrow room from the colonel, sitting on an unevenly upholstered daybed, were two large men, D. Francisco, the host, and D. Federico, a former teacher, Republican army captain, and now small businessman. The two men looked uncomfortable, with their knees higher than their belt lines. When they got up to greet me and then sank down again on the daybed there was much creaking of springs, much laughter, and some joshing between them as to the eventual division of responsibilities in case the couch should collapse entirely. D. Francisco motioned me to the handsome ottoman which stood in the remaining free corner of the room, arranged the coffee table so that it would be equidistant from all four of us, poured us each a cognac, and invited me to begin the conversation.

I knew that D. Francisco had been a member of Lerroux's party during the 1920s. Alejandro Lerroux, who styled himself "the historic Republican," had built up a large following among lawyers, small businessmen, and civil servants. After April 1931 many of Lerroux's followers, including D. Francisco, had been disillusioned by his obstructionism, general pomposity, and the rapidly accumulating evidence of political jobbery. D. Francisco in 1933 had transferred his allegiance to the newly organized CEDA, the Confederation of Autonomous Right parties, one of whose leaders was a widely admired lawyer and professor in Seville. In recent years, out of a combination of strong feelings—hatred of the dictatorship, disgust with the blind conservatism of his clients, and bitter disappointment with the United States—he had become sympathetic to the communists. I knew also that he had practiced law in Seville throughout the Republican years, and so I asked him whether there had been serious problems of public order in the city.

"Perhaps, on the average, four or five *atentados,* assassinations or attempted assassinations, per year, on the waterfront, among the labor factions."

"Then how is it," I asked, "that not only the conservative press, but *El Sol* too, talked about serious problems of disorder? In going through *El Sol* for the five-year period 1931 to 1936 I read two feature articles on the subject as well as any number of short references to violence in Seville, either the city or the province."

"El Sol would emphasize the problem," he replied, "perhaps even exaggerate it. The Republicans felt responsible for everything that was wrong in Spain. Liberal journalists were among the harshest critics of the government."

Colonel C. broke in at that point to speak of the punctiliousness and acute self-criticism of the minority of officers who had been genuine enthusiasts of the Republic.

"Listen," D. Francisco resumed, "I will never forget the speech of José Díaz at the funeral of Dr. Ferrara. You know who Díaz was, secretary general of the Communist party during the Civil War. Díaz came from Seville. He was a stevedore, something of an autodidact, and a magnificent orator. There were, as I said, four or five shootings a year near the docks. This Dr. Ferrara was one of the intellectual leaders of the party here when they were very small, probably not more than a hundred strong, calling themselves the Committee of Reconstruction. But Ferrara was widely known and loved, and his funeral became a kind of protest demonstration against factional violence. Díaz devoted his whole speech to calming down the excited workers. He quoted Lenin against terrorism and insisted repeatedly that the workers mustn't think in terms of revenge, that violence simply played the game of the bosses."

"Díaz could have said all that," I replied, "and could have meant it without the slightest reservations. But wasn't the Seville waterfront infested with anarchist *pistoleros* and labor spies? Wouldn't the communists have to reply to fire with fire, no matter what their theoretical views on terrorism?"

D. Federico had nodded vigorous agreement while I had spoken, and he now turned to D. Francisco. "I remember Díaz too, a man with an almost religious respect for intellectuals, at that time at least. The desire for schooling and the respect for intellectuals was one of the distinguishing marks of the communists. I don't think you or I would have known it if they had organized any *atentados* of their own. They would have gone to any lengths to prevent their educated supporters from knowing about violence."

"Of course," conceded D. Francisco, "they weren't the type of Christian martyrs. They didn't just let the FAI run them out of town. But the whole business of disorder is exaggerated anyway. Why there are ten times the number of murders in New York and Chicago than there ever were in Seville. Who talks of making a revolution against the United States government because of the problem of public order?"

D. Federico spoke again. "What I remember from those years is not so much violence, but hatred, palpable class hatred. Not just between workers and employers, but a whole society dividing up into friends and enemies. My wife and I were both public-school teachers in a village near here. The workers considered us one of theirs. The priest and the rich hated us."

"Tell him what happened to you in July 1936," said D. Francisco.

Federico shrugged his shoulders in a gesture of reluctance, then looked over at me, and seeing my expectant expression, consented to be more "personal," he said, than he had intended to be. Nothing had happened in their village during the first lightning days of the military rising, during which Queipo de Llano had secured Seville. The Right had won the February election in this village, and the mayor was a Catholic conservative. Early in August the mayor had received a telegram from Seville ordering him immediately to arrest several persons, among whom was Federico. The blood purge of everyone remotely identified with the Left was already in full swing. The mayor sent a message obliquely warning him to leave town. He had fled to the Sierra Morena and crossed the lines to join the Republican army near Córdoba. His wife and children had gone to Seville to live with her family. His crimes he listed as the following: membership in the moderate Republican party of Diego Martínez Barrio; his profession as a teacher; his failure as a reserve officer to join the military rising.

I was interested to know what proportion of officers he thought had been loyal to the Republic. From his slightly puzzled hesitation I could tell that the question had never occurred to him, certainly not in numerical terms. He began to calculate aloud. "At least two thirds of all the officers must have been in loyal territory when the war began, simply because the big cities, Madrid, Barcelona, Valencia, Bilbao, all stayed with the Republic. Then, let me see, at the end of the war when I was imprisoned in Montjuich, the professional officers were separated from the other prisoners, and there were at least fifteen hundred professionals there. There were similar military prisons in Valencia, Murcia, Alicante, Cádiz, Badajoz, Ciudad Real, and two in Madrid. If you could find out how many officers were held in each of these prisons in 1940—but *hombre,* how to find such information in Spain?"

Everybody laughed. "The fact that an officer was physically in Republican territory on July 18 doesn't prove anything about his loyalties or his participation in the war, does it?" I asked.

"Lots of people crossed the lines, in both directions, during the first days," D. Francisco pointed out. "There wasn't any real front. I know of many sad sacks who were passed over in promotions during the Forties because they didn't make it to the fascist lines quickly enough to prove their ardor, or because, worse yet, they spent the war in the relative comfort of the Madrid embassies. The Argentine, Mexican, Finnish, Dutch, and other legations too were full of platonically committed Francoist officers."

"Still," insisted Federico, "forty percent of the officer corps must have been loyal. I am thinking too of the Casa de Campo in November, when the fascists first arrived before Madrid. All the militia units had professional officers."

Colonel C. smilingly shook his head in the negative. He had been arrested in Tetuán on July 18 and had been imprisoned rather than shot because of his decorations for outstanding valor in the Moroccan war. "Very few career officers were loyal. When you speak of the Casa de Campo and the prisons after the war you must be including the reserve officers like yourself, and the thousands of new officers commissioned by the Republican army during the war. You may think the latter were separated from the former in the prisons," he continued in a tone of gentle irony, "but for the victorious authorities you were all the same *canaille.*"

Federico readily granted the erroneous basis of his rough calculation, protesting only the high caliber of the new officers, who acted like professionals. "Ah, now we are talking about something else." The colonel launched into a long disquisition on the Spaniard as a first-class soldier: his endurance, his ardor, his bravery. After which I asked him for an estimate of the number of career officers loyal to the Popular Front Republic on July 18.

"Very few, a handful only. In the large garrison in Tetuán we were so few that everybody knew exactly who we were, like some kind of freak. No, I would say that about forty percent joined the rebellion from the beginning, and most of the rest waited a few days, or weeks, to see how things developed. Then they joined the rebel ranks, and some of them incurred suspicion, as D. Francisco said, because they did not join more quickly. The defense of Madrid was more like guerrilla warfare, and the Spaniards have a hereditary genius for such war; witness the defense of Saragossa in 1808. The first time the Republic showed it had field units led by trained officers was in February 1937 at the Jarama. That was after the Republic had had five months to train the first generation of its own officers."

Whether out of respect for the colonel as a man or because of the convincing nature of his statements, both Francisco and Federico accepted without further debate his judgment as to the extremely small proportion of career officers serving the Republic. The three then exchanged personal reminiscences of various *hombres decentes,* decent men, whom they had known among the military caste. Suddenly Federico turned to me.

"I will tell you about the death of a great Spaniard, the Civil Guard general Antonio Escobar Huertas, shot at dawn in the castle of Montjuich, February 7, 1940." As he pronounced the name he had held up his hand, pointing his index finger toward the ceiling and enunciating slowly. At that moment I could see him in my mind's eye as the teacher he had formerly been, giving the class a sign of caution, and pronouncing slowly the proper names in one of those "dictation" sessions so dear to the French and Spanish school systems.

General Escobar, a fervent Catholic, had been on duty in Barcelona on July 18. He had put his wife and daughter on a ship for Italy while he and his older son remained to serve the Republic. A younger son who had earlier joined the Falange fought and died on the Nationalist side. General Escobar himself had been wounded during the Barcelona street fighting of May 1937. He vowed to visit Lourdes if he recovered, and when he was again well enough to move, he made the pilgrimage, with the full permission of the Negrín government. Afterward he served the Republic to the end, was imprisoned and court-martialed for "military rebellion" by the now victorious government which had been born of a military rebellion. According to Federico, Cardinal Segura had interceded unsuccessfully against the sentence of death.

For six weeks before his death he did not know which night he would be shot. At midnight he would shave and put on a fresh collar. When finally he was informed, an hour beforehand, he confessed and took communion. "He took his cross with him, told the firing squad that he would kiss the cross and raise it as the signal to fire. Thus he died, and he honored me by leaving me that cross, which I hope I will be able to show you in my home while you are still in Seville."

I told him that I felt honored by the invitation, and indeed by the attention and serious discussion which all three men had given me. But I was pressed for time now on my last day in Seville. I had two important visits still to make during the course of the afternoon. We all shook hands, and I could only hope that my haste did not leave them, despite their expressions of full understanding, with an impression of discourtesy.

After a quick look at the city map I rushed off to the home of Manuel Giménez Fernández, who had been ill, and whose daughter asked me to wait some minutes after I arrived. When he eventually appeared, he was in bathrobe and slippers, breathing heavily, and trailing the odor of several medicaments. But he no sooner began to speak than I felt myself to be in the presence of one of the most intelligent, energetic, and enthusiastic human beings I had ever met. Professor Giménez Fernández had been the principal lieutenant of Gil Robles in the leadership of the Catholic bloc of the Republican Cortes. He was an ardent Catholic, a professor of history, a lifelong Republican, and in the 1950s and 1960s a leading personality of such opposition as was tolerated by the dictatorship. I wanted to ask him my usual questions about public order, about Church-State relations, and also since he had been Minister of Agriculture, I wanted to discuss the agrarian problem with him.

He spoke with great rapidity and assurance on all subjects, and I later felt particularly indebted to him for an important qualification he had made in discussing the problem of public order in the 1930s. There was, he said, no real problem of public order until well into the spring of 1936, but from the very first days of the Republic there had been an increasing problem of *desasosiego,* of intranquillity, of not knowing what to expect in the way of legislation and social change. This restlessness had frayed the nerves of all classes of the population by 1936, and people had come to feel that, one way or another, a host of unresolved problems would have to be vigorously resolved. They were prepared for strong, even temporarily authoritarian, government but not, he insisted, for civil war and military dictatorship.

With regard to Church-State relations he excoriated the Azaña government for its anticlerical policies while at the same time protesting his affection and respect for Azaña the man and the parliamentary leader. I did not contest his judgment, but after mentioning such things as the attitude of Cardinal Segura and the Vatican refusal to recognize the new regime and to receive the Republican ambassador, I asked him what the Republic ought to have done.

"Instead of attacking the Church at home and arousing fierce opposition by their utter ignorance of real public opinion, they should have gone quietly to the Vatican and asked that all the bishops in Spain be replaced."

I was too startled to reply. On the one hand his answer, and the anecdotes he went on to relate as illustrative of the anti-Republican passions of the hierarchy, seemed a sweeping confirmation, from a Catholic leader, of the general charges leveled by the non-Catholic Republicans. On the other hand, given the history of papal conflicts, public or private, with numerous European and Latin American governments, how could anyone seriously suppose that the Vatican would oblige a barely established, anticlerical government by replacing all the bishops? My efforts to suggest the impracticality of such a solution made no impression upon my host.

When we turned to agriculture I asked him his opinion of the wheat import policy of 1932. At that time, faced with rapidly rising domestic prices and with constant reports of a poor harvest to come, the Azaña government had used precious foreign exchange to import wheat. The policy had been praised by the Left and by urban interests as preventing inflation and bread shortages. It had been bitterly attacked by agricultural interests as having disastrously cut the price of domestic wheat.

"The wheat import was a *disparate,* a stupid blunder, completely unnecessary, and of course it ruined the small cultivators, not the big growers."

"But," I said, "the reports of anticipated shortage, and even some of the requests for importing as a solution, came from conservative rural areas."

"Propaganda. The government didn't know what was happening in the countryside, that's all. There was no shortage."

"I don't see how you can say there was no shortage when the press was full of it, when prices were rising and grain being hoarded for speculative purposes."

He relented so far as to admit that there had been a real shortage in the fall of 1932. But, he said, though the government was well intentioned, they were fooled by the speculators, and they imported at least three times too much wheat, thereby ruining the small growers. "The proper solution would have been to find out the true size of the harvest before importing." It was already clear that my interlocutor did not relish contradiction, so that I did not point out the obvious difficulty of learning the true size of the harvest when a large proportion of the growers were doing everything in their power to deceive the public and the government. But again I was troubled by the sheer impracticality of Sr. Giménez's propositions.

On the question of land reform the "credibility gap" was still larger. I had asked him to elucidate certain technical clauses in land legislation of 1935 of which he had been the author. After very helpfully explaining points of law and vocabulary he went on to claim that as a result of these laws small farms had replaced the large estates in most of Andalusia. I knew how little land had been transferred to small holders in 1935, and how many legal obstacles to final title existed as a result of some of the very clauses we had been discussing. I also knew from a French agronomist who had been studying land distribution in Andalusia as of 1960 that social patterns remained virtually what they had been as of 1930, that if anything the gap in living standards between landlord and peasant had become greater in the past two decades, and that the only real solution available to the Andalusian villager was to emigrate to Madrid or Barcelona to work in a factory.

But I could not say this to the warm enthusiast and true *caballero* sitting before me. The conversation moved to his memory of personalities in the Cortes. He spoke with great warmth of men such as Miguel Maura, Gil Robles, and Prieto, all of whom I was to meet myself, and whose memories of particular caucuses dovetailed closely with what Giménez Fernández told me. In particular I valued his circumstantial account of opinion with the CEDA bloc. Apropos of the atmosphere in 1936 he related how in late April he had polled the CEDA deputies as to their attitude toward the Republic. Out of 115, 101 had voted to work within the Republic rather than to seek either a military or a monarchist solution. That caucus vote had been a condition of his continuing as a CEDA leader. He did not seem to be impressed by my doubts as to just how significant the vote was in the circumstances. I suggested that many doubters might have voted to work with the Republic because at the moment such a vote was really a vote of personal confidence which he had demanded. My words struck him as an unwarranted reflection on the honor of his colleagues.

D. Manuel Giménez Fernández was indeed a *caballero,* a true gentleman defending a record of generous intentions, frank dogmas, and honorable relationships with his political friends and opponents. But I was sorely troubled by the sheer misreading of the facts in connection with religious and agricultural questions which had been his very province in active politics. Upon checking my newspaper sources and Cortes reports for 1935 I later concluded that in the matter of land reform he had simply mistaken his own intention and his verbal pleadings for accomplished fact. With regard to the wheat imports and the clerical problems, his views were probably an oversimplified version of what he had really thought at the time. The pity of his situation, and that of thinking Spaniards generally, was that for twenty years they had been deprived of all access to honest information. They had to live with their memories distorted by propaganda and repression, and without the corrective of open political discussion. I felt here, as on many other occasions, that in undertaking to write a history of the Republic and the Civil War I was not simply undertaking a scholarly obligation but a moral duty to come as close as humanly possible to the truth, the whole truth, and nothing but the truth concerning events which had been deliberately distorted for a whole generation of Spaniards.

After leaving D. Manuel I paid one last short visit, to one of the grand old men of Spanish historiography, Professor Ramón Caraunde, who had pioneered in the economic history of the Spanish Empire. He greeted me with friendly courtesy toward a younger colleague, but I received the distinct impression that to him what I was doing was not history. There are many historians to whom nothing is history until it is several centuries past. It is undoubtedly true, as such men will argue, that until the archives are opened and until enough time has elapsed to judge controversial events without passion, the history of any complex set of events will be incomplete. But it is equally true that unless one speaks to the participants while they are still alive, one loses much of the human context. More important, there is no guarantee whatever that those things which are best documented from the past are necessarily the most important things which occurred. I was sorry that we could not better communicate with each other, but remained convinced that my interviews were indeed an essential element of my work.

At 10:45 p.m., in a state of intellectual exhilaration and emotional exhaustion, I took the train for Madrid.

10

At Work in Three Archives

Every historian dreams of being able to use collections of documents which have not been available to his predecessors and which may supply important new facts and perspectives concerning his subject. I was no exception. It is true that since I was not writing a biography, or treating exhaustively the history of a single political movement or government bureau, such special collections of documents were not of the highest importance to me. My main materials, inevitably, were the printed books on the Spanish Republic and Civil War, the Spanish and European press for the 1930s, and the oral testimony of participants. Before coming to Spain, I had concentrated entirely on books, and during the year 1960–1 I was devoting most of my time to the press and to interviews such as those I had just completed in Saragossa, Barcelona, and Seville. But in the course of the year's research I did work briefly in several archives, the most important of which were those of the International Red Cross, the Spanish Socialist party in exile, and the Archivo Militar of the Spanish government. Very different technical problems, intellectual values, and human relationships were involved in each instance.

I wanted particularly to see the Red Cross archives because I had heard the most conflicting oral testimonies concerning prison conditions and treatment of prisoners of war. The subject seemed very important to me as an index of the human quality of the leadership on each side. I had written beforehand to the offices of the International Red Cross and had received a friendly but entirely noncommittal reply. When I arrived in Geneva in February 1961, the first impulse of M. Jequier, the officer to whom I was directed, was to refuse all permission to consult documents. He explained to me that IRC personnel, all of whom were Swiss, made regular visits to political prisoners in both the communist and Western countries; and that they, as citizens of a neutral country, were the only ones who could obtain information about the treatment of prisoners, and who could sometimes bring accurate news to families who had heard nothing for months. Obviously there was a price attached to this privileged position in the world community. The IRC must guarantee that there would be absolutely no publicity concerning its activities except such as the host governments themselves might decide to release. IRC delegates must scrupulously avoid all activities that might carry the slightest political implications.

The Spanish Civil War had in fact been a crucial event for the IRC. Up to that time its activities had been limited to wars between countries, most notably to the delivery of mail and gifts and to the exchange of prisoners between the Allies and the Central Powers in World War I. The Spanish conflict was the first civil war in which the IRC had played a role, and that role had become the precedent for its greatly expanded activities since World War II. Experience in Spain had shown the extreme susceptibility of both Republican and Nationalist officials. It had been difficult to persuade the Largo Caballero government that the IRC could be truly neutral because the most influential Swiss newspapers were generally favorable to the Nationalist cause and because the Swiss government, although discreet, seemed also to anticipate and to favor the victory of General Franco. In the Nationalist zone the mere words "international" and "red" created the suspicion of communism, and there was also considerable prejudice against the delegates as Protestants. In both zones IRC personnel were frequently accused of espionage, and in both zones officials had resented the entire role of the IRC, implying, as it inevitably did, that outsiders were necessary to guarantee the humane treatment of prisoners. M. Jequier made it clear that difficulties of this sort had arisen in many countries since 1945. He wanted to be sure that nothing I might publish could embarrass the IRC in the Congo, in Cuba or Greece, or in Eastern Europe.

I did not find it easy to answer M. Jequier's doubts. I was immensely impressed by the critical importance for civilized mankind of several current missions of which he spoke. I would have agreed, then or now, that the work of the IRC was infinitely more important than anything I might be able to write with the help of IRC documents. But I did urge upon him the fact that the Spanish Civil War had ended twenty-two years ago, that most Spaniards were by now anxious to let bygones be bygones, and that the constant occurrence of revolutions and civil wars could be depended upon to prevent anyone in 1961 from being excessively preoccupied with what had happened in Spain from 1936 to 1939. I argued also that the truth should be known, especially about controversial matters, provided that enough time had elapsed so that revelations concerning the past would not hamper present activities. Fortunately I could point to the fact that one of the delegates of the time, Dr. Marcel Junod, had already published a book in which he had referred specifically to his experiences in Spain.

In the light of Dr. Junod's book and of the passage of twenty-two years, M. Jequier was willing to reconsider his original negative. I said that I would gladly observe whatever restrictions he felt necessary concerning the quotation of material, and we made the following agreement. I could quote from the unpublished mimeographed IRC reports on medical equipment and exchange of prisoners. I could take notes on any of their materials relevant to Spain that I wished to read while in Geneva, but I would not attribute to IRC documents any political or military information that I might glean from that reading, and I would not mention the names of anyone not already mentioned in Dr. Junod's book.

The IRC archives were better arranged than most private document collections I had seen, indeed were better cared for than many of the unshelved materials in major university libraries. There was no catalogue, but the papers were filed in boxes by country and by period. Although the boxes were not dustproof, they benefited from the exemplary cleanliness of the basement in which they were stored. None of the containers was overcrowded, so that there was little danger of papers becoming crushed or torn. The documents provided detailed information about prison furnishings and diet, prisoner health, sanitary and medical conditions, and the negotiations for the exchange of prisoners between the two sides. For the most part they confirmed, and made more precise, things which I already knew from a variety of other sources. In this sense, perhaps, the IRC need not have felt so cautious about allowing me to read them in the first place.

The most important thing was not the novelty of the material, but its dependability. Unpublished reports may or may not be more valuable than published ones, depending on the circumstances of their composition. If the confidential nature of a report makes it easier for the writer to expound embarrassing or unpalatable truths, it also makes it easier for him to express private prejudice or omit vital facts without fear that his work will be subject to public verification. No matter how numerous his sources or how detailed his factual knowledge, a historian is constantly forced to make value judgments based on the general context of a document: the extent to which it reflects intelligence, expertise, moral or political commitment. The most impressive characteristic of the IRC reports was the complete absence of propaganda intent, together with expert technical knowledge of law and of public health practices. I was able to conclude that medical care and sanitary practices had been excellent on both sides, and that readiness for prisoner exchanges had been much greater on the Republican than on the Nationalist side.

I also had a most valuable conversation with Dr. Junod himself. From his book I knew that he had negotiated with both Nationalist and Republican officials and that he had visited prisons in both zones. I had surmised that he had enjoyed greater credit among the Republicans than among the Nationalists, and he readily confirmed my impression. Given the fact that twenty-two years had passed, he was willing to discuss matters which he had not included in his book. I wanted to ask him particularly about the unofficial prisons which had been established in Barcelona by the Servicio de Inteligencia Militar. This intelligence service, staffed almost entirely by communists and fellow travelers, had reproduced on Spanish soil the ideological and physical methods of the Soviet secret police. I had plenty of evidence concerning the tortures practiced in these prisons and their strict subordination to Soviet rather than to Spanish governmental control. I wanted to know whether he had visited these prisons, and whether in his opinion the Republican government was fully aware of what was going on in them.

Dr. Junod was very precise in his reply. He had visited the prison of Santa Ursula, in Valencia, where certain prisoners were regularly beaten on SIM orders. After the fall of Barcelona he had seen a SIM torture chamber equipped with a great metal sphere in which the prisoner was placed, and which was then hammered as a gong, thereby driving the prisoner to the verge of insanity through noise and vibration. It was his opinion, of the truth of which he could not be positive, that the principal Republican officials concerned with prison conditions—José Giral, Julián Zugazagoitia, and Manuel de Irujo—all knew that there were prisons which they were unable to control but did not know how many such prisons there were, or the worst abuses which occurred in them. Dr. Junod was sure that the combination of his Swiss nationality and his generous distribution of American cigarettes to local prison officials had permitted him to know more accurately than did the government both the total numbers and the general treatment of prisoners. He felt that Prime Minister Negrín must have known more than the other ministers, but that while the war lasted, and while his government depended completely on Russian military aid, he was determined to avoid all conflict with the Soviets.

Working in Geneva was a revealing experience for several reasons not directly connected with the International Red Cross archives. I had just spent five months in a country where

I had had to show my passport in every bank and every hotel and where, even with the official letters of introduction supplied to me by the Foreign Ministry, I had had to explain my purposes to uneasy and cautious librarians. In Geneva, except for the very understandable reservations of M. Jequier about the potential effects of my work on the IRC, no one asked me such questions. At the hotel they wanted my passport number, but they accepted the information orally without examining the document themselves. It took several days for my reflexes to become accustomed to the situation. When I went to the offices of the *Journal de Genève,* I was fully prepared to explain why I needed to see certain articles published in 1937 by the ex-President of the Spanish Republic, Alcalá-Zamora. No explanations were necessary. Minor employees, without feeling any necessity to check with their superiors, showed me the file for 1937 and invited me to make myself at home. When I found other items of interest and wished to stay there after hours, they did not hesitate to leave me alone, and simply informed me how to get out of the building after the front door had been locked.

The next day, when I went out to the university library in search of a pamphlet by a Swiss Protestant theologian, I automatically took something to read, since in both French and Spanish libraries I was used to long questionnaires and then further delays before any books would appear. In this case, when I told the librarian in the reading room, which room I had reached without having anyone challenging my right of entry, that I was only in Geneva for a few days and that I wanted only to see this particular pamphlet, he undertook to bring it to me without any formalities whatsoever.

I had come from a country where one could not step into the street without seeing armed men in several varieties of uniform. Here, between work sessions I walked in a city where it was hard to find even a traffic cop, let alone an armed policeman or a platoon of soldiers. In Spain I had involuntarily become accustomed to the constant censorship of books and newspapers. Here I could buy any paper I liked, and in comfortable coffee houses where they mount the newspapers on rollers for their customers I could read as many more as I wished. I had come from a country in which the government identified national loyalty with the speaking of a single language. In the streets of Geneva I heard French and German all the time, with nobody whispering or pointing a suspicious finger. I am aware of all that can be said about the stodgy conservatism of the Swiss, but in that week I felt, somewhat as the citizen of a dictatorship—any dictatorship, Right, Left, or colorless—must feel, the sudden, almost giddy, sense of relief at escaping from an atmosphere of constant caution and surveillance, and the wonderful, unfamiliar sensation of going about one's business without political interference.

From Geneva I went to Toulouse, in order to go through some fifteen years of *El Socialista,* the weekly organ of the Spanish Socialist party in exile. Under the Republic the Socialist party had unquestionably been the most important single political party in Spain. It had had the largest membership, the largest core of votes, and the greatest continuity of leadership. During the first three decades of the twentieth century it had developed steadily as a party which cut across class and regional lines, grouping university intellectuals, the liberal professions, white-collar and industrial workers. Beginning in the late 1920s and increasingly during the Republican era, it had also included a large contingent of both landowning peasants and landless agricultural workers. Its major leaders—Julián Besteiro, Indalecio Prieto, and Francisco Largo Caballero—had all played key roles in the organization of the party prior to 1931 and in the government of the second Republic.

El Socialista contained invaluable information for a student of the Republic and the Civil War. There were substantial articles on such topics as the founding of the first trade unions, the first elections of Socialists to municipal office and to the Cortes, Socialist leadership in the widespread strikes of 1917, and the split occasioned by the founding of the Third International. Each year there were anniversary articles commemorating the deaths of Besteiro and Caballero, such key events as the Sanjurjo *pronunciamiento* in 1932, the October revolution of 1934, and the Popular Front elections of February 1936.

There were frequent discussions of subjects in which the Socialists had been particularly interested: school building, irrigation and dam construction, electrification, and the "pedagogic missions" into the poverty-stricken countryside undertaken by university students during summer vacation.

I had to apply entirely different critical standards to this material than to the reports of the International Red Cross delegates. The articles had been written to place on public record the constructive accomplishments of the party, to uphold the morale of the exiles, and to reverse the dictum of Shakespeare's Antony, that "the evil men do lives after them; the good is oft interred with their bones." But on most questions the propaganda intent did not deform the truth. When an engineer wrote about dam construction or urban planning, when a doctor wrote about public health problems and services, when a professor wrote about curriculum reform, each of them was interested in presenting the truth for future use, and each of them knew that his audience included many colleagues who would not hesitate to write a polemical and detailed reply if they found the presentation inaccurate.

Thus articles on technical, impersonal subjects tended to be quite reliable and to be further corrected by letters from readers. Essays about individuals tended to give the truth, but not the whole truth. The party had been very bitterly split into three segments after the electoral victory of the Right in 1933. Besteiro had felt that the party should not collaborate further with "bourgeois" governments but should continue its educational and electoral efforts until it could command an independent parliamentary majority. Prieto had leaned toward continued electoral and governing alliances with the Left Republicans. Largo Caballero had become disillusioned with parliamentary methods as such and had moved toward a revolutionary position. These fundamental divergences continued through the Civil War. Besteiro had confined himself to municipal social services in besieged Madrid and to the search for peace. Prieto had actively served each of the wartime governments. Largo Caballero had been Prime Minister during the eight months in which the Spanish workers and peasants had felt themselves most deeply committed to the Republic, and during which the Republic had converted its raw militia into a trained army.

From the columns of *El Socialista* it was clear that the rival factions desired to bury the hatchet. Articles about individuals stressed their contributions to the common cause and were completely silent about the factional struggles. Thus it was possible to document Besteiro's services as Chairman of the Constituent Cortes without mentioning his virtual rejection of the Popular Front. It was possible to celebrate the ascetic scruples of Caballero without mentioning his extreme jealousy of Prieto. In some ways this meant that the historical articles in *El Socialista* were more valuable than the factional polemics which had filled the rival Socialist newspapers in the years 1934–6. But of course anyone depending solely on *El Socialista* would receive an incomplete, and much too rosy, picture of Socialist party history.

At the editorial offices of *El Socialista* I felt myself to be a welcome guest. The tables and shelves were all uneven, the piles of back newspapers were all dusty, there was no heat, and no light bulb stronger than about twenty watts. The staff, composed of middle-aged typesetters who had been militants in one of the oldest and strongest Socialist trade unions, had the solid, bureaucratic look of trade-union officials everywhere. But beneath the bureaucratic air were passionate, proud memories of the Spanish struggle, an almost pathetic faith in the ultimate triumph of human enlightenment and social justice, and an embarrassingly respectful attitude toward professors. They were proud that I was using their archives, they spent hours happily searching for missing issues, and they did not try in any way—as did most Spanish librarians—to influence my selection of materials.

We talked a great deal, not so much about the Civil War as about their experiences in exile. When the defeated army had crossed the border in February 1939 the French police had herded them into improvised camps along the seashore between the frontier and Perpignan. As of 1961 these Socialist veterans were willing to admit that the flood of refugees had presented the French authorities with a totally unprecedented problem, but they remembered bitterly the humiliation at the time; and then, more serious, the eager cooperation of the French police with Francoist authorities trying to get them to return to Spain, and later with the German occupiers of defeated France. They were scornful of the French as soldiers. Why, they boasted, we Spaniards fought Hitler for two and a half years, and these people collapsed in six weeks. When I said that no real comparison could be made between Hitler's five thousand aviators and gun crews in Spain and the army of several hundred thousand which poured into France directly from its home bases, they replied by claiming that the toughest fighters in the French maquis had been Spaniards.

Since this was not a seminar in history, I did not argue the matter. The bread of exile is bitter indeed. These were men who, before 1936, had belonged to the aristocracy of skilled labor in a country where bourgeois standards and education had never penetrated society as a whole, and where workmen had been proud of their status as such. They recalled a constitution whose preamble spoke of a "Republic of workers of all categories," and they had been partisans of Largo Caballero, the only workingman ever to become prime minister of a democratic government. They had never become adapted to the more pragmatic, distinctly less idealistic tone of life in France, and they did not want to become adapted to it. Also, after three years of war in Spain and five years of concentration camps and guerrilla fighting in France, they had lost their skills and habits of workmanship. At the same time they grudgingly admitted that after 1945 the French had given them residence and work permits, and they were positively boastful of the French education and the successful professional careers of their children and their friends' children. In the end we agreed that the much-maligned Fourth Republic and the centuries-old French tradition of political asylum were merits to be recognized in that tired, slightly cynical society wherein they personally would never feel completely at home.

From Toulouse I returned to Madrid to complete my reading of the Spanish press for the 1930s, and also with the hope that I might finally receive permission to work in the Archivo Militar. Altogether I visited the archives four times between October 1960 and May 1961. On the first two occasions, in the fall, I had gone there with the late Willard Smith, who also held a Fulbright research fellowship and who was doing research for a book on the Primo de Rivera dictatorship. We had both received strong verbal encouragement from the officials at the Fulbright Commission, but we had not received letters of introduction. Sr. F. had told us that permission could only come from the Ministry of War, but that the officers at the archives would undoubtedly smooth the way for us. Willard was anxious to examine materials bearing on the role of the Defense Juntas of 1917 and on the struggle between the artillery corps and the dictator in 1926. While these were not exactly neutral subjects, especially from the viewpoint of career officers, they were certainly not as controversial as the Civil War. It was quite conceivable that the ministry might want to say yes to Willard and no to me, not only because his research was less controversial than mine but because his previous writings had not identified him as a "pinko." We therefore agreed in advance that he should take the initiative in the conversation.

The colonel on duty at the archives was a short, stout man who treated us with great friendliness, but who was also very nervous and noncommittal. Willard spoke eloquently of his enormous admiration for Primo de Rivera and of the high qualities of mind and character of Spanish officers, for which he regretted that he found little parallel in the United States. The colonel almost purred. The archives were rich in documents on the Primo era, and it would be a pleasure to serve a historian who appreciated the fine traditions of the Spanish military. He would write to the Minister of War, and if we would come back in about two weeks he hoped there would be good news for us.

Knowing that things take time in Spain, and not wanting to appear importunate, we waited three weeks before our second visit. The little colonel was again all smiles, but no, he had not heard yet from the ministry. We said that we understood, and Willard waxed lyrical about a retired colonel whom he had had to dinner several nights earlier. I mentioned that I had met General Martínez Campos, who had been a general staff officer and who had explained to me a number of important aspects of Spanish military organization; also General Kindelán, who had been chief of the Nationalist air force; and that both these officers had encouraged me to work in the Archivo Militar. The colonel nodded rapidly. Yes, there were very valuable materials which, once I saw them, would completely revolutionize my conception of foreign intervention in the Civil War. The documents would prove to me how unimportant had been the Italian and German contributions to the Nationalist side, and how, on the contrary, the International Brigades and the Russians had been the only forces worth talking about in the Republican camp. I agreed that this was somewhat the reverse of my present impression, but that I had come to Spain to learn and that I was most anxious to see any and all documents bearing on foreign intervention on both sides. The colonel reminded us nervously that permission had not yet been received, but he hoped that shortly after Christmas, at the latest, we would be able to see a portion of the archives.

During the winter months Willard made several visits, during which he was shown briefly a few not-very-crucial documents. But he did not receive permission to do any reading on his own. I therefore had very little hope of ever seeing anything of importance, and I did not want to waste time or to irritate people fruitlessly. However, I felt a professional obligation to make at least one further effort on an individual basis; in mid-April I returned alone to the archives. The little colonel seemed pleased and excited to see me. He could assure me now that the minister was aware of my request, but he was out of town at the moment and would make a decision just as soon as he returned to Madrid. Since the colonel seemed to be happily animated rather than nervous, and since I was no longer trying to be unobtrusive for Willard's sake, I decided flatly to name my own figures on foreign intervention and to see what response I would draw.

"You remember, colonel, that when I was here several months ago, you told me that documents in your archives would revolutionize my concept of foreign intervention. I have kept that statement in mind, and I am more anxious than ever to be able to check my other sources with those in your archives. On the basis of Italian and German sources, plus other confirmation in press and diplomatic dispatches, I now believe that there were between fifty and seventy thousand Italians and about five to six thousand Germans serving in the Nationalist ranks. I have no ax to grind in this matter. If I am wrong, show me."

"The Italians hardly counted for anything," he replied. "Many of ours laughed when they ran away at Guadalajara. I can show you official documents on the withdrawal of volunteers in 1938 which prove that there were not more than ten thousand Italians. And these Italians were not trained soldiers. They were volunteers, easily demoralized, without real discipline. As for the Germans, a few specialists, instructors to teach our officers how to fire anti-aircraft and antitank guns, and a handful of volunteer aviators. But that story, which has appeared in all anti-Spanish histories, that the Germans bombed Guernica—that is a lie spread by the Reds, who burned Guernica themselves and then tried to blame the Nationalists."

I did not attempt to reply to what I recognized immediately as sheer mythology. By referrnig to the token withdrawal of Italians in 1938, he simply ignored the fact that the great majority had not been repatriated until after the Franco victory in 1939. As for Guernica: an unimpeachable Basque priest had seen the town just after the bombing, Captain Adolf Galland of the Condor Legion had written of it in his memoirs, Field Marshal Hermann Goering had discussed it in his prison cell prior to the Nuremberg war crimes trial. It was probably true that Franco was angered rather than pleased by this German action, but it was typical of his dictatorship simply to repeat the same stale lies year after year.

Meanwhile the colonel had opened a safe and was looking for the document which would prove to me that not more than ten thousand Italians had ever fought in Spain. He could not locate it, and then suddenly recalled that one of his colleagues had it in another office. The colonel telephoned the colleague, but he had not yet come in. His desk was now piled high with typewritten dispatches that he had removed from the safe in the course of his search. Clearly legible to me at a distance of a few feet was a report, entirely in caps, dated May 1938, stating that military intelligence estimated the total of the International Brigades as between thirty-five and forty thousand.

"Would it be all right," I asked, "if I took a look at that report on the International Brigades?"

The colonel wheeled around, grabbed the dispatch, and after seeing what it was, looked at me triumphantly.

"Here," he shouted, "evidence from our military intelligence, not newspaper propaganda. There were forty thousand foreign communists fighting for the Reds, and they were the only real troops they had. Why don't you print that, and not repeat the slanders of the international Red press?"

I replied that any number of accounts favorable to the Republicans published in France or the United States had estimated the total number of International Brigade fighters at thirty to forty thousand. He seemed stupefied, and asked me whether I would use those figures. I said that of course I would, that I had no intention of hiding the truth, whether it turned out to be ten thousand or a hundred thousand. Again he seemed positively stupefied by my words, and covered his perplexity by hastily gathering up all the papers and returning them to the safe. He told me that he found it very interesting to talk with me, that he hoped I would not become impatient, that there were many documents in the safe that he would like to show me, but that we must await word from the Minister of War. Would I still be in Madrid for a few weeks? Yes, I would, and we shook hands on the proposition that it would be worth one more visit after the minister had returned to Madrid.

My fourth and last visit took place late in April. This time the colonel was distinctly embarrassed. He apologized for the continuing delay, but the permission had not arrived yet, I said that I would be leaving Madrid in about two weeks, that this was really my last opportunity, and might it be possible for him to call the Ministry of War. No, he said, the minister knew of my request, and one did not remind a general who was known for his efficiency and decision. Might I not return to Madrid the next year? Surely something could be arranged then. Meanwhile, this morning, it would give him great pleasure to show me the exhibition of war trophies which had just recently been completed. He conducted me into a spacious rectangular room which must have measured at least one hundred by forty or fifty feet. Along three walls and lengthwise down the center of the room stood glass-covered exhibition cases. There were regimental flags, Carlist and Falangist banners, relief maps of the terrain around Bilbao, Teruel, and Madrid; photos of the siege of the Alcázar, of victory parades in the main cities, of air aces, of General Franco receiving both military and civilian delegations. Most memorable was the mural which covered the entire fourth wall. It represented General Franco dressed as a white knight and haloed, on his knees before the Cross. To each side of him were ardent, idealistic-looking soldiers and churchmen, and stretching into the background, a worshipful mass of followers. *"Nuestra cruzada,"* our crusade, said the colonel briefly.

After we had spent a suitable time admiring the exhibits we returned to his office and he offered me a cup of coffee. It was the end of April, just a week after the dramatic, unsuccessful *Putsch* in North Africa in which Generals Challe and Salan had threatened to overthrow the De Gaulle government in order to prevent the conclusion of a peace treaty between France and its former colony Algeria. The colonel felt sorry for France. Like Spain in 1936, he said, France in 1961 needed a regime which would combat the disrupting effects of materialism and ideological confusion. The military are the rightful guardians of national tradition in any society; in fact, said the colonel, that should be their principal peacetime function. It would have been better for both metropolitan France and for Algeria if the generals had won, but they had not been decisive enough, they had lacked Franco's iron will, and their troops, of course, had been undermined by communism just as had the civilian population of France.

I listened politely, almost without comment, and he went on to speak of the Eichmann trial in Jerusalem. The Israeli intelligence service had executed a fantastic coup in tracing Eichmann to Argentina and kidnaping him under the eyes of the Argentine police. But really, the charges were incredible. Did I not think so? Who was going to believe that the Germans had murdered six million Jews?

"Haven't you read about or seen pictures of the crematoria?" I asked. "We didn't need the Eichmann trial to prove that these things happened."

"Propaganda," he said decisively. "Mind you, I admire the Jews. We have no anti-Semitism in Spain. Many Jews have come back to Spain and they live here very quietly, in complete freedom; they have their synagogues, everything. But you know, the Jews are very rich. They own all the movies in Hollywood. They can get testimony on anything."

I thanked the colonel for his hospitality and for his efforts to secure me a permit to work in the Archivo Militar. As I walked home I felt disappointed not to have learned anything concrete from my several visits. Undoubtedly there was a great deal of material there which could enable a future historian to document much more accurately and precisely than anyone has so far the internal politics and the military history of Spain. But he would have to have really free access, not just have an occasional document waved in his face, or alluded to without demonstration, as in the cases of both Willard Smith and myself. I wondered also what use approved Spanish historians might have made of the archives. I had compared the 1940 and 1958 editions of Manuel Aznar's *Historia militar de la guerra de España* without finding any major differences between the two.

But if I had learned no new facts, I felt that I had learned something about fascism from the evident fellow feeling of the little colonel toward both the mutinous French generals and the Nazi "victims" of postwar trials from Nuremberg to Jerusalem. An important part of the emotional substratum of fascism was the mutual sympathy of humiliated military men. The colonel was not a bad fellow; nothing that he said gave me the feeling of fanaticism or race hatred. But his sympathies lay with the Italian officers who had felt cheated by the results of World War I and with the German officers who dreamed of revenge by any means. He had suffered personally from the low esteem in which his compatriots held the army when they had been free to express themselves. In the Algerian *Putsch* he had instinctively sided with the factious officers who felt that their services to France had given them the right, even the duty, to overthrow a "corrupt" civilian government which was about to "give away" part of the sacred soil. But from the colonel's manner I was convinced that the territorial issue and the talk about materialism, were not the crucial matters. Identification with humiliated military men was the common denominator, the emotional basis of all his expressed political sympathies. As for a truly valuable use of the archives: like many things in Spain, it would have to wait for a thoroughgoing change of regime.

11

The Act of Composition

In early September 1961 the reunited Jackson family moved into a beautiful, but not very practical, old stone house on the edge of the village of Les Molières, about twenty miles southwest of Paris on the road to Rambouillet. The Social Science Research Council had generously extended my fellowship for a second year, and the French government, looking toward the publication of her doctoral thesis on Marcel Proust, had awarded my wife a grant-in-aid. Our house had been built in several stages. In the seventeenth century it had been a bakery, and the oven was still visible, although that portion of the building had long since been used only to store lumber and coal. In the nineteenth century the house had been greatly expanded as a restaurant, and what had been the restaurant was now our living room. Below the kitchen ran an underground stream, which had served as a wine cellar and natural refrigerator. Above the former restaurant were three bedrooms, one of which had a trap door into the kitchen. The earthen walls of the ground story were constantly damp as a result of osmosis from the underground stream, and we could use the living room only on Sundays, with a large wood fire burning, with our chairs drawn around the fire, and with scarves on to protect us from the drafts and the damp. We lived principally in the kitchen and the bedrooms, and heated these four rooms, plus the bathroom, by means of two oil-burning space heaters of the sort we were familiar with from our Vermont winters.

For some years prior to our arrival, the house had been lived in during the summer only, and the fact that it was not really equipped for year-round occupancy was responsible for the bargain rental of ninety dollars a month, very low indeed for anything large enough to house a family of four within twenty miles of Paris. Three decades earlier the house had been the summer home of the poet Patrice de la Tour du Pin, and its present owner, a cousin of the poet, was a professional army officer. According to the renting agent, our proprietor was a bitter opponent of President De Gaulle's peace negotiations with the Algerian nationalists and had, among other things, helped Jacques Soustelle, one of the top leaders of the Secret Army Organization, to escape to Switzerland when the French police were trying to arrest him for armed rebellion. I was pleased by the various associations of the house: with a three-hundred-year-old bakery and a nineteenth-century cafe; with a fine if little known poet; with Jacques Soustelle, who was known to me not only as one of the intellectual fascists of the dying French Algeria, but more importantly as an excellent anthropologist and student of the Aztecs. Our renting agent was a man of the Left and was therefore enormously delighted at the thought that the tenant of La Tour du Pin would be writing a history of the Spanish Republic.

Despite its practical inconveniences, La Tour du Pin was very much home to all of us for ten months. My wife could get to Paris easily to consult her thesis director and to work at the Bibliothèque Nationale. The girls played jacks, rolled in the grass, and climbed trees with their village classmates. There was an old peasant named Père Tassiot who grumbled at all the children, and whom they called *gros patapouf*. Kate and Rachel were afraid of him at first, but quickly realized that the whole thing was a game, indeed that Père Tassiot would have been a very lonely old man if he had not been able to get a rise out of the village children with his grumbling. For the girls English had become a foreign language, and I was obliged to converse with them in my fairly fluent, but very badly accented, French. I had always thought of a different language as signifying a different form of thought, a different way of reacting to and communicating about life. This had been one of our reasons for taking our doctoral studies in France—to become bilingual. In my daughters, studying in French schools for the second year, I was constantly startled by the contrast of manner, intonation, and choice of topics and phrases between their rapid, smoothly modulated Parisian French and their explosive, brusque New England American.

I worked in one of the upstairs rooms, at a window which looked out across the grounds of the Club Hippique des Molières. As I made outlines and typed drafts, I could watch the trainers teaching their beautiful, mettlesome horses to pose proudly, as if on exhibit; to walk with their tails arched perfectly, to canter with a completely even motion. The horses were also being trained to jump hurdles, a form of instruction at which they all balked, and which was accompanied by much verbal abuse and occasional beating. The girls, who loved animals, were much distressed, both by the actions of the trainers and by the generally rough way in which most of their companions treated dogs, cats, and sheep. It was difficult to explain to them that the horses were being trained at great expense for highly competitive races, and that farm people think of animals more for their practical value than for their quality as pets.

I spent many desperate hours at that window, watching the trainers discipline their horses while I tried to convert my formless materials into a disciplined narrative. It was painfully discouraging to realize how many large questions remained only partially answered after years of reading and months of interviewing witnesses. To what extent had votes been counted honestly, and elections conducted in an atmosphere of free speech? How extensive was the wealth of Church orders, whose stocks and real estate were frequently held in the names of private persons? How many elementary schools were built by the Republic? What real changes were accomplished in the training, the supply, and the promotional standards of the army? What was the relation between wages and the cost of living between 1931 and 1936? What proportion of career officers welcomed the military rising in July 1936? And how many officers fought on the side of the Republic? I felt that I could give qualitatively accurate answers to these questions, but I was unhappy at the relative paucity of dependable quantitative data. The only way to proceed was to tailor my narrative to the materials available, and to explain in the footnotes and the critical bibliography the precise limitations of my data.

At the same time I realized only too well how it happens that many of the finest, most scrupulous scholars never quite manage to finish their books because the limitations of their evidence inhibit them from producing any publishable version of their researches. This psychological problem, I might add, often adversely affects the tenure decisions made in colleges and universities. Because of the understandable emphasis on publication as the only objective means by which a scholar can be judged by people who do not know him as a personal colleague, it frequently happens that tenure committees reward quantity over quality, thereby giving a premium to those who are more "productive" but often less complete and accurate in their writing.

Quite aside from disappointment at the incompleteness of my data, I had to struggle with an organizational problem which had not arisen in my earlier writing. On the whole, my note packets were arranged topically rather than chronologically. My Master's and doctoral theses and my various articles had all dealt with particular topics, such as the ideology of Joaquín Costa, the sources of Spanish anarchism, or the significance of Erasmist thought in sixteenth-century Spain. These topics, of course, had to be treated within a historical context, but I had not had to present a general historical account of a whole era in order to write such articles. They had been addressed to an audience of specialists whose background knowledge could be assumed. In fact, it had been important not to waste words on a general account but to arrive as quickly as possible at the new data and interpretation that I would be offering to a scholarly audience.

My present task involved much more in the way of background and synthesis, and the audience which I pictured was not primarily a group of professional Hispanists but educated laymen who would be interested in solidly documented history but who need not know anything about modern Spain before reading my book. It quickly became clear to me that I would have to use a far more chronological and sequential narrative form than in my previous writings. I took note packets which were labeled Church, Army, Agrarian Question, Monarchists, Socialist Party, etc., and rearranged them under roughly chronological headings such as Constitutional Period (April–October 1931), Azaña Era (October 1931–October 1933), Center-Right Government (November 1933–October 1934), Asturian Revolt and Its Aftermath (October 1934–late 1935). This procedure did not in itself solve the organizational problem. A day-by-day account would not be any more unified and comprehensible than a series of topical essays on different aspects of the Republic. In fact, the greatest formal weakness of the existing histories, those of Melchor Fernández Almagro, Joaquín Arraras, and Josep Plá, was that they supplied a mere chronicle of events. What I had to do, ideally, was combine the chronological with the topical. The reader must always know the sequence of important events, whether those events regarded principally the Church, the agrarian situation, or any other specific phase of Spanish society. But he must also be able to see continuing threads of significance, and not simply watch a daily newsreel pass before his eyes. Curiously enough, nothing is more static in its effect on the mind than a purely chronological presentation of events which are unrelated except as to their sequence in time.

Gradually then, I combined the sequential and the topical approaches, after which the question still remained: in what order to treat the various topics within each chronological period. Here it seemed best to begin with the national political situation, since the description of politics inevitably tends to be chronological, and also introduces the reader to personalities and parties with which he can readily identify the other aspects of a given period. After the treatment of politics came economics, subdivided as far as necessary for clarity and with problems treated in the order of their estimated importance. After economics came cultural and ideological topics, subdivided according to geographical region and social class, and again treated in the order of estimated importance. The above scheme sufficed for the background of the Republic and for the period April 1931–July 1936. But the outbreak of the Civil War introduced two new complications: the diplomatic and military role of foreign powers and the separate political-economic development of the two halves of Spain at war. It was thus necessary to organize specific chapters dealing with international intervention and with the internal history of each zone, and to combine in these chapters, as in the earlier ones, a chronological and topical approach.

Second only to the task of organizing the narrative was the problem of political terminology. The Spanish Civil War aroused passions, both within Spain and in the world at large, comparable in violence and ardor to those aroused by the French and Russian revolutions. There was absolutely no trace of consensus as to the political and moral significance of the events when they occurred. There was no such consensus when I was writing, and I doubt whether there will be any general consensus on the subject a century from now. How was I to label the forces in presence without being guilty, by my very choice of words, of "stacking the cards" as to emotional and moral connotations? If I employed the terms "reds" and "whites" everyone would know whom I meant, and I would be dealing even-handedly with the parties, but only in a crude, pejorative sense, as if one were to discuss the civil rights question in the United States in terms of "niggers" and "whiteys." If I used the terms "Marxists" or "communists" for the one side and "fascists" for the other, everyone would also know whom I meant, but I would be perpetuating a common violation of the truth, since those terms, widely as they were used, do not refer accurately to more than a small proportion of the forces in each camp. They would have the additional disadvantage of suggesting to the reader that the issues in Spain were identical with the general European confrontation between fascist- and communist-led forces.

Newspaper usage of the time offered various labels which had the virtue of applying specifically to Spain: "Rebels,"

"Insurgents," and "Nationalists" for the supporters of the military rising; "Loyalists" and "Republicans" for those who resisted the military rising. I did not like "Rebels" and "Loyalists" because they imply a greater element of legal deliberation than I thought was present in the choices made by those who were in a position to choose, and who had the will to choose, which side they would support. These terms would also, I felt, make the question of "legitimacy" appear to be simpler than in fact it was. The main factor in the situation was indeed that activist officers and monarchists had deliberately undertaken to overthrow the government which had arisen out of reasonably free parliamentary elections in February 1936. To this extent, "Rebels" versus "Loyalists" would be justified. However, the legitimate president of the Republic, Alcalá-Zamora, had been ousted from office on the thinnest of legal pretexts in April 1936. Much of the Left, which claimed to represent legitimacy in its defense of the Republican government during the war, had supported a revolutionary uprising in October 1934 against the legitimate government of that era. Much of that same Left had also, between February and July 1936, refused to share governing responsibility with the moderate Republicans, and had in fact harassed them only slightly less than had the monarchists and fascists. It thus seemed to me that as a historian I should not award unquestioned legal honors to the Left, but should acknowledge the virtual absence on July 18 of governmental authority, and the arrival of a revolutionary crisis in which men could make honorable and thoughtful decisions as to which side they would support, but on the basis of social programs and ideologies, not of political legitimacy.

My consideration of different terms was also complicated by the fact that the political situation was very fluid in both zones during the first months of the war, but that from about November 1936 there was a perfectly clear form of authority in Franco Spain and an increasingly clear trend of development in Republican Spain. It thus seemed to me that "Insurgents" would be the appropriate term for those who had supported the military rising, and that this term should be applied to them during the months of uncertainty between the rising itself and the firm establishment of General Franco's personal ascendancy. And it does not have the pejorative, or even slightly humorous, overtones of the term "Rebel." For the same period I decided to use the admittedly clumsy phrase "Popular Front zone" to refer to the portion of Spain which had declared its loyalty to the Republican government. Between July and November that government had exercised only nominal authority in much of its territory. The true common denominator of both the civilian political administrations and the military units in anti-Francoist Spain was adherence to one or another of the parties composing the Popular Front. Hence "Popular Front" zone, or forces, gives an accurate denomination without implying a greater degree of loyalty to legitimate institutions than in fact existed.

Finally, for the period after November 1936 I used the terms "Nationalists" and "Republicans" to characterize the two camps. In "Nationalist" Spain the government steadily proclaimed the primacy of Castile over the several minority nationalities. It governed with the support of those economic, religious, and military forces which have traditionally formed the backbone of the most conservative governments in Europe since the eighteenth century. While nationalism is by no means a monopoly of conservatives and military men, it is much more integral to their ideology than to that of the Left. For the other camp the term "Republicans" seemed to me the most accurate single word available, since from November 1936 onward the revolutionary elements were in steady retreat, the government increasingly reaffirmed the aims and program of the reformist Republic, and the Caballero and Negrín cabinets acted as much in the spirit of the reformist Republic as it was physically possible to act under wartime conditions.

A final organizational problem concerned the treatment of especially controversial aspects of the eight-year period: the complete distortion of the Republican era by the uncontested propaganda versions published under official auspices since 1939; the interpretation of contested elections; and the determination, even approximately, of how many people died as a result of the Civil War, and what specific form those deaths had taken. One of the constant dangers in composing a detailed account of a controversial event is that the author will be simultaneously trying to anticipate the objections of a dozen hostile critics—and will thereby tend to confuse or at least irritate the ordinary reader who does not feel himself involved in the polemics of either scholars or politicians. I did not want to clutter my narrative with such polemics. At the same time I did not want to give the reader the impression that all the evidence was clear and simple. More important, I have always felt that a historian has a moral obligation to the truth. By sheer force of repetition over two decades, many outright lies had come to be accepted as true even by democratic and revolutionary opponents of the Franco dictatorship. An English historian of Laborite affiliations had been fooled by much of this propaganda and his book had become a best seller on both sides of the Atlantic. It thus seemed to me imperative not merely that I embody my own researches in a published narrative, but that I directly expose some of the worst examples of this propaganda. The solution to this problem was to incorporate these detailed and controversial discussions in three separate appendices to the general history. They would thus be not only available, but emphasized for those who were interested, and they could be omitted by others.

While writing the first draft of my book in Les Molières, I continued to interview important personalities, this time among the exiles living in Paris. Personal contact with two of these men was especially significant: Manuel de Irujo, former Minister of Justice under both Caballero and Negrín, and a leader of the Basque Autonomists; and the late Diego Martínez Barrio, Prime Minister and member of several moderate Republican cabinets, and President in exile of the Spanish Republic.

In late 1961, D. Manuel de Irujo was dividing his time between the Basque Delegation headquarters in London and Paris. I had two long conversations with him in his sparsely furnished Paris office. He was a ruddy, energetic, enthusiastic human being who communicated with great pleasure and fluency. Although we talked about the entire range of war and politics between 1936 and 1939, he kept constantly returning the conversation to two main themes: personalities and justice. He had deeply admired both Caballero and Negrín, feeling perhaps greater affection for the former and greater respect for the latter. Caballero he characterized as a *fraile sindical,* a trade-union monk, who would have felt guilty of larceny if he had accidentally walked out of a cabinet meeting with an office pencil. (I had heard much the same thing from Indalecio Prieto, who told me with a combination of wry amusement and respect how in October 1934 Caballero had been frightened of arrest, not because of what the police might do to him but because he might be caught with party funds which at the time he was unwillingly carrying on his person.)

According to Irujo, Caballero's whole aim as Prime Minister had been to rebuild the authority of the democratic state under conditions of full political liberty for all those not actively implicated in the military rising. For this reason he had resisted Communist efforts to have the POUM and other anti-Stalinist factions suppressed, had refused to remove loyal military men because of their past membership in Rightist organizations, and had supported Irujo's demand that no priests should be kept in jail simply because they were priests. Irujo was proud that he had been able to free all imprisoned priests early in 1937, and that the Popular Tribunals in the same period were increasingly acquitting, and reversing earlier decisions, in cases of persons accused of espionage by malicious neighbors or political enemies who could offer nothing but hearsay evidence. He had also decreed that at the discretion of the prison directors, political prisoners could be temporarily released on their word of honor for family ceremonials such as christenings, marriages, and funerals. He claimed that no escapes had occurred under this rule, and stated explicitly that both Caballero and Negrín had approved his initiative.

He was pleased also by the recollection of his relationship to the anarchist chief García Oliver, who had been his predecessor as Minister of Justice. García Oliver had, among other things, permitted postmortem marriages, eliminated the toga and biretta from the courts, and decreed the transfer of birth and marriage registers from the courts to the municipal governments. When Irujo, at this time minister without portfolio, protested to Caballero, the latter replied: "You are quite right, Irujo, but first we must win a few battles." By the time Irujo took over as Minister of Justice, García Oliver had become convinced that his "reforms" had not worked out well; he came to Irujo's office to acknowledge the fact and to offer full cooperation for Irujo's court and prison plans.

Negrín, he thought, was without question the ablest statesman produced by the Civil War crisis, a man of political stature comparable to Churchill or De Gaulle. Although he was a member of the Socialist party, he had not been a Marxist or a trade-union official. Consequently he lacked intimate psychological contact with the party as a whole, and this was a serious source of tension during, and especially after, the war. He had proven his great administrative ability as chairman of the faculty committee which built the University City in Madrid. He had really discovered his political vocation only under the impact of the war, however; he had conceived of himself as a bourgeois democrat but had been ready to sacrifice anyone and anything, including himself, to keep the Republican forces in the field until, inevitably, a general European war would break out and the cause of Republican Spain would be merged with that of the Western democratic powers, which in 1937 and 1938 were refusing to aid the Republic. His physical courage and his self-possession in adversity made him an inspiring war leader in contrast with personally fine but essentially defeatist leaders such as Azaña, Prieto, and the Catalan President Companys. Without yielding anything as to his ultimate plans, he would cooperate as far as was necessary with the Soviets and the Communist party in order to win the war. For the same reason, faced with civilian defeatism in mid-1938, he had permitted the Communist-dominated Servicio de Inteligencia Militar to circumvent the Minister of Justice, a practice which had led to Irujo's resignation in August.

There was a certain filial element in the attitude of Irujo toward both Negrín and Caballero. He credited the former with impeccable motives and the correct analysis of the international situation despite the profound disagreement about standards of wartime justice which had caused his resignation. While speaking of Negrín's abrupt, often imperious manner of dealing with colleagues and of his antipathy to both Catalan and Basque regionalism, Irujo also referred repeatedly to the great personal tenderness of his Christmas messages after the war. This is of course a kind of gesture which, in an ambitious executive personality, may be merely sentimental, or intended to improve what we now call the "image." But I was inclined to accept Irujo's interpretation because Negrín was throughout his life a thoroughly independent man with none of the "other-directed" qualities which throw doubt on the genuineness of personal expressions. He was also a man who hated to make speeches or write letters. A brief gesture from him meant more than a flood of prose from others.

Even more striking was Irujo's filial affection for Largo Caballero, who must have been more than twenty years his senior. He characterized as "paternal" Caballero's efforts in cabinet meetings to keep the ministers from getting on one another's nerves and his desire to understand the Basque and Catalan movements, to which he had admittedly paid little previous attention. In late 1945 Largo Caballero had returned to Paris after four years in a German concentration camp. He was ill, and knew that he must be close to death. Irujo described him as anxious to see as many as possible of his surviving cabinet colleagues. He was preoccupied with the errors of what he now considered his "too abstract" form of thought. He wanted Irujo to know that he thought he had been too dogmatic in the spring of 1936, and that Spain needed national and class reconciliation more than it needed any particular form of economic or political system. His words, as Irujo reported them, were quite different in tone from the very bitter memoirs which he had written while in Germany, and which were published in Mexico after his death. Nor could I follow all the details, because D. Manuel's voice was obstructed by tears. But I knew from his entire manner that he thought of Largo Caballero as having embodied all that was most noble, and perhaps most naïvely mistaken, in the Spanish Left.

The second major Republican figure whom I was able to consult in Paris was Diego Martínez Barrio, who had been Prime Minister of the interim government which had supervised the Cortes elections of October 1933—elections which commentators on both sides acknowledge to have been the most honestly conducted elections in Spanish history thus far. He had also been president of the Cortes in 1936. He had come from a very modest family in Seville, his father having been a construction worker. He was a thirty-third-degree Mason and had been one of Alejandro Lerroux's principal lieutenants in the Radical Party. In 1934 he had founded a small centrist party of his own after separating from Lerroux in opposition to the latter's reinforcement of the Civil Guard and his readiness to protect the educational privileges of the Church. At no time, however, was he an anticlerical demagogue. He was neither a colorful personality nor a distinguished orator. He was known for his moderation and his devotion to government by persuasion; he was thus available, both in peacetime and during the Civil War, for delicate missions of compromise.

In 1961 he was suffering from a serious heart condition, but he had consented to see me one afternoon at his home in St. Germain-en-Laye. My appearance, however, took him by surprise. He had expected me on the same day a week later. There was much vociferous argument between him and two secretaries as to who had received my letter, what date it had mentioned, and where the letter had been filed. Neither secretary could locate the letter. In addition, my arrival had interrupted a dictation session in which he was answering official letters from Mexico. Everybody hoped I would not mind waiting a few minutes. He returned to his dictation, and the session took up the better part of an hour, partly because the male stenographer did not know shorthand, partly because the president had to rest for a few minutes between letters.

Meanwhile, I wondered how I could best excuse myself. I knew that this was in fact the agreed date for the interview, but my host was a very sick man who ought not to have been using his voice at all. His wife interrupted once to give him an injection, and she tried unsuccessfully to have him cancel the rest of the afternoon's plans. He sat reclining deeply in a leather arm chair and wrapped in a heavy woolen blanket, although it was quite warm in the room. His expression was morose but determined. Sparing himself any unnecessary physical movements and pausing whenever his breath was short, he went on dictating doggedly, without so much as replying to his wife's plea. At last the letters were finished. When he turned toward me I apologized for having come the wrong day, asserted that I did not live far away, and that I would be glad to come back another time. He measured me slowly, as if to register the features of one more conspirator who was trying to keep him from his work. "Since you are already here," he said, raising his naturally arched eyebrows, "you may as well stay."

Despite this unpromising start, we had a most fruitful conversation about the several elections of the Republican period. He insisted on their fully representative quality, despite the fact that they were all unquestionably marred by violence and faulty vote counting. As Prime Minister during the 1933 election he had ordered the Civil Guard and the police to abstain completely from intervening in electoral meetings. He had removed one civil governor who thought that his job was to "arrange" the results as in monarchical times. He had refused suggestions from the Left that the elections be annulled, and he had remained in office afterward until the new Cortes could meet to choose its own majority leader, and hence Prime Minister. He said he had kept the police out of the election in the belief that the distortions caused by sporadic violence and threats of violence were much smaller than those which would have resulted from police intervention. The temperamental excitement of the Spaniards should be taken for granted, likewise the readiness of the police and the old-time politicians to tabulate the results in advance if given the opportunity; of the two dangers, the first was distinctly the lesser. On the other hand, since the actual results were a disagreeable surprise to the Left, and since extremists talked of annulling the vote, he had decided, with the full support of President Alcalá-Zamora, to remain in office for several weeks until the tally was final, the main complaints had been investigated, and the new Cortes had been able to meet. He was very proud of the public statements made by Dr. Marañon and other prestigious intellectuals to the effect that these had been the most honestly conducted national elections in Spanish history.

He also insisted on the legitimacy of the Popular Front election of February 1936. The Prime Minister, Portela Valladares, had also, like Martínez Barrio in 1933, guaranteed freedom of press and assembly and had kept the forces of *orden público* strictly on the sidelines. The most militant Left leaders were still in jail, and during the campaign a number of civil governors had expressed their gratitude to Portela for the electoral freedom and relative absence of violence. In the five days following the election the leaders of the defeated Right parties had all published statements explaining their defeat, but even if every accusation of fraud had turned out to be correct, the overall result would not have been altered. But also, as in 1933, there was extremist talk of annulling the elections, this time from the Right, and Madrid was filled with rumors of a military coup. Under these circumstances, said Martínez Barrio, Portela had done a great disservice to the country by insisting that the new majority take office immediately.

As he said this I was suddenly reminded of a conversation in Madrid the year before. D. Javier Morata, who had been the mayor of Madrid at the time of the Popular Front election, had also been very critical of Portela's haste in resigning office the day after the Popular Front victory. He had told me to read an article by Martínez Barrio which had appeared in the Madrid edition of *ABC* on February 23, 1937—an article commemorating, in wartime, the first anniversary of the Popular Front electoral triumph. Morata, a Lerroux partisan, hence a former colleague but now political foe of Martínez Barrio, had been in the Prime Minister's office when the latter had, in a tone of panic, announced his resignation. Morata vouched for the complete accuracy of Martínez Barrio's version of the incident. I now, in October 1961, asked Martínez Barrio if he knew how and why Portela had resigned in February 1936. He told me a story which, an hour later, I was able to check against my notes of the Morata conversation and the 1937 article. What he had said to me checked perfectly with what he had written twenty-four years earlier in an article which one of his political opponents had recommended to me as fully accurate.

Such memory and such honesty were enormously impressive. I had had hundreds of conversations with former officials and military officers of both sides in the Civil War. In the majority of cases I could credit the honesty of intention, and I had received a great deal of information which was consistent with my documentary sources, even if I could not check on all the details. But it had also been clear to me that many of my interlocutors' memories, especially if they had been leaders and if they had been publicly pilloried by one side or the other, had been deformed by their passions. In some cases the desire to defend their public record distorted their memory of what had really occurred. In others the result of two decades' propaganda within Spain and concurrent polemical debate in exile had obscured the actual events. I remembered also the number of times I had tried to tell students for whom examination cheating was not a moral issue that honesty is a matter of habit, and not a quality that one applies or sets aside according to circumstances.

On December 4 I had a twice-postponed second interview with Martínez Barrio, this time in Paris, where he had come for the winter, and where his apartment was only one story above ground level. I used the opportunity first to check on controversial items about which he would have an opinion based on direct experience: the size of the International Brigades, the role of the Masons, the nature of Lerroux's Radical Party and the results of the split, the exact attitude of Azaña in 1932 when briefly there had been some question of a military alliance with France. Most interesting on this occasion was his commentary on my earlier conversation with Miguel Maura concerning the church burnings of May 11. Maura had emphasized the sense of shock and urgency within the cabinet. He had attributed the failure of his colleagues to let him call out the Civil Guard to the opposition of Largo Caballero, who, he said, had voted first, and whose vote obliged the other Socialists, Prieto and de los Ríos, to vote against using the Guard.

Martínez Barrio slowly shook his head in the negative. He began by characterizing Maura as "a conservative with the temperament of a Jacobin." He then recalled the seating order at cabinet meetings, and stated that Largo had sat five places back on the left and that therefore he would not have been the first person to vote. As for reasons why no Socialist would vote to call out the Civil Guard, he recalled that the Radicals were opposed to such a move on May 10 and that obviously the Socialists would not favor a police action which the Radicals did not favor. As for the atmosphere of urgency, he agreed that the cabinet was indeed nervous—anticlerical violence would have made any Spanish government nervous. But he remembered that his party chief, Lerroux, the Foreign Minister of the provisional government, had left for Geneva after the cabinet meeting, a departure he would surely have postponed if the cabinet members had anticipated the development of a major crisis. Except on the question of Caballero's vote, the two versions were not necessarily in conflict with each other. The cabinet on May 12 authorized the use of the Civil Guard, and it is reasonable to suppose that in the two days previous they had been simultaneously shocked and uncertain about how gravely to interpret the burnings. The particular indications of Martínez Barrio's extraordinary memory and objectivity were the details he gave about the voting order and Lerroux's departure for Geneva.

After we had discussed the May crisis, my host told me that he had written his memoirs, that they were not to be published during his own lifetime or while Franco was still in power, but that he would like to read me a short passage. He pointed to the top shelf of his bookcase and asked me apologetically if I would mind handing the volume to him. The passage he read concerned his own return to Seville just before

May 10, 1931. The new government was less than a month old. He had received a big welcome, as the only Sevillano in the cabinet and as a local boy who had "made good." It had been the proudest moment of his life so far. Then, to his great surprise, shortly after the public demonstration, Cardinal Ilundáin had appeared at his home, alighting from his auto and walking into the narrow street where Martínez Barrio's family lived. He had been overwhelmed by the cardinal's gesture, by his nobility of manner and his readiness to make the first approach toward a minor member of the new government, and by his expressed desire for the negotiation of an amicable arrangement between the Church and the Republic. He asked Martínez Barrio's opinion of what the Church might expect from the Republic. The latter had felt unable to say, and nothing had come of their meeting except a feeling of mutual respect between the two as individuals. In May 1936, Martínez Barrio met the cardinal once again, when, as president of the Cortes, he was leaving for Madrid to function as provisional President of the Republic between the impeachment of Alcalá-Zamora and the election of Manuel Azaña. Cardinal Ilundáin came to see him off at the railway terminal. He regretted that his offer of amicable negotiations in 1931 had not been acted on, and so did Martínez Barrio. Closing the volume, he went on to say that the mishandling of the Church question had been the greatest of the Republic's errors. He himself had always been a Mason and his beliefs had always been laic. He believed now, as always, in religious liberty and in the strict separation of Church and State. But he regretted bitterly that the Republic had not tried to win the goodwill of a Cardinal Ilundáin while that goodwill had been offered.

Less than a month later, on New Year's Day 1962, Martínez Barrio died of a heart attack on a family outing. I attended the funeral in St. Germain-en-Laye along with perhaps two hundred Spanish Republican exiles. The service was entirely laic, without religious blessing and without music. We stood bareheaded before the flower-banked grave and listened to four brief, moving speeches by Jean Cassou, the French art historian and longtime advocate of the Spanish Republic, and by representatives of the government in exile, the Catalan and the Basque delegations. All of them emphasized D. Diego's humble origins, his honesty and decency, and his conciliatory ways without sacrifice of principle. I do not know whether the service was emotionally satisfying to the family and friends. I felt overwhelmed by the atmosphere of hopelessness, of grief without transcendence, of death in exile, experienced by people of religious needs and temperament, without religious comfort.

At home that afternoon I ran a high fever. Having always been subject to sinus headaches, I was doubtless paying the price for having stood bareheaded in the penetrating damp of a Paris winter morning. The radio that same evening carried a performance of the Verdi *Requiem,* the intensely dramatic Requiem Mass dedicated to the memory of the noble, humane poet Alessandro Manzoni. I remembered Martínez Barrio reading to me of his brief meeting with the Cardinal Archbishop of his native Seville. I recalled the religious nostalgia of the "Generation of 1898" and the religious idealism of the Krausists. My head was filled with memories of the ethical thought of Immanuel Kant and the poetry of Friedrich Schiller. The great Germans of the Enlightenment and the early nineteenth century had felt the unsatisfactory nature of both traditional Christianity and philosophical materialism. They had been searching for metaphysical principles which could form the sure groundwork of a generous, universal human ethic freed of both traditional superstition and material self-interest. I felt more consciously than at any time in the past the emotional locus of my relationship to the Spanish liberals. We were both the spiritual grandchildren of Kant and Schiller. For them the intermediate generation were the Krausists and Francisco Giner de los Ríos. For me the transmission had come through a German-Jewish father who had been a lifelong socialist, a reader of Lessing, Schiller, Heine, and Marx, not so much the Marx of *Das Kapital* as the Marx of prophetic social protest. I realized, twelve hours after the funeral, the crushing weight of the double, albeit proud and voluntary, exile suffered by the Spaniards among whom I had stood that morning: exile from their homeland, ruled by the dictatorship, and exile from their Church, which had taken the side of the oppressors. I felt too that Verdi, with his admiration for Garibaldi and his profound understanding of Othello, would have meant his *Requiem* to celebrate the memory of such men as the Spanish Republicans. I was about half way through the first draft of my history at this time. I felt a renewed determination to make it worthy of the events about which I was writing, and I knew that the memory of Martínez Barrio would spur me to seek both the factual truth and a humane interpretation.

12

Seeking to Interpret Contemporary Spain

During the years of my work on the Republic and the Civil War, Spanish intellectuals both in the peninsula and in exile were conducting a fundamental debate concerning the interpretation of two thousand years of Spanish history. The debate was clearly motivated by the experience of the Civil War, even though very little of the discussion bore directly on that disaster. These publications of the 1950s differed markedly from the essays and treatises published in the years following the Spanish-American War of 1898. While the post-1898 literature often demonstrated considerable factual knowledge of the Spanish past, it was concerned overwhelmingly with the Spanish spirit, ideals, and state of mind. In the 1950s the spiritual preoccupation was also very strong, but the discussion was based much more firmly on the facts of Spanish history. It focused primarily on the results of the eighth-century Arab conquest of Spain and the slow, painfully achieved Christian Reconquest, which was finally completed by Ferdinand and Isabella in 1492. But it constantly stretched backward to Roman and Visigothic times and forward to the Counter Reformation, the Bourbon era, and the catastrophic experience of the 1930s.

The protagonists of this great debate were two exiled professors, D. Américo Castro, author of *The Structure of Spanish History,* and D. Claudio Sánchez-Albornoz, author of *España, un enigma histórico*. Professor Castro was a Romance philologist, a literary critic of great depth and insight, and a spiritual disciple of the German philosopher Wilhelm Dilthey. Professor Sánchez-Albornoz was a medievalist whose research and writing had broken ground for a virtually new field of Spanish historiography: the economic, legal, and social history of the small Christian kingdoms in the early Middle Ages. Both men had been university professors of international reputation before the Civil War. Both had been conservative, nonparty Republicans, serving the new government in curriculum and administrative reform but avoiding as far as possible direct political involvement. As a result of the Civil War, Professor Castro had settled in the United States, and Professor Sánchez-Albornoz in Argentina. Each had produced a monumental interpretation of Spanish history based upon two decades of research and teaching in Spain, two decades of exile, and profound emotional responses to the Civil War. I knew the compelling nature of both works, not only from my own reading but from the responses of my advanced students at Wellesley College.

For D. Américo Castro the ethos of Spain could only be understood as the result of the constant interpenetration and symbiosis of Islam, Judaism, and Christianity during the nine hundred years from 711 to about 1600. Before the Arab conquest there had been inhabitants of Spain who were the biological ancestors of the Spaniards, but there were no "Spaniards" as such, just as there were no "Italians" in Italy under the Roman Empire or under the succession of barbarian kings in the early Middle Ages. During the centuries of coexistence, Islam had contributed the absolute monotheism of a religion which possesses neither Trinity, saints, nor such semidivine figures as Moses and David. Arabic had been the lingua franca of the most civilized portion of the world, and the entire philosophical and scientific heritage of Greece, Persia, and India had become available through the work of Arabic scholars. Middle Eastern forms of agriculture, architecture, ceramics, and textile manufacture had flourished in Spain. Social life had been greatly influenced by the sensuality and polygamy of the Arabs, and such complex Islamic ideals as tolerance and holy war had taken root.

The Jews had been much less numerous than either the Islamic or Christian communities, but they had played vital roles in economics, diplomacy, science, and literary culture. They were particularly distinguished in both Muslim and Christian courts as physicians, astronomers, cartographers, economic administrators, and diplomats. Their presence all over the Mediterranean world and in Europe made them the natural intermediaries among the merchant classes and the rulers of the Muslim and Christian worlds. As poets and scholars they tended to adopt Arabic under Islamic domination, and they were, according to the philological evidence adduced by Castro, virtually the creators of Castilian literary prose in the twelfth and thirteenth centuries. Under the pressure of steadily rising anti-Semitism in the fifteenth century a large proportion of the Jews had converted to Christianity, but they continued, as so-called New Christians, to perform the same functions, and with the same distinction, as they had in earlier centuries. The Jews, according to Castro, had been an endogamous community with powerful social and legal sanctions against intermarriage; one of his most controversial claims was that later Christian concern with blood purity, i.e., with "hidalgo" ancestry, had been largely a form of reaction to, and imitation of, medieval Jewish custom. The medieval Christians had been soldiers, farmers, and priests. With the development of the Reconquest those who could afford it had become a caste of overlords, living on the tribute of subject Muslim princes and later on the income of vast landed estates in southern Spain. The Cid had been the prototype of the war captains of the Reconquest and the conquistadors of America.

Both the conscious ideals and the intuitive assumptions, the entire *morada vital,* "vital dwelling place," of the Spaniards had resulted from the nine centuries' interaction of Islam, Judaism, and Christianity. The unique synthesis had created that Hispanic man noted for his "personal integralism," i.e., his powerful affirmation of the self in a world of psychological and economic insecurities, his religious fanaticism, his combativity, his dignity, his sense of command, and his frank inaptitude for modern science and capitalism. The personal and religious traits were a blend of elements from all three religious communities. The scientific and economic backwardness resulted from the series of conscious rejections by the dominant Christian community between the late fifteenth and the early seventeenth centuries: expulsion of the Jews, Inquisitorial persecution of the New Christians and the forcibly converted Muslims, expulsion finally of the *moriscos,* the nominally Christian descendants of those converted Muslims. Through these actions Christian Spain deprived itself of those human groups which had provided the bulk of economic administrators, scientists, skilled agricultural workers, and urban artisans.

As one might assume from reading the above summary, the tone of Castro's book is frequently anguished. On the one hand he can glorify the Spaniard's personal "integralism" and claim for it a moral superiority to the money-grubbing virtues of the bourgeois world. He can inveigh against the excessive materialist spirit of both the capitalist West and the Marxist East. But in pain and sorrow he must recognize the inadaptability of his Hispanic man to the world as it has developed since the sixteenth century. And, by implication more than by direction, he cannot help contrasting Spain of the last three centuries unfavorably with the Christian-Muslim-Hebrew Spain of the Middle Ages.

For Sánchez-Albornoz as for Castro, the Middle Ages are crucial for interpreting Spanish history. But for him the interrelationship of the three religious communities is much more one of struggle than of symbiosis. The Spaniards as we know them were formed spiritually by the Reconquest: by eight centuries of frontier warfare in a country of rude mountains and desert-like plateaus, and by constant religious struggle. Sánchez-Albornoz is well aware of and expresses great pride in the cultural glories of Spanish Islam. But in describing the historical formation of the Spanish people, he places all the emphasis on the Christian rejection of the sensuality and despotism of the Arabs and on Christian (for him evidently justified) hatred of the Jews as exploiters. By implication at least, the cultural radiance of Córdoba was more significant for the later European Renaissance than for the internal development of Spain. Taking direct issue with Castro's claim that "the Visigoths were not Spaniards," Sánchez-Albornoz shows, documents in hand, the tenacity with which the medieval Christian kingdoms modeled their laws on those of the Visigothic era, and he emphasizes constantly the survival of Roman law in both secular and religious life.

At no time was there a true synthesis of Christian, Hebrew, and Islamic elements, nor would such a synthesis have been desirable. The task of the Spaniards, i.e., the inhabitants of the Christian north and the subject Christian peasantry of Andalusia, was to resist the blandishments and the power of Islamic Spain. Against economic, cultural, and for a time demographic superiority, the Christians must pit their virtues as hard-working, uncorrupted farmers, artisans, and soldiers. The greatest single superiority of the Christians was their capacity to develop democratically based, law-abiding governments with recognized limits on royal power, divisions of authority, and local liberties. The Christian community, characterized by mutual responsibilities and rights from top to bottom, triumphed eventually over an unstable, despotically governed community despite the cultural superiority of the latter. In the opinion of Sánchez-Albornoz, religious unity was also the necessary condition for national unity and internal peace. Hence it was correct and inevitable that the Muslims and the Jews should be expelled, as literally foreign bodies, from the territory of reconquered Spain. The Spaniards who were formed by the eight centuries' struggle against the Islamic invader were a warlike, religious, highly individualistic and legalistic nation of frontier farmers, ranchers, soldiers, priests, missionaries, and colonial administrators. That portion of their ethos not directly attributable to the Reconquest owed far more to Roman and Visigothic influences than to Islamic or Hebrew influences.

Neither of these comprehensive interpretations can be accepted as a whole. No contemporary historian could defer to Castro's cavalier manner of deducing the psychology of whole eras and peoples on the basis of a fairly small number of literary documents which he chooses to claim as fully representative. Few if any contemporary historians can notice the blatant ethnic prejudices of Sánchez-Albornoz without subsequently questioning the basis of many of his specific judgments. However, the many excellent reviews in European and American journals, the additions and corrections added by the two protagonists, and the thoughtful, nonpolemical essays by various third parties have tended to clarify the great contributions and point out errors and exaggerations.

At least as important as the strong contrasts between the two men's views are the common denominators of their interpretation. Both men find Spaniards more religiously exalted, more passionate, or "integral," in their spiritual reactions generally than are other Europeans. Both men see the Spaniards as a nation of farmers, soldiers, priests, and colonizers. They appear to agree also on the supposed incompetence of their compatriots in economic management and in the exact sciences. Both men focus their attention on Castile and give only fleeting attention to the Catalans or other groups not completely assimilated with the dominant Castilian culture. Both men are alternately defensive and proud when referring to the economic and cultural contrast between Spain and Western Europe. These common denominators of the Castro and Sánchez-Albornoz interpretations also characterize the historical interpretations of other recent intellectual giants: Marcelino Menéndez y Pelayo, Ramón Menéndez Pidal, José Ortega y Gasset, and Miguel de Unamuno. For this reason alone, and regardless of polemical motives, it seemed to me essential to test my own understanding of the Republic and the Civil War by reference to the major theses expounded in the great debate which I have just summarized.

I asked myself to what extent it would be proper, in 1931, to define the Spaniards as a nation of farmers, soldiers, priests, and colonizers. Certainly the great majority still depended on the land for their living. Also, to an astonishing degree, the legal, social, and technological characteristics of Spanish agriculture remained much as they had been for centuries. Castilian peasants had the same proud, hard-working, independent, and contentious natures which they had shown during the Middle Ages. In Valencia the traditional water tribunals continued to govern the irrigation of the citrus orchards and truck farms. In Andalusia a mass of semiserfs continued inefficiently to cultivate the estates of absentee landlords. Spain was a nation not only of people living on the land, but of people exploiting the land in a thoroughly traditional manner.

Were they also a nation of soldiers and colonizers? In this respect the situation had greatly altered. They had remained soldiers and colonizers through the eighteenth century, as long as they had ruled an immense American empire; and they had largely reproduced in America the forms of land tenure, municipal government, and military administration which Castile had developed during the reconquest. But after 1830 the empire had been reduced to Cuba, the Philippines, and a few bits of North Africa; and in 1898, Spain had lost Cuba and the Philippines. The monarchy decided to maintain a large military establishment, and the middle class persisted in demanding governmental administrative jobs as in the days when there were colonies to administer. But there were only peninsular Spain and the smaller portion of Morocco in which soldiers and administrators could exercise their talents. Spain continued to export people, as emigrants, to the territories of her former empire, but there were no proper occupations for the traditional classes of soldiers and administrators. The Carlist wars, the *pronunciamientos,* and the ministerial crises of the century preceding 1931 were not caused by surplus soldiers and would-be administrators, but the excess energies of these two groups certainly contributed to the instability of Spanish political life. Thus Spain in 1931 was no longer a nation of soldiers and colonizers, but the expectation, and the remembered habit, of numerous military and administrative employments was still very strong, especially among the lower middle classes, for whom these functions had represented dignified careers open to talent. At the same time the new groups in Spanish society, i.e., the business middle class and the anarchist and socialist working classes, were either hostile or indifferent to the residual soldier-colonizer tradition.

Were the Spaniards still a nation of priests? To define this question a little more precisely, in terms of what both Castro and Sánchez-Albornoz meant: Were the Spaniards still ardently orthodox Catholics, as at the end of the Middle Ages? And did they still identify religious unity with national unity, and Catholicism with the world role of Spain? Here I found it necessary, and by no means easy, to distinguish between nostalgia and fact. As of 1930 it seemed quite clear that well over half the population of Spain was completely indifferent to the Catholic religion. Figures for attendance at Mass and confession and the taking of communion were extremely low, in villages as well as in the cities. Aside from the Carlists, the Basque Nationalists, and a large but undeterminable proportion of middle-class women, very few Spaniards took religion seriously on a day-to-day basis. Certainly neither national unity nor the very minor role of Spain in international affairs depended visibly on Catholicism. On the other hand, the writings and the lectures of many intellectuals, including quite a few of those on the Left, continued to underline the intimate relationship of Catholicism not only to national unity and imperial glory but to the highest Spanish achievements in literature and art. When the Republicans moved to separate Church and State, large numbers of previously indifferent Spaniards suddenly discovered that they did identify Spanishness with Catholicism, and all over rural Spain parents angrily withdrew their children from schools in which, by government order, the crucifix was no longer to be displayed. From April 1931 to July 1936 the most divisive single political issue was precisely the question of the relationship between the Catholic Church and the Spanish people.

From this fact, however, I saw no reason to conclude that Spaniards were still Catholics of the sort that they had been in the sixteenth century. The nostalgia of conservative intellectuals arose largely from the fact that Spanish art and literature of the last century had not been particularly inspired by Catholicism. Many reasons can be adduced for a Spanish presence in Morocco, but they hardly include the creation of a Hispanic-Catholic world empire as in the sixteenth century.

Castilian conservatives might claim that national unity depended upon religious uniformity, but most thinking Spaniards by 1930 favored religious liberty, de facto if not de jure; and Basque and Catalan Catholics would by no means accept the exploitation of their religion as a means to enforce Castilian centralism.

When Manuel Azaña stated in the Cortes that Spain had ceased to be Catholic and when Miguel Maura warned that a republic could perhaps be built without the Catholics but never in opposition to the Catholics, both men were correct. Spanish culture had ceased to draw its inspiration from Roman Catholicism, and considerably less than half the population were practicing Catholics. But just as truly, a large Catholic minority continued to identify Spanishness with Catholicism, and direct attacks on the Church aroused a strong defensive reaction among many people who never went inside a church except at marriages and funerals. On the basis both of my reading and of my personal experience in Spain, I slowly came to the conclusion, of whose validity I am not completely certain, that the Spaniards are no longer a nation of Catholics, but that instinctively they remember themselves as such, that they identify their highest past achievements with Catholicism, and that they suffer moral anguish through having lost their Catholic faith without having found any satisfactory replacement therefor.

A different but closely related question is whether the Spaniards are more religiously exalted, more "integral" in their spiritual reactions than other Western peoples, and whether, as a corollary to this characteristic, they are more ready to sacrifice their material interests and more ready to shed both other people's blood and their own in struggles of an ideological nature. The argument for this thesis runs somewhat as follows. The Spaniards conducted an eight centuries' crusade to wrest their homeland from the Muslim invader. Convinced that there was only one road to salvation, and also that national unity could be based only on religious unity, they insisted on the conversion or expulsion of the non-Christians just as soon as they were physically powerful enough to make their will prevail. In the creation of religious unity at home and in the wars of the Counter Reformation abroad, they deliberately and knowingly sacrificed their material interests to their spiritual drives. In the three centuries' history of their American empire they placed their religious interests ahead of their economic interests. In the nineteenth and twentieth centuries they have admittedly turned away from the Church, but anticlerical violence in itself is a form of religious passion. Finally, the violence of internecine labor struggles in the twentieth century and the character of anarchist, Carlist, and Falangist blood purges during the Civil War testify to the continuing tradition of religious exaltation and violence.

The evidence to support the above line of thinking is abundant, but there is much contrary evidence as well. During most of the eight centuries which are labeled "Reconquest," Christian and Muslim princes fought a great deal more among themselves than against each other. The historically known behavior of the Cid, of Fernán González, and of many less famous war captains hardly supports the notion of ardent religious conviction as the basis of their political and military exploits. In the early centuries Christian princes were often undecided as to whether it was more advantageous to levy tribute on a Muslim prince or to occupy and administer his lands. In the later centuries the kings of both Castile and Aragon-Catalonia protected their Jewish and Muslim subjects against clerical pressure for their conversion or expulsion. The Inquisition was a favorite instrument of Queen Isabella and Philip II, but it was actively opposed by many nobles, clerics, and municipal officials. Some of the military chiefs and the majority of the priests and monks who accompanied Spanish armies in Europe and America were primarily concerned with religion, but most of the troops thought of themselves as making a living, either as professional soldiers of the emperor in Europe or through conquest and settlement in the Indies. As for anticlerical and labor violence, there is no evidence that these phenomena in Spain were any more "passionate" than pogroms in czarist Russia, anti-Semitic riots in Central Europe, or white American resistance to integrated schools and housing for American blacks. If we are going to insist on the exaltation and violence of the Spaniards, will we not end up by discovering that Russians, Poles, Germans, and Americans are equally exalted and violent? If we look at the evidence for many countries, what we find is a tendency for human beings everywhere to become fanatical and violent whenever their deep-seated class fears or their religious or ethnic prejudices are aroused.

Is there perhaps greater validity to the thesis of Spanish inaptitude for rational economics and the exact sciences? Here it is absolutely necessary not to generalize about "Spain" but to distinguish the different portions of the peninsula. The agricultural-warrior kingdoms of Leon, Castile, Navarre, and Aragon never developed a strong commercial or professional middle class. In both peace and war they borrowed the services of Jews, Muslims, and Frenchmen. From the middle of the thirteenth century Castile was overwhelmingly the dominant political unit within Spain. The Castilian court and nobility employed Jews, and to a lesser extent Muslims, as doctors, scholar-translators, cartographers, diplomats, economic and financial experts. These non-Castilian servants of the Castilian Crown transmitted Oriental philosophy and science to Spain and fulfilled the most important economic functions in the country.

After the establishment of the Inquisition and the expulsion of the Jews, New Christians continued to fulfill the scientific, economic, and literary functions which the Jews had previously fulfilled. In the sixteenth and seventeenth centuries New World bullion and the expansion of Atlantic commerce led to the steady growth of commercial capitalism in Holland, England, Germany, and northern Italy, but the Castilians seemed unable to make similar use of their economic opportunities. The gold and silver of America built Dutch and German prosperity but not Spanish prosperity. In the eighteenth century the enlightened despot Charles III imported German farmers and artisans in an effort to encourage economic development in Spain. When railroads were built and mines exploited in nineteenth-century Castile, the capital, methods, and engineering and management personnel came from Western Europe and England.

It thus seems to be a clear historical fact that in the areas ruled by Castile leading economic and technical functions remained principally in the hands of foreigners. The Christian conquerors arriving from the north during and after the thirteenth century came as soldier-administrators, for whom the military overlordship of a prosperous economic community was a prestigious way of making one's living. The same vocation as soldier-administrator applied to the Netherlands and Italy in the sixteenth century, and to the American empire from the sixteenth through the eighteenth centuries. In the nineteenth century those who had wealth to invest placed it in railroads and mines, under foreign management. Across these six centuries this particular category of Spaniard convinced himself of his moral superiority to Jews, Muslims, New Christians, *moriscos,* European bourgeois, English shopkeepers—to anyone who exercised the middle-class functions which were by definition inferior to the functions of the soldier-administrator. Naturally, such a frame of mind helps to explain why Christian Castile has appeared to lack proficiency in modern economics and science.

However, it is necessary to bear in mind that Castilian culture was the dominant, but not the only, culture in Spain. Andalusia of the eighth through the twelfth centuries developed a sophisticated commercial economy, produced a variety of manufactures with the best technical methods known at the time, used currency and credit, and engaged heavily in the Mediterranean and Oriental trade. There were sizable Christian communities in Muslim Andalusia, and Christians engaged in the same advanced forms of commerce and industry as their neighbors. In the later Middle Ages the political development of Aragon-Catalonia was accompanied by the expansion of manufactures, banking and insurance, commercial shipping, and international trade with Africa, Italy, Greece, and the Orient, based principally in Barcelona and secondarily in Valencia and several smaller Levantine and Balearic ports. Largely as a result of sixteenth- and seventeenth-century Castilian efforts to dominate Catalonia politically and to exclude Catalan merchants from the American colonial trade, Catalonia suffered a long economic eclipse. But in the nineteenth century Catalonia and the Basque country shared in the European industrial revolution. Though both provinces depended largely on foreign capital (as did the German and American industrial revolutions in their early decades), they produced their own engineers and managers, and the Basques in particular developed banking and corporate structures on a par with those of northern Europe and England. There is then no reason to speak of a general Christian Spanish inability to apply modern economics and science.

Reflecting on the two profound interpretations of Castro and Sánchez-Albornoz, and thinking specifically of Spain since 1930, I retained as fundamentally valid the following generalizations: (1) that a specific feature of Castilian culture was the soldier-administrator tradition; (2) that in the context of Spanish history this tradition implied a neglect or scorn for "bourgeois" activities; (3) that the Catholic religion, while no longer providing a major stimulus to Spanish culture, retained a strong nostalgic hold on the Spanish middle class and peasantry.

Many aspects of the history both of the Republic and of Franco Spain can be better understood in the light of these generalizations. Noticeably, the Republicans, as middle-class civilians, felt themselves insecure when they tried to govern Spain in 1931. It was abundantly clear that the officer corps was accepting the new regime *provisionally* and that they had not even begun to think in terms of civilian supremacy. Civil servants, judges, and municipal officials simply did not accord to Republican ministers the respect they had shown royal ministers or captains general. Plans to reduce the size of both the officer corps and the civil service visibly upset those classes of the population which had automatically, for centuries, thought in terms of government military or administrative posts. For the most intelligent Republican leaders, such as

Azaña and Maura, and for the parliamentary Socialist Prieto, economic development and education were the primary tasks of Spain. Only by overcoming the soldier-administrator tradition could a free, prosperous, civilian-ruled, "Europeanized" Spain be created. For these tasks the cooperation of the Catalans and Basques was essential, since they were the two minority peoples within Spain who had already achieved European levels of literacy, technical education, and economic management.

The Republicans thought also that the greatly diminished religious and cultural role of Catholicism should be reflected in the institutions of Spain, i.e., that religious liberty should be officially proclaimed and that the Catholic Church should not hold a privileged position in any civic or educational functions. From the first days most of the Church hierarchy looked upon the Republic as an enemy. They advised the Vatican not to recognize the new regime, and they let their royalism be known, some discreetly, others melodramatically. It was to be expected that they would resist the loss of their privileged status, but the Republicans, in pressing for immediate separation of Church and State and proclaiming their intention to secularize the entire school system, unquestionably underestimated both the size of the actively Catholic minority and the inertial loyalties of many people who no longer practiced the Catholic religion.

The continuing importance of the soldier-administrator and Catholic traditions is equally clear in the history of the Franco regime. General Franco himself is a superb example of the former: an able, self-confident soldier and administrator whose rise from modest beginnings has included a brilliant military career in Morocco; the rescue of his country from "chaos" and "Bolshevism"; the skillful use of, and decisive arbitration among, both military and civilian experts; the acquisition of a large fortune through means not yet known in detail; the marriage of his daughter into the nobility; the re-establishment of the political primacy of Castile; and the steady support of a Church which meant nothing to him until he became the dictator of Spain. The Cid and Fernán González would recognize him as the most successful of their spiritual descendants!

Meanwhile the Church has bent every effort to re-establish its former religious and cultural primacy. It has jealously guarded its position as the official church of Spain, while consenting to a degree of liberty of private worship for Protestants. It has made great proselytizing efforts among all classes of the population, and during the 1940s it could point to impressive increases in church attendance. In recent years many younger priests have supported left-wing working-class demands and the regional movements in Catalonia and the Basque country. Catholic magazines have published some of the best recent literature in both fiction and nonfiction. Catholic student organizations cooperate frequently with both the student and the labor Left. Both conservative and liberal Catholics are aware of how many Spaniards had become indifferent or hostile to the Church before 1931, and they are determined to restore the older reality in which the Church was largely consubstantial with the Spanish people.

In much of my personal contact with Spaniards, I came to realize how profoundly typical were the syndromes of attitudes underlying both the Sánchez-Albornoz and the Castro interpretations. I met many conservatives among both supporters and opponents of the regime who shared Sánchez-Albornoz's fierce Catholicism; his ambivalent feeling toward the "Semitic" contributions to Spanish culture; his thinly disguised prejudice against the Jews; his pride in the toughness, asceticism, and capacity for exaltation and suffering of the Castilian peasants; his justification of Catholic unity and Spanish destiny as understood by Queen Isabella and by Philip II. At the same time I met many liberals and Leftists who shared Castro's nostalgia for the "Spain of the Three Religions," the era stretching from the accession of Ferdinand III (Saint Ferdinand) in 1217 to the death of Henry IV in 1474, in which the dominant concept of national unity under Castilian auspices was the co-existence of the three religious communities under the protection of Catholic rulers. This culturally pluralistic

Spain had been deliberately destroyed by Isabella and her successors. The great literature of the thirteenth through the fifteenth centuries had flourished on the free intermingling of Islamic, Hebrew, and Christian elements. The most beautiful and profound works of the sixteenth and seventeenth centuries, "the Golden Age," had been those which, through Erasmist idealism, through mysticism flowing from all three religious traditions, and through humor, had escaped the confines of official ideology and authoritarian government.

As an aid to understanding the Spaniards, I also found especially powerful Castro's concept of the "vital insecurity" of the Spaniards. For one thing, the co-existence of the three religions had resulted from a precarious, ever-shifting balance of power rather than from an ideal of tolerance. Within each religious community there were intellectuals who preached true tolerance, and merchants and rulers whose prosperity depended upon it. But there were also religious officials and a potentially fanatical lower class ready to be incited on religious grounds against the other communities. At the same time the two hundred and fifty years of cultural pluralism was also an era of dynastic civil wars, of bitter struggles between cattle ranchers and farmers and among powerful, undisciplined families of the nobility. At no time in the almost eight hundred years separating the Arab conquest from the triumph of Ferdinand and Isabella did Spain enjoy stable laws or stable economic and social structures. All these forms of instability tended to produce by reaction a mentality of "vital insecurity" and self-affirmation, of "personal integralism."

However, deeply as I admired Castro's characterization of the Spaniard's "vital dwelling place," I could not remotely follow him in such statements as that "a people, like a tragic hero, has an inescapable destiny." Both he and Sánchez-Albornoz, and indeed the overwhelming majority of their predecessors and commentators, insist on reifying cultural traits, giving a quasi-biological or religiously transcendental significance to their descriptions of men's thoughts. They thus make ideas the motive force of history, and as in the case of Castro, quite joyously flaunt their scorn for the concrete details of economics and politics. Their interpretations of the Spanish Middle Ages tend to become fixed molds by which to interpret the present and anticipate the future.

The enduring cultural traits of Castilian Spain, which I have discussed in this chapter, developed out of an enduring syndrome of conditions: rude climate and mediocre soil; thin population density; frontier warfare; rivalry between farmers and herdsmen; rivalry between kings and nobles; lack of commercial and industrial development, with its corollary of low educational and technical standards. As these conditions change, the "vital dwelling place" will change. Frontier warfare and the rivalry of kings and nobles are already affairs of the past. Industrialization and public health services are bringing about a rapid rise in population. Economic development and rapid communications make much less significant than in the past such factors as climate, soil, and rural isolation. They also encourage the improvement of technical education by providing economic incentives to literacy and professional training. The Second Republic made a significant start in the direction of educational and economic development and the free political institutions which have accompanied such development in almost all Western countries. That start was hampered by the world depression of the 1930s, and cut off by the victorious military revolt which owed its triumph largely to the fascist powers.

In the person of General Franco the oldest Castilian traditions have once again triumphed in the form of military dictatorship. But even during this dictatorship, whose most powerful supporters hope to restore the Catholic, hierarchical Spain of the past, Madrid has for the first time become an industrial city; more than half the Spanish population live by industry or urban services rather than by agriculture; university students learn far more economics and applied science than did the students of thirty or forty years ago; thousands of Spanish workers prove their aptitude for skilled industrial jobs in the factories of Germany and Switzerland; and millions of tourists show all classes of the population what European life is like in the middle of the twentieth century. The objective conditions within the "vital dwelling place" have been changing in the last half-century more rapidly than they changed in a thousand years. The force of industrialization and urbanization, the economic and political example of the Common Market nations, the reorientation of the Roman Church under Popes John XXIII and Paul VI, are creating a new Spain underneath the surface of the dictatorship. That new Spain will result from the interaction between the new objective conditions and the traditional frame of mind as expounded by Castro and Sánchez-Albornoz. Much as I learned about the background of twentieth-century Spain from these two giants of Spanish scholarship, I must insist that the value of their work lies in the analysis of cultural traits belonging to a specific, long-enduring past, but that their interpretations, focused nostalgically on medieval Castile, should not be used as the framework of an "eternal Spain" into which the new elements of the late nineteenth and twentieth centuries must somehow be fitted.

13

A Continuing Commitment

Originally I had read the works of Castro and Sánchez-Albornoz as part of my effort to understand in depth the twentieth-century Spain about which I was writing. Subsequently the exposure to their intellectual dilemmas whetted my curiosity about medieval Spain. I had often been puzzled by the apparent inability of different ethnic and religious communities to co-exist peacefully in a given territory. The history of the Ottoman Empire in the Balkans, the French Empire in North Africa, and the Jews almost everywhere before the late nineteenth century seemed to indicate that religious differences, perhaps precisely because they are not subject to rational tests, are the most intractable differences between peoples. Despite the fact that both French culture and Muslim ideals are universalist, nonparochial and nonracist in nature, there was never any significant cultural or biological interpenetration between the Christian and Muslim communities in French North Africa. Nor, farther east, was there ever any stable, fruitful interrelationship between the Muslim and Hindu communities in India. And only because of the marked decline in religious faith has there been considerable assimilation between Christians and Jews in the modern West.

It is very easy to exaggerate or idealize the degree of cultural interpenetration among the three great religious communities of medieval Spain, and as I have indicated in the previous chapter, contemporary emotions tend to color all interpretations of the Spanish past. But when full allowance has been made for exaggerations, the fact remains that nowhere else have Christians, Muslims, and Jews lived peacefully together, assimilated biologically, and enriched one another's cultural life to the extent that they did in the Iberian peninsula between 711 and 1492. In this perspective Spain becomes a fascinating historical laboratory for the study of interfaith and interracial associations. There were detailed, manifold relationships of peace and war, commerce and marriage, cultural imitation and rejection, intellectual cooperation and rivalry. Because the connections were far more complex and subtle than in any other society for which we have evidence, the study of medieval Spain must inevitably enrich our knowledge of human adaptability and prejudice in the presence of contrasting religious and ethnic communities. Though for several years after completing *The Spanish Republic and the Civil War* I did not have any time to concentrate on the study of the Spanish Middle Ages, I knew that I would seize the first opportunity to do so. Meanwhile, to familiarize myself with the spirit of the three cultures I read the poetry of Gonzalo de Berceo and the Archpriest of Hita, the miscellany of medieval documents edited by Sánchez-Albornoz, and such Arabic and Hebrew poetry as was available in translation in the European languages I could read.

While writing about the Spain of 1931–9 I had deliberately minimized my discussion of both precedents and subsequent influences. Indeed the strongest prepublication criticism of my manuscript by scholars consulted by the Princeton University Press was that apparently I had not used the available theories of revolution. This criticism was accurate. I had been motivated by the desire to narrate the events as they were felt by Spaniards, within their own frame of reference. I was convinced that too much of the literature concerning both Right and Left political parties and the Civil War explained Spanish events mechanically, as a repetition of various phases of the French or Russian revolutions. I was perhaps reacting too strongly against the wholesale use of such analogies, but I preferred to err on the side of too little interpretation rather than overinterpret in terms of concepts which referred overwhelmingly to French or Russian experience.

Actually a number of large general questions occurred to me, all of which I would like to pursue, either in my own work or as suggestions to offer students in my seminars. For example: What valid analogies might be drawn between the experience of the intellectual and middle-class Republicans of Spain in 1931 and that of similar groups in the short-lived French republic of 1848? To what extent might one compare the depoliticization of disillusioned liberals and workers after 1848 in France, Germany, and Austria with the similar phenomenon after 1939 in Spain? Could one, in the Spanish instance, speak of a "white" countryside versus "red" cities as in the cases of the 1848 revolutions or the Paris Commune of 1871? Looking at the successful Right rather than at the defeated Left, could the dictatorship of General Franco, infinitely more powerful than that of any nineteenth-century Spanish general, be fruitfully compared with those of the Conde-Duque de Olivares in the seventeenth century or the royal favorite D. Alvaro de Luna in the fifteenth century?

Thinking as much of the present and future as of the past, might the historic function of the Franco dictatorship be in any way analogous to that of the crudely unifying and modernizing nineteenth-century dictatorships of Rosas in Argentina and Porfirio Díaz in Mexico? When I observed the Franco dictatorship myself in 1950 and 1960, I was most impressed by its heavy-handed, completely negative character and by the muted hostility of the population. In 1968 the situation appeared somewhat different to me. The standard of living had risen considerably. The people seemed apolitical, nervous and uncertain rather than hostile toward the dictatorship, and the regime had developed not a cohesive or constructive program, but a much more supple style of control, based upon such things as the withholding of passports, of export and import licenses, of land and capital for new enterprises, of access to higher education—rather than upon prison and torture.

I began to wonder whether I was witnessing the gradual development of a new type of dictatorship, composed of the following ingredients: (1) an improved material life which would remove the main economic cause of past revolutionary unrest; (2) physical control of the people through several large and pampered police forces, but with violence minimized in favor of economic or intellectual harassment; (3) spiritual control through censored press and television, and through the careful maintenance of one official Church. Such a dictatorship would never be safe from succession struggles whenever the dictator might be incapacitated, but as a form of regime it might prove far more lasting than the 1930s' fascism out of which it evolved, and it might provide a model for other new nations achieving a minimum of economic prosperity in the absence of established democratic traditions. Franco had always claimed that his regime, far from being a throwback to fascism or Nazism, was an "organic democracy" which had resolved the problem of "atheistic communism" in Spain. There was nothing that any Western European or Anglo-Saxon could call democratic about his government, and the "atheistic communism" which it had defeated was largely a figment of the imagination. But the combination of rising standards of living, muted ideology, and completely authoritarian rule by a military and economic oligarchy might prove to be a syndrome that will appear in many countries in future decades.

I was also deeply interested in the subsequent influence of the Spanish Left on the European world. For a whole generation of men now in their fifties and, despite the "generation gap," for idealistic college students, the Spanish Civil War was the "last crusade," the final ideological cause in which individual heroism had played an effective role and in which the lines of battle had, by and large, separated the humanist, socialist forces of the "future" from the militarist, reactionary forces of the "past." Certainly in comparison with the alignments and war aims of World War II and the several frontier conflicts between the communist and American-dominated empires (Greece, Korea, Southeast Asia) the Spanish Civil War was a moral crusade on the part of both the Popular Front and the fascist Right. I recognized that emotionally as well as intellectually I identified my hopes with the cause of the Spanish Left, but I refused the adjective "last." It seemed to me that the use of this term constitutes a surrender to Orwellian nightmare visions of a humanity rendered helpless by the technical complexity of society and the enormous means of control available to governing elites. But there have been other eras, such as the late Western Roman Empire, in which inertia, unwieldy size, and emotional and imaginative exhaustion convinced many sensitive people that there were no alternatives to the spiritual impoverishment and depersonalization of life.

I do not see that kind of inanition in the contemporary world. At the same time, much of what appears to me most hopeful since 1939 shows traces of the Spanish Civil War. The French, Italian, Central and East European resistance movements to the Nazi occupation were led largely by veterans of the International Brigades and involved the same alignments and ideals as had the Spanish Popular Front. The regime of Marshal Tito has never been as dogmatic and sectarian as the Stalinist puppet governments of the postwar era, and the relative success of the Yugoslav communists in maintaining a broad front of Leftist forces surely owes much to the Spanish experience of many of the Yugoslav leaders. In the Poland and Hungary of October 1956 and in the Czechoslovakia of January to August 1968, the calls for a humanized socialism, for worker management, for freedom of expression, for an end to secret police power are all reminiscent of the best efforts of the Catalan regional government and of the non-Stalinist forces in the Valencia government during 1937 and 1938. In the Cuba of Fidel Castro the swift and thorough land reform, the emphasis on popular education and participation, the alliance of intellectuals, workers, and peasants, and the avoidance of Stalinist governing methods all owe something to the example of Popular Front Spain. As long as such events occur in the communist world and as long as vocal minorities in the West protest against the "one-dimensional" society of affluence, I personally shall not conclude that the Spanish Civil War was the "last" great cause. Rather was it the heroic forerunner of contemporary struggles against the dehumanizing traits of both capitalism and communism.

Thinking both of the Spanish past and the contemporary

world, I find there are many important topics to which I could devote more than a lifetime of research and writing. The problem of a continuing commitment is not one of enthusiasm or ideas, but one of time. Like almost every professor of my acquaintance, I have seen my daily tasks multiply in almost geometric proportions during the past ten years. I used to teach a Hispanic World course to four or five students and general European history to about twenty-five students. I graded all papers and examinations myself, had at least a speaking acquaintance with all my students, and could still find ten or twelve hours weekly in the library to do new reading unconnected with my immediate teaching. Now I teach Hispanic and European courses to groups of one hundred and or more, and I cannot possibly know personally or grade the writing of more than a small proportion of each class. Instead of going to the library I write letters of recommendation or attend committee meetings. Whereas a decade ago I would be asked by a dozen students to write on their behalf to one or two institutions, there are now several dozen students needing five or six letters apiece, because of the increasing number of graduate schools and government agencies offering fellowships.

More important than the quantitative increase of daily work is the mood of the campus. Draft-card burnings, drug parties, sit-ins, deliberate insults to all constituted authorities, the courting of violence in order to dramatize (I do not use the word "resolve") political issues are not just normal student rebelliousness. My optimistic neighbors like to think that these acts are the equivalent of sowing one's wild oats, and my pessimistic neighbors grumble about the younger generation having had it too easy and not knowing what real work is. I am painfully certain, both as a historian and as a human being in daily contact with disaffected students, that their rebellion today reflects a new and little-understood crisis in American life. The United States, a young, expansive, incredibly vigorous, consciously optimistic nation devoted to the pursuit of happiness, has in the past decade lost its innocence. When students took up the cause of labor or demanded public works programs in the 1930s they were dealing with problems which could be resolved by economic and legal means, and whose existence did not undermine their basic optimism about human nature. When in the same years they responded to the rise of Nazism, their enemy was external, and their own country was on the side of the angels, as they had been taught in their textbooks and churches that it had been in all its international conflicts. When in the 1950s they worked for civil liberties and civil rights, they again thought that the problem was simply to fulfill the long-standing and legally stated ideals of the American Constitution.

The near failure of the civil rights movement and the war in Vietnam have shattered the kind of positivist optimism which underlay the earlier expressions of youthful idealism and rebellion against the status quo. Every American student who has worked in the civil rights movement now knows that there are bitter, deeply rooted prejudices in the hearts of American white men and black men which cannot be reached by appeals to reason, justice, or legality. A large proportion of students, perhaps now even the majority of them, know that in Vietnam the United States is, at best, conducting an old-fashioned imperialist "sphere of influence" struggle with the communist world, and, at worst, is demonstrating, through its napalming of whole villages, the ignorant brutality of a giant who does not know his own strength and who is incapable of imagining the human costs of his actions. Beyond both dramas lies the possibility, never before envisaged by Americans, that the United States is not a model for the hopes of mankind and that American optimism has itself always been shallow; that perhaps the original sin of the Old Testament and the "tragic flaw" in the heroes of Greek drama represent, truthfully and ineluctably, the profound inability of human beings to live by the ideals of justice, tolerance, and love.

Because I never shared the easy optimism concerning the "American way of life," and because I had been opposed to American intervention in Vietnam under Presidents Eisenhower and Kennedy as well as under President Johnson, I did not personally experience the same shock and disillusionment as I have seen in a whole generation of students since roughly 1962. But the effect on my emotions and on the use of my time was nonetheless powerful. I had always made financial contributions to civil liberties and civil rights causes, and as a professor of history at Knox College, I chaired a municipal committee attempting to obtain an open-housing ordinance in the city of Galesburg, Illinois. I had never sought to involve myself in public debates, but now I took part in Vietnam teach-ins. In the privacy of my office I tried, mostly by simple listening, to comfort desperate students and, not infrequently, desperate colleagues. Believing neither in final religious nor political solutions to human anguish, but also enjoying life and thinking of men as slightly improvable though not perfectible, I offered no dogmas, wishing only to combat cynicism and hopelessness. I believed that the most important aspect of individual life is honest workmanship, in work which one loves and which one has to some degree freely chosen; and that if a high proportion of the human race could achieve a modicum of that kind of satisfaction, the quality of existence would improve, and with it the chances that men would find life more worth cultivating than destroying. I said such things to students who were thinking of dropping out of college or to colleagues who could not finish their doctoral theses, all of them individuals whose day-to-day effectiveness was being ravaged by the moral crisis of their powerful and prosperous country.

Meanwhile I was having trouble following my own advice. Honest workmanship, in work freely chosen, would have meant the regular investment of at least part of my time in the research and writing of history. For about three years I found it impossible to turn my attention in that direction. Problems of teaching, of advising, of institutional expansion, and of community politics absorbed all my energy. At a conscious level this unceasing round of activity seemed to be not only worthy but necessary in the circumstances. Inwardly, however, I felt a growing tension at engaging virtually all my time outside the classroom in tasks for which I was temperamentally unsuited, however much they might represent the immediate significant challenges of my personal environment.

I desired ardently to write again, and I knew that this was indeed the freely chosen work which I could best accomplish. In *The Spanish Republic and the Civil War* I had hoped to do what no Spaniard, because of impassioned memories and because of book censorship, could do: produce an objective, nonpolemical account of the living experience of the Spanish people in the 1930s. Many reviews and letters from inside Spain encouraged me to feel that for a considerable audience I had achieved that aim. At the same time, in all my classroom teaching I tried to offer some credible, sympathetic sense of how life might have been enjoyed, endured, and interpreted by different classes of people in different eras. Originally I did this to combat the smugness of some students about (con)temporary American superiority and the despair of others over the apparent helplessness of all men in the atomic age. The study of history could be used, almost therapeutically, to widen students' awareness of alternatives, of the variety and open-endedness of human experience.

Gradually I have come to think of perspective, of comparative understanding and interpretation, as my most important task. This represents a considerable shift of emphasis in relation both to my training and my previous writing. In all branches of scientific and humanistic learning the tendency of the past century has been for researchers to concentrate increasingly on carefully limited areas of specialization. This trend has been as powerful in history as in any other field. Yet it seems to me that history can, and should, lend itself equally to the perhaps paradoxical-sounding specialization in general perspective. Of course this involves risks which are avoidable for the scholar who sticks to the area of his particular competence. Perspective demands the constant comparison of many situations; one must give precise attention both to the analogies and the contrasts and make the most careful allowance for the differences in the amount and accuracy of the information available about the situations under comparison. No one can possibly know as much about world history as he can know about several decades in the history of one nation. But writers as different as Bertrand Russell, William McNeill, Geoffrey Barraclough, and Stuart Hughes have shown that with the enormous resources of bibliography and data now available, one can deal in broad perspectives almost as accurately as one can deal with special topics.

The ideal of perspective as a primary responsibility has become the unifying ideal of all my work. It has helped me resolve the dilemmas between teaching and writing, between immediate public commitment and long-term research projects. There is no tightly definable program for the continuing quest, but I think its main elements are now clear to me: an enduring special interest in Spain; a determination to teach perspective, to myself and to others; an underlying faith that the teaching and writing for which I am best fitted will in fact be meaningful to others as well as satisfying to me; and finally, that the terrible stresses of the day will themselves, in the long run, improve the quality of that freely chosen work.

A NOTE ABOUT THE AUTHOR

Gabriel Jackson was born in Mt. Vernon, New York, and was graduated from Harvard in 1942. He received an M.A. from Stanford in 1950 and a PhD. from the University of Toulouse in 1952. He has taught at the Putney School, Goddard College, Wellesley College, Knox College and, since 1965, at the University of California at San Diego, where he is professor of history. He has received fellowships from the Social Science Research Council and the American Council of Learned Societies. Mr. Jackson is the author of *The Spanish Republic and the Civil War, 1931–1939,* which won the American Historical Association Prize in European History in 1966 and *The Spanish Civil War: Domestic Crisis or International Conspiracy.* He lives in La Jolla, California, with his wife and two children.

A NOTE ON THE TYPE

The text of this book was set on the Linotype in a face called Times Roman, designed by Stanley Morison for The Times *(London) and first introduced by that newspaper in 1932.*

Among typographers and designers of the twentieth century, Stanley Morison has been a strong forming influence, as typographical adviser to the English Monotype Corporation, as a director of two distinguished English publishing houses, and as a writer of sensibility, erudition, and keen practical sense.

This book was composed, printed and bound by Kingsport Press, Inc., Kingsport, Tennessee.

Typography and binding design by

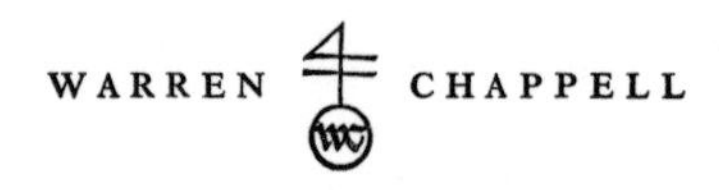